12-9-63

World Mission Studies

---- ✿ ----

THE GROWTH OF THE CHURCH
IN BUGANDA

THE GROWTH
OF THE CHURCH
IN BUGANDA

An Attempt at Understanding

JOHN V. TAYLOR

SCM PRESS LTD

BLOOMSBURY STREET LONDON

First published 1958

© SCM PRESS LTD 1958

Printed in Great Britain by
T. & A. Constable Ltd., Edinburgh

To my Wife

CONTENTS

LIST OF ILLUSTRATIONS

STUDIES IN THE LIFE AND GROWTH OF
THE YOUNGER CHURCHES

UNDER this general title a series of studies is at present being undertaken by the Missionary Studies Department of the International Missionary Council and the World Council of Churches—with special reference to those churches which have come into being in Asia, Africa and Latin America during the last two centuries. The intention is, not to present a general survey of the churches, but rather, in a number of clearly delimited, selected situations, to make studies 'in depth'. This is a search to understand, at a deeper level than a general survey can attempt, what it means for individual Christians or local churches to stand at a particular point of time in a given situation; how do they respond to the different factors in this environment and what influences and determines this response? What, in fact, does it mean to be the church—in this situation at this time? To this end the central element of this series consists of a number of 'case studies' or studies 'in depth'. The present volume presents the first such study, undertaken during 1956 in Buganda at the invitation of the Bishop of Uganda, the Rt. Rev. Leslie Brown.

We are greatly indebted to the Rev. John V. Taylor for his readiness to undertake this work and to all those, in Uganda and elsewhere, who have helped in making it possible. We are especially grateful to the Church Missionary Society, London, who made Mr Taylor available to us for this study.

E. W. NIELSEN

London

AUTHOR'S PREFACE

THE field-work in connexion with this study, undertaken in 1956, was concentrated upon a few 'parishes' in Buganda. The old kingdom of Buganda is, of course, only a part of the modern territory, comprising many tribes, which has been named after it in the Swahili form, Uganda. What follows, therefore, applies sociologically and ecclesiastically to the kingdom of Buganda alone. Its value lies precisely in this element of concentration, and, eventually, in the contribution it makes to the overall series of studies, from which it is hoped certain major themes will be seen to emerge.

In Kabubiro village, of the 'parish' of Makindu in Kyagwe county, a young man had quarrelled with his father, left his home and built himself a small hut of mud and thatch a few hundred yards along the path. A year later he took a job in a place nine miles away, and his hut became vacant just in time for me to move into it. There I lived, sharing as fully as possible in all the work and experiences of my neighbours' daily lives, visiting every home, listening to their gossip and learning their thoughts and concerns. It was with great reluctance that I left that community after three months, but it seemed necessary to spend also some short periods in three other villages—Kasawo in north Kyagwe, Masulita and Buloba in Busiro county—in order to make comparisons and guard against generalizing from local idiosyncrasies. I also spent several weeks as the guest of Africans living in Kampala, members of the new professional class.

Though I was able to speak the language of Buganda, there were still the obvious weaknesses of a one-man study. I endeavoured to overcome these as far as possible by co-opting a panel of African consultants, men and women of various walks of life, all of whom showed a lively interest in the study and were able to take an objective view of their situation. As the work progressed I came to rely more and more on this group to correct my misunderstandings and suggest new lines for investigation, and I gratefully acknowledge my debt to them. On a smaller and more local scale I owe more than I can say to the group of friends which was formed in each village as an unofficial advisory committee, with whom I checked all my tentative conclusions, and whose arguments with one another as to what exactly was the truth threw more light on the dark places than all my previous study had done. It is my hope that the discussions went on even after I had left, and that the research, by becoming contagious, led ordinary members of the local church into self-knowledge and a fuller discovery of their own strength and weakness.

I am very conscious that in two respects the book that I have written gives an incomplete picture.

It concentrates unashamedly on the rural rather than the urban situations. This is, of course a partial distortion, for the few towns of Uganda are rapidly developing all the aspects of industrialization. Some would affirm that the real destiny of the country, and of the church, lies there rather than in the rural parishes, though Dr Kenneth Ingham in his recent study of *The Making of Modern Uganda* is satisfied that 'the heart of Uganda is still in the villages and scattered shambas'. My excuse for this perhaps one-sided emphasis is that a number of very thorough sociological studies of Kampala and Jinja have appeared in recent years, and interest all over Africa is being focused upon the processes of rapid urbanization, so that the problems of the church in the growing cities is in no danger of being overlooked. The life of the villages, however, has been much less taken into account; yet it might well be argued that, in Buganda at least, the real roots of even the town-dwellers run down into the soil of the clan lands and draw up vitality from the half-forgotten ways and wisdom of the cultivators.

The second serious omission is that not much has been said directly about the African clergy. This will appear the more strange inasmuch as the Anglican Church in Uganda so early built up its own indigenous ministry, and its African bishops and clergy today carry almost the whole pastoral and administrative responsibility of the diocese. There are two reasons why I have not devoted more space directly to them and their work. In the first place I have sought to convey the 'peasant's eye view' of the church, and the fact is that in the experience of the ordinary village Christian the ordained clergy do not play any greater part than they appear to do in this book. At the same time I have tried to imply, through many small incidental references, the nature of the task and the resources and the problems of the pastors and rural deans. My second reason for hesitating to write more directly of them is mainly a matter of personal relationship. Before undertaking this study I was on the staff of the Anglican theological college at Mukono, Kyagwe, and many of the clergy have been my students. They might most naturally have resented the appearance of their old tutor in the role of an investigator and critic of their work. Instead they gave me, wherever I went, a most generous welcome and shared with me with a disarming frankness the failures as well as the triumphs of their ministry. My gratitude for this trust is only equalled by my respect for their devotion. Without their help I could never have got very far with my enquiry. But such a relationship carries with it certain obligations, and a natural diffidence makes it impossible to include in this study what would unavoidably be a personal description of individual friends.

At the risk of irritating readers who are not acquainted with Buganda, I have used vernacular terms rather frequently, mainly as a reminder that the English equivalents are only approximations to the real meaning of words. In such cases I have employed the most recent orthography unless there was a particular reason against doing so. I have, however, been inconsistent in the spelling of proper names, partly to avoid making them appear more difficult than is necessary, and partly because many of them also occur in quotations from the past when the new orthography was not in use. In the case of a few words, such as *lubaale*, a hero god, I have used the new spelling on my own account, but have reproduced them in quotations according to the authors' spelling. Occasionally the use of a vernacular plural may confuse readers, though I have tried in every case to make the meaning clear. It may, however, help to note that singular or plural is indicated by a prefix, and that

  personal nouns which begin *mu-* in the singular, begin *ba-* in the plural,
  other nouns which begin *mu-* in the singular, begin *mi-* in the plural,
  and nouns which begin *ki-* in the singular, begin *bi-* in the plural.

Proper names may also be confusing until it is realized that a child does not necessarily take the surname of its father. People may have one or two vernacular names; most of these are selected from the names traditionally associated with the particular clan of the father, but some very common names, such as Mukasa, are the names of hero gods and can be given to children of any clan. Characters in this book may therefore be referred to by one or sometimes two African names, e.g. Mukasa Naganafa; but if they are baptized they will also have a Christian name, often from the Bible. This, however, may not be immediately recognizable to European readers, owing to the transcription into Bantu usage by which *l* and *r* may be interchangeable, and a vowel is required after every proper consonant. So, after his baptism, Mukasa Naganafa will be known as Samwili (i.e. Samuel) Mukasa, or Samwili Mukasa Naganafa.

I am deeply grateful to the many Africans who gave generously of their time and hospitality to help me towards understanding. To select only a few names would be invidious, but I cannot forbear to mention one, Erusoni Wandera, who for four months put himself unreservedly at my disposal and offered me an unstinting friendship.

Dr A. I. Richards, then of the East African Institute of Social Research, and now at Newnham College, Cambridge, gave me the benefit of her wide experience, and later read through my manuscript and made a number of stimulating suggestions. Dr Lloyd A. Fallers, who was then the head of the East African Institute of Social Research, gave both guidance and encouragement, and Mr Anthony Low of Makerere College shared most generously his expert knowledge of the history of Uganda. I am indebted to Mr John Goldthorpe, also of Makerere College, for permitting me to be present at a number of student seminars. My thanks are specially due to the Bishop of Uganda, the Rt. Rev. Leslie Brown, and to the Diocesan Council, for their invitation to the International Missionary Council to conduct the study, in the first instance, and for the welcome and encouragement they extended to me personally. Miss Ferrier, the librarian, and Miss Belcher, the archivist, at the headquarters of the Church Missionary Society, responded to my request for help with a readiness and patience which gave an added pleasure to that part of the work.

I particularly wish to thank Mr H. B. Thomas for his most valuable help. He read through my first draft, correcting and polishing with meticulous care, and finally offered to see my manuscript through the press, in my own absence from Great Britain. For such unsolicited kindness from one who has already filled his retirement with more activity than most younger men would care to undertake there are no words that can adequately express my gratitude.

In dedicating this book to my wife I am sensitive of those other dimensions of help which are beyond recording or assessment; and I salute the patience with which she endured first the long separation of the field-work and then the overwhelming ubiquity of authorship.

J. V. T.

London

I

THE HISTORY

'If distance, like time, still throws a strange halo of glory round the saints of God, there is in the present day a steady determination to see through the golden haze, and to realize the facts as they are. Nothing is gained by living in a world of dreams, even though the awakening reveal but a sordid and a common-place world, whose men and women are essentially human, and only too evidently of like passions with ourselves. The scene is not all bright, as we would fain have painted it . . . but neither is it all dark, as the superficial critic would have us believe. And a careful study of the actual condition of Christian life in Uganda leaves one profoundly conscious that God is in it of a truth, and expectant of the future with a hope that is born not of blind enthusiasm, but of reasoned conviction.' Bishop J. J. Willis of Uganda in his charge to the Missionaries' Conference, 1913.

Mutesa I and the Dormant Church

ISTORY, as a living force, consists not simply of what has happened but also of what men have believed to have happened. Legend, being somewhat larger than life and simpler than the whole truth, may generate dynamic impulses which determine men's activities for many centuries. In Uganda the story of the birth of the Christian Church has become stylized into just such a piece of folk-lore which is shaping to a considerable extent the thought and conscience of people in that country.

The tale as popularly recounted, goes something like this: Kabaka Mutesa the first, having already begun to lose faith in the old pagan gods, was deeply impressed by his friendship with the explorer Stanley and by the Christian teaching which he received from him; so he decided to invite missionaries from Europe to bring the new teaching to his people. He therefore instructed Stanley to issue the appeal which brought the British missionaries to Uganda. He was confused, however, by the contradictory teaching of the French Roman Catholics who arrived shortly after and so he never himself became a convert. Yet he readily allowed his chiefs to adopt the new faith and encouraged them to read in the missionaries' classes. Christian teachers, therefore, came to Uganda with the royal sanction, whereas other Europeans, and in particular the colonial administrators of Great Britain, arrived as uninvited intruders. That is the myth, and it is still a potent factor in the developing story of the Uganda Church. How much of it is true?

The answer to that question depends mainly upon an understanding of the elusive personality of Mutesa himself. What was he like as a man? What did it mean to be the Kabaka? And what was the historical environment in which he had to make his decisions?

He was the thirtieth ruler of Buganda in a dynasty which had started probably, in the fifteenth century, when invaders, formerly presumed to be Hamitic but more probably Nilotic, moving south-west into the region of the great lakes, had conquered the Bantu inhabitants and mingled with them, setting up dynastic royal houses over five or six neighbouring kingdoms in the crescent between the great lakes. For the past century his four predecessors had been extending the dominance of Buganda over these other kingdoms and by the end of his reign all but distant Ruanda were paying regular tribute to his officers.

In Buganda itself his absolutism was such as is difficult in these days to comprehend. He was the source and centre of all the vitality and activity of his kingdom. Speke was told early in his visit in 1862 that 'Uganda is personified by Mutesa and no one can say he has seen Uganda until he has been presented to the king'. The supernatural status of the Kabaka and his relation to the cult of the *balubaale*, or hero gods, is not easy to define and is dealt with more fully in a later chapter. It is, however, important to grasp that every dead Kabaka was thought to belong to the same order of beings as the *balubaale* themselves. The living Kabaka was, therefore, in relation to the gods, more than a priest. It is significant that the Kabaka Tebandeke, at the end of the seventeenth century, had killed off the official mediums and combined kingship and priesthood in himself. But when his cousin, Kabaka Ndaula, succeeded him he separated the two functions in perpetuity, and this so far from weakening the position of the king, enhanced it; for to be possessed by the *lubaale* Mukasa is to be his agent, whereas the Kabaka claimed to be potentially his equal. Moreover, from that time the Kabakas maintained not only their spiritual independence of the priest, but also their physical superiority over them, by leading periodic raids to plunder the temples of Mukasa. The Kabaka therefore was able to be a law unto himself, independent of the traditional cultures, without in any way endangering the solidarity of the tribe. For the religious sentiments, which elsewhere function as the cement of that solidarity, were in Buganda focused upon the royal dynasty itself. The most important of the *balubaale* seemed to be concerned more with the support and guidance of the king than with their own power and prestige. Reverent dependence upon ancestral spirits, though still supremely important in the daily affairs of the family group, was of small account on the clan level because it had become absorbed into the cult of the dead kings. A Muganda's links with his family, his clan, or even his chief, were none of them inviolable, for all intermediate loyalties could be changed, provided only his allegiance to the Kabaka remained unbroken. This meant that people could readily adopt new ideas provided they did not conflict with the hierarchical political structure that was centred upon the Kabaka; and that the Kabaka himself could experiment in new

religious beliefs and ceremonies without shocking his people or destroying the solidarity of traditional society.

If the Kabaka was indeed 'the cock of Buganda', 'the queen ant',
what was the social structure by which his centrality was maintained?
It has been inaccurately described as a feudal system, but actually he
was at the centre of two separate networks, each of which bore some of
the features of mediaeval feudalism. As *Sabataka*, he was the overlord
of the heads of clans. There are about thirty-six traditional clans in
Buganda, each under the headship of a *mutaka*, or 'owner of the soil'.
This man usually owns, lives on and is buried on the original clan hill,
which in many cases is reputed to have been given to a traditional
ancestor by one of the earliest Kabakas. Each *mutaka* is the patriarchal
head over all the burial lands of his clan and these freeholds could not,
in the old days, be alienated. Even the Kabakas could not, officially,
requisition these clan grounds, though some of them, out of animosity
or jealousy towards a particular clan, did occasionally effect the destruction of a whole branch of a clan and confiscate their estates; but the
appointment of every new *mutaka* or clan head, and the choice of every
new heir to clan property, had to receive the royal ratification.

Any *mutaka* might, as occasion arose, delegate to a chosen repre-
senative some task of stewardship or administration, and such stewards
were known as *batongole*. The Kabaka, also, as supreme master of the
clan heads, had many *batongole* whom he commissioned to fulfil some
special task—it might be some military appointment, or the raising of
tribute, or the stewardship of some tract of royal land. If he wished to
reward them he presented them with land, either from his own royal
estates or, occasionally, requisitioned from the clan lands of some
unfortunate Mutaka. These gifts, or *butongole*, were purely *ex officio*
holdings and, usually, non-hereditary.

In the earlier centuries the administration of the six counties of the
original Buganda was in the hands of the *bataka* so that the county
chieftainships were always held by the heads of particular clans.[1] They
and their deputies, together with the great *batongole* of the Kabaka,
formed the *Lukiiko* or Council of State, under the headship of the
Katikkiro, who was the Kabaka's right-hand man and held the wand of
judgment as Chief Justice of Buganda. But at the beginning of the
imperial period of Buganda's history, that is, from the mid-eighteenth
century, it became necessary to choose the chiefs mainly for their
military prowess, since the main task of each was then to raise and maintain a fighting force; and so from that time the Kabakas ignored the old

prerogative of the clans and, appointing the men of their own choice, became the centre of an entirely independent system of administrative officers. Conquest added the three huge counties of Kyagwe, Singo and Buddu to the original Buganda, and these, with the Kayima, the county chief of Mawokota, brought the total of county chiefs up to ten. Each of these was assisted by a number of district chiefs who were responsible for the traditional subdivisions of the county, and these also were appointed by the Kabaka. Eventually the word *batongole* was loosely applied to all these officials who were directly responsible to the Kabaka, including the county chiefs.

These were the 'new' men who, unable to rely on hereditary privilege, had to win and hold their powers by their skill, first as generals in the field and then, more and more, as courtiers at the palace, for everything depended on the favour of the Kabaka. The result was an extraordinary rat-race of rivalry and intrigue, the sycophancy of the chiefs continually inflating the fickle despotism of the Kabaka. There was a change of ethos in Ganda life not unlike that which took place in Italy when the old Roman republic became the empire. Out in the *byalo*, the country homesteads of Buganda, life went on with many of the traditional virtues unimpaired. But, unlike the old *bataka* who were rooted in their clan lands, the new chiefs were spending more and more time at the capital, where the precarious prizes were to be won or lost. There they came to report the success of their raids and to bring their tribute of cattle, ivory and slaves; there they set up their establishments, each with a great household of retainers modelled on the palace itself. Compared with the earlier period, when one man might remain as Mugema[1] or Kangawo throughout five reigns, the chieftainships now changed hands so rapidly that the people of a county might scarcely know their chief before he was replaced. Failure in their task, or the slander of rivals, or even some carelessness in etiquette, might throw them in a moment into the arms of the executioners; then their pardon must be bought, if possible, with presents of cattle, or, best of all, with the gift of their daughters for the royal pleasure. For it is only in this imperial period that the enormous harem of wives and concubines became a feature of the palace.

Their sons also were an acceptable gift, as pages in the royal household, and since most chieftainships were no longer hereditary, the most hopeful method of seeking promotion for one's child was to *siiga*, or to send him into service at the court. If one was too lowly to aspire to a place at the palace for him, then he could be given to one of the chiefs; there was always a chance that the chief, in his turn, would pass him on to the Kabaka. To be a *mugalagala*, or page, at the palace was a gamble with high stakes. A mere youth, if he showed ability and won the royal favour, might win a chieftainship or be made admiral of the canoe fleet which commanded the lake. On the other hand he might be put to death if he so much as showed his naked legs as he ran on an errand. Sometimes, therefore, a chief who feared to risk the life of his own child would give one of his captive slaves, saying that it was his son. Then, if fortune smiled, the slave boy might become a chief; this possibility, of course, gave rich opportunities of slander to a great man's rivals, a form of attack that is not unheard of even to this day.

The career of a young page in the household of the King or of one of the great chiefs was by no means shadowed entirely by personal fears and hopes. In many ways it resembled the life of a great boarding-school, with its disciplines and conventions, its pride of membership and *esprit de corps*, and it provided an education for leadership through daily contact with all the affairs and personalities that gathered at the centre of the nation's life. At Mutesa's court there might be four or five hundred pages at one time in the charge of the major-domo, and though not all of them had much contact with the Kabaka, yet there is plenty of evidence that many became deeply attached to their master. The same would be true of the households of the Queen Mother and Royal Sister, the Katikkiro and the Kimbugwe (the four great notables below the Kabaka himself), and those of the chiefs also. In all these establishments were to be found, in their several degrees, first the various heads of staff, such as chief cook, janitor, brewer, drummer, executioner and so on[2]; then the wives and concubines of the harem, of whom the chief wife or Kaddulubaale held a position of considerable power, together with two others, known as Kabejja and Nasaza; then the pages; and lastly the slaves. The great household, with its 'cluster' of retainers and dependents, swarming, as it were, around the head of the house, was a dominant pattern in Kiganda society which, throughout all the changes of the past eighty years, emerges again and again even to the present day. Its significance for the development of the young Christian Church will shortly be seen.

In spite of the absolute despotism and sacrosanctity of the Kabaka it is not to be supposed that his position was unassailable. This may appear illogical to Western minds, but it is typical of the dialectical structure of African society which Max Gluckman has described with penetration in his *Custom and Conflict in Africa*. The Kabakaship of Buganda will never be understood unless it is realized that, while being absolutely pivotal to society, it has usually been maintained only in great insecurity. During the eighteenth century five kings had been killed by their relatives and two others deposed, so when Semakokiro came to the throne in about 1797 he had had all the rival princes burned to death, and this custom was followed by each of his successors. When the Arabs at Suna's court remonstrated with him over the casual slaughter of a score of victims for some trivial offence, the King had declared that he had no other secret for keeping his subjects in awe of him and for preventing conspiracies.[3] Mutesa's position, also, was anything but secure. On the death of his father there were many of the chiefs who preferred one of the older princes to the young Semunju, as he was then called, and he had to make good his position by force of arms before he could be crowned. It was his skill in this emergency that won for him the name 'Mutesa', the Counsellor; yet it was apparently not until the sixth year of his reign that he was sufficiently established to be able to fulfil the ratification ceremonies of 'eating Buganda'.[4] Jealousy and intrigue remained, however, just below the surface. Dr Felkin, the C.M.S. missionary, reports that in 1879 the chiefs were angry because he was treating Mutesa's sickness, for they were hoping for his death, and at that time one of his sons had begun to collect firearms for a revolt. The following year Pearson wrote that Mutesa 'has not such an absolute power as is generally supposed, and is in fear of his chiefs, who are also one afraid of another'. Four or five of them had privately threatened the Kabaka that if he did not receive the priests of the *balubaale* and restore the old religion they would depose him and place one of his sons on the throne. Pearson adds: 'They possess the power over the army and could do so easily'.[5] Throughout his reign, therefore, Mutesa only maintained his position by a skilful balance of power, playing one faction against another.

But his statecraft and diplomacy were to be tested by what seemed a far greater threat to his security than any that his predecessors had dreamed of. Great powers that lay beyond the horizon of that inter-lacustrine world appeared to be reaching out their hands towards his kingdom.

The first of these was the commercial empire of Zanzibar. There had been casual Swahili trade as far inland as Karagwe in the early nineteenth century when Semakokiro of Buganda sent ivory down to the trading post there in exchange for blue cotton cloth, copper wire and shells. But it was not until Seyyid Said, the great Sultan of Oman and Zanzibar, had captured Mombasa in 1837 that the Arabs began to work the mainland trade in a systematic way. Within seven years, if his own account is true, Ahmed bin Ibrahim, the Arab who was to have the greatest influence upon Uganda, had made his first journey to the capital of the Kabaka Suna II, travelling round the west side of the Lake. He was followed by Saim, the half-breed, whose party of Arabs and Swahilis, with their firearms, helped Suna's army to defeat the neighbouring Basoga. The desire to command a monopoly of the new weapons became, from that time, a major consideration in the diplomacy of the Kabakas. Shortly afterwards, Isa bin Hussein, a soldier of fortune from Zanzibar, arrived with his gun and was made Suna's personal bodyguard and given land in Buddu. During the last six years of the reign Zanzibar traders arrived more frequently. One of these, Snay bin Amir, later reported to the explorer Burton at Tabora that 'Suna greatly encouraged the Arab merchants to trade at his capital: all came away loudly praising his courtesy and his hospitality'. Once the doors were opened, the Baganda were much quicker to learn the shadowy outlines of the world that lay beyond than Europeans have generally supposed. 'The conversation', said Snay, 'began with a string of questions concerning Zanzibar, the route, the news. . . . Suna proved himself a man of intelligence; he enquired about the Wazungu or Europeans, and professed to be anxious for a closer alliance with the Sultan of Zanzibar.'[6]

Suna died of smallpox before that wish could be gratified, and during the first few years of Mutesa's reign the kingdom was too unsettled over the question of the succession for the Arabs to venture there. But by 1861 Kafuro in Karagwe was being used as the permanent advance post from which merchants worked either the Bunyoro or the Buganda trade. By 1867 the Sultan was preparing to send a special gift to Mutesa, who in 1870 sent back some 150 Baganda with ivory and a young elephant as a return present. They came back to Buganda with guns, gunpowder and spirits from the new Sultan Seyyid Barghash, and further exchanges between Mutesa and Zanzibar took place in 1877 and 1879. Meanwhile Mutesa was developing his canoe transport across the lake so as to avoid the long trek through Karagwe, and an Arab half-caste called Songoro had begun to build a dhow on Ukerewe Island with an eye on the lake traffic.

The Baganda had soon learned, however, that the fascinating new powers which the foreigners had to offer were linked in some way with new religious observances. This was not a strange thought to a Kabaka of Buganda, though it was, perhaps, startling for his chiefs to find innovations being proposed by anyone but the Kabaka himself. Ahmed bin Ibrahim, on his third visit in 1854, had remonstrated with Suna over his intention to put a score of people to death in one of the ritual executions. Suna admired his audacity and submitted to instruction in the first four chapters of the Koran. Mutesa, also, early in his reign, put himself under the tuition of several teachers of Islam, together with about eight of the notables of the palace. They began to learn to read the Koran and to observe some of the fasts and the hours of prayer. Apolo Kagwa, indeed, says that Mutesa kept Ramadan for ten years, and he seems to have been more committed to Islam at this period than ever he was to Christianity in later years. One Muganda who embraced Islam at that time says:

> 'Mutesa himself, anxious to please the Sultan of Zanzibar, of whose power and riches he had been given an exaggerated account, declared that he also wanted to become a Moslem. Orders were given to build mosques in all the counties. For a short while it looked as if the whole country was going to embrace the religion.'[7]

The Arabs have been charged with introducing many evils into Uganda; but though they have been responsible for much that corrupts society, yet undoubtedly they deserve the credit for first compelling the Kabaka to ask the question: 'Where is there a God greater than I?'[8]

It was they who first had courage to proclaim that the wanton destruction of human lives was a sin against the Creator, though, ironically, they thereby set up a standard of values by which Mutesa himself was one day going to judge them, and find them wanting.

Meanwhile, we must ask what it was that made Mutesa so anxious to be on good terms with Zanzibar. The answer lies in another direction. Less than two hundred miles to the north, beyond the eastern domains of Bunyoro, the Nilotic tribes of Acholi, Lango and Chua had been ravaged since about 1860 by unscrupulous traders advancing south from Gondokoro, the outpost of the Egyptian power. They included two Maltese and several Arabs from Khartoum. In that year also Giovanni Miani, the Italian explorer, broke through into the Acholi area, and in 1864 Samuel Baker and his wife crossed the Nile into Bunyoro and reached Lake Albert. To Mutesa these events must have appeared as a steady advance towards his kingdom and he had, as yet, no grounds for discriminating between explorers and traders. The arrival of the exuberant Captain Speke early in 1862 did little to mitigate his fears. He gave the impression that he was a prince of England, who had come to open up a direct route northwards between his country and Buganda[9]; but princes, surely, were the precursors not of trade but of conquest; and this man's importunate anxiety to make contact with Petherick (who was reported to have reached Bunyoro) looked like a predesigned manoeuvre. The Queen Mother had said to Speke, 'We hear men like yourself come to Amara from the other side and drive cattle away.' (Was this a reference to the Maltese at Faloro?) To which he had answered:

> 'We never fight for such paltry objects. If cows fall into our hands when fighting, we allow our soldiers to eat them, while we take the government of the country into our own hands.' A little later in the conversation he had boasted, 'If they have patience for a year or two until the Ukori (Acholi) road is open, and trade between our respective countries shall commence, they will then see the fruit of my advent, so much so that every Mganda will say the first Uganda year dates from the arrival of the first Mzungu (white) visitor. As one coffee-seed sown brings forth fruit in plenty, so my coming here may be considered.' After which it seems probable that he misinterpreted their reaction, when he added: 'Putting their hands to their mouths, they looked askance at me, nodding their admiring approval.'[10]

By about 1870 Egyptian traders had quartered themselves not far from Mutesa's capital at Banda, in Kyagwe, and although he had treated them 'like dogs' so that they had 'slunk back abashed' from his country[11], he had sent word by his caravan to the Sultan of Zanzibar to say that he greatly feared Egyptian expansion and looked to the development of his trade link with Zanzibar as a means of protecting himself against the north.[12]

Mutesa was not to know that European opinion was strongly roused by the revelations of the slave trade on the Upper Nile which appeared in the writings of Petherick, Speke, Grant and Baker, nor that Ismail, the Khedive of Egypt, had seized this opportunity to tender himself as the champion of liberation through the permanent occupation of Equatorial Africa. What he did know was that Sir Samuel Baker in 1872 advanced through Acholi into Bunyoro and proclaimed the annexation of that country to Egypt. When he was attacked by the Banyoro he burned their capital and, retreating over the Nile, built three military forts across Acholi. Mutesa decided to deal with Egypt, for the time being, on the same terms as he had with Zanzibar, and so early in 1874 he sent a large present north to the Khedive. Charles Gordon, who had succeeded Baker as the agent of Ismail, found this awaiting him when he arrived at Gondokoro and promptly sent the American, Colonel Chaillé-Long, to Mutesa's court to return the compliments. The road from the north, which Speke had promised, appeared to be open and, before Chaillé-Long left, the Kabaka had signed a paper declaring that the road to Zanzibar was to be closed thenceforth and that all ivory trade should go to Gondokoro. Whether Mutesa had calculated to stir Zanzibar to action by this declaration it is impossible to determine; but certainly that clash between the two powers on which he was depending did in fact take place the following year.

It was really a conflict between Gordon and Sir John Kirk, the British Consul at Zanzibar. Each was committed to the suppression of slave trading in Equatorial Africa; each was attempting to do so by extending and strengthening the effective control of the interior by the sovereign with whom he was associated. During 1875 the Khedive attempted to put into operation a plan, which Gordon had proposed, to annex a port on the coast of East Africa and make direct contact with Uganda from there. But Kirk and the Sultan protested to the British Government; so, after standing off from the coast for three months, the Egyptian fleet re-embarked the expeditionary force which had been landed at Kismayu and returned to Egypt. Meanwhile Gordon was advancing again up the Nile with the intention of strengthening his outposts on the northern frontier of Bunyoro, 'using them as a base for further operations against Kabarega at Mruli, and ultimately, if necessary, against Mutesa of Uganda'.[13] He had already sent forward his lieutenant, Linant de Bellefonds, to obtain a favourable treaty with the Kabaka. But a few days before the Frenchman's arrival, H. M. Stanley had been welcomed at Kazi on the lake shore and had marched into Mutesa's new capital at Rubaga.

Stanley was, of course, a bird of passage, whose primary concern was his reputation as a great explorer. But he also cared sincerely about the slave trade, and now, like Kirk and Gordon, he pinned his hopes on a great sovereign. His candidate was Mutesa himself. After his first interview with the 'Foremost Man of Equatorial Africa', Stanley had written in his diary:

> 'Mutesa has impressed me as being an intelligent and distinguished prince who, if aided in time by virtuous philanthropists, will do more for Central Africa than fifty years of Gospel teaching, unaided by such authority, can do. I think I see in him the light that shall lighten the darkness of this benighted region; a prince well worthy the most hearty sympathies that Europe can give him. In this man I see the possible fruition of Livingstone's hopes, for with his aid the civilization of Equatorial Africa becomes feasible.'[14]

Stanley's story of his relationship with Mutesa during his two visits to Buganda in 1875 is no doubt coloured by his own enthusiasms. Yet even when allowance has been made for all his self-esteem, there remains the extraordinary fact of the influence which the two men had on one another. The explorer's first visit lasted only from 4 to 17 April, and was confined to the environs of Rubaga. Yet the famous letter to the *Daily Telegraph*, calling for 'a pious practical missionary', was written during this time. He then completed his circumnavigation of the Lake and returned by way of the western coast with Frank Pocock in August. Finding Mutesa at war against Buvuma Island, he marched eastwards across Buganda to meet him. At Makindu, in south-east Kyagwe, he was greeted by the King's messengers who presented to him a walking-stick, a signal act of friendship. They finally met at Ugungu on 23 August and spent a considerable time in camp on both sides of the Nile before returning to Rubaga.

A great deal of their conversation together was concerned with matters of religion. One of Stanley's servants was a sixteen-year-old boy from Nyasaland, Dallington Scopion Muftaa, a liberated slave who had been educated by the U.M.C.A. With his help Stanley made a Kiswahili translation of portions of the Bible, and another of his men wrote them out in the Arabic characters which Mutesa's Moslem instructors had taught him to read. On his first visit Stanley gave him only the Lord's Prayer and the Golden Rule; but during the longer stay he made a selection of Bible events from the Creation to the Crucifixion and a complete gospel of Saint Luke. When Stanley finally moved on early in 1876, he left Dallington behind as a sort of secretary-chaplain to the Kabaka, at Mutesa's own request.

What are we to make of all this? There are strong grounds for believing that Mutesa looked upon the white man simply as the most powerful ally against Egyptian aggression and the source of that technical mastery which promised untold power. To welcome his religion might be merely incidental to being initiated into all his other wisdom. Captain Speke had revealed the direction to which Mutesa's thoughts were continually returning. Before he reached the capital, messengers had met him saying the Kabaka 'would not take food until he saw me, so that everybody might know what great respect he felt for me. In the meanwhile, however, he wished for some gunpowder.' Later, when Speke was trying to get the evasive Mutesa to send men to fetch Grant from Karagwe, he reports how the King, probably forgetting he had put a question, hastily changed the conversation and said, 'What guns have you got? Let me see the one you shoot with.'[15]

When Stanley arrived he found about two hundred musketeers in the

Kabaka's bodyguard; but it is not the mere supply but the source itself which now intrigues the King. He says, in one of their discussions in full court,

> 'A great many Arabs, some Turks, and four white men have visited me, and I have examined and heard them all talk, and for wisdom and goodness the white men excel all the others. The Arabs bring cloth, beads and wire to buy ivory and slaves, they also bring powder and guns; but who made all these things? I have seen nothing yet of all they have brought that the white men did not make. Therefore, I say, give me the white men.'[16]

Later in the year this white man proved his value by intervening in the Buvuma war with an ingenious invention of a floating fort which brought victory to the Baganda.

Mackay, one year after his arrival in Buganda, records how Mutesa asked him one day why the missionaries had come. He replied that it was in response to the Kabaka's appeal to Stanley. But Mutesa answered that he understood that they came to teach his people how to make powder and guns, and what he wanted was men who would do so.[17]

The obvious conclusion is that Mutesa, who regarded all religions as means, not as ends, welcomed Christianity as he had once welcomed Islam because he wanted to discover, and make use of, the secret of the power of those who professed that faith; but he would turn against Christianity just as readily, as soon as it appeared to require of the Kabaka anything resembling submission to its standards or cultus.[18]

Yet this, while certainly true, does not appear to be the whole of the truth. Mutesa's is not a personality that can be contained in a simple formula, least of all one that emanates from European minds. Certain other facts have to be reckoned with. There is the strong tradition among the Baganda themselves that early in Mutesa's reign there was a widespread loss of confidence in the old structure of paganism. There was an atmosphere of disillusionment and expectancy abroad. One sub-chief, early in Mutesa's reign, had, according to his stepson, 'always believed that the Baganda had not the truth, and he sought it in his heart. He had often mentioned this to me, and before his death he told me that men would one day come to teach us the right way.'[19]

Several stories are widely told of Mutesa's own disillusionment with the existing regime.

He gave instructions that on his death his body was to be buried entire, instead of having the jawbone separated and enshrined in its temple. He was at great pains also to exhume the bones of many of his ancestors and to bury them at the places where their jawbones had been preserved. This unusual concern would appear to have arisen from the Islamic teaching about the resurrection of the body.

Again, there is the strange mellowing of the personality of the Kabaka after the advent of Christianity. He ordered that the customary slaughter of wives and retainers should not take place at his burial. The frequency of the holocausts of sacrificial victims grew less as his reign proceeded. And Mackay wrote that from the time of Stanley's visit 'people in Buganda dated the commencement of leniency and law in place of the previous reign of bloodshed and terror'.[20] This more merciful behaviour has been variously attributed to fear of the white men and the effect of his last illness; but all the evidence of history and psychology is that the terrors and diseases of tyrants lead them not to moderation but to greater ferocity.

It seems more reasonable to accept at its face value the statement Mutesa made to C. T. Wilson within the first few weeks of their acquaintance, 'When Speke was here I was a heathen, but now I know better'.[21]

The character of Mutesa remains an enigma. And it is good that thus early in this study we should be confronted with the irrational and contradictory nature of human personality. For if one Muganda, about whom so much has been written, defies analysis, how shall we understand the growth of the Uganda Church? This is not to abandon the quest at the start, but to remember how many dimensions there are in the object of our study. For the human spirit and its response to God cannot be contained within the laws of any of our sciences.

Eighteen months, however, were to pass after Stanley had gone from Buganda before the arrival of the first missionaries. During this time not only was Mutesa promoting religious debates between Dallington Muftaa, his Christian secretary, and the venerable Sheikh Ahmed bin Ibrahim, who had been his father's tutor in Islam, but the threat from the north was reaching its climax. At the time when the seven C.M.S. missionaries sailed from Britain, Gordon was sending Nuehr Aga, his Egyptian emissary, with 160 soldiers to occupy Buganda, and in May 1876 the Khedive announced that Gordon had annexed all the territories round the Lakes Victoria and Albert. This was something of an overstatement, seeing that Mutesa was virtually detaining the Egyptian force as his prisoners. He had sent a letter to the Sultan of Zanzibar asking for his assistance in arms and ammunition to help him to resist aggression, and he now hoisted a flag as a sign of his Christian faith and of his country's independence, and refused the Egyptians' angry orders to haul it down.[22] At the end of July Emin Bey (later Pasha), the German doctor who was one of Gordon's lieutenants, was sent to negotiate with Mutesa. The Kabaka allowed the Egyptian soldiers to withdraw but gave no reply to Emin's suggestions for a treaty, appearing to be more interested in the Book of Revelation. Meanwhile Gordon himself pressed on to Nyamyongo, the furthest point south that he ever reached. But, upon Emin's return he decided to withdraw. The following spring he accepted a new appointment as Governor-General of the Sudan, but agitation in England on Mutesa's behalf, and the arrival of the missionaries in Buganda, effectively prevented any further attempt by Egypt.

In June 1877, Lieut. Shergold Smith, the leader of the C.M.S. party, with the Rev. C. T. Wilson, set out from Kageyi at the south of the Lake to sail north to Buganda. In that country there awaited them the man who, being (as Speke had called him) 'the religion of the Baganda', could throw open the doors to any new faith he chose to welcome and yet could never ultimately submit himself to any god. They were going to a man politically hard-pressed and looking for new sources of power to support him. They were going, moreover, to a court that had already entertained seven white men before them and which was by no means unaware of the wider world around it. For example, at Samuel Baker's request Mutesa had sent a caravan of Baganda far into Tanganyika to relieve Livingstone, and it was Baganda who carried the news of Livingstone's death nine hundred miles from Tabora back to Gordon at Gondokoro. The last person to see Livingstone alive was a Muganda boy, who had told his tale at the Buganda court; and in the King's entourage was a young man from Madagascar who had visited France with the Sultan of Zanzibar. In every sense the doors were open.

As the missionaries sailed northwards across the Lake there awaited them in Buganda, in the palace of the Kabaka and in the great establishments of the nobility, those 'clusters' of retainers, womenfolk and slaves which were the natural feature of that society, and which were also, in the economy of God, the household churches in which the Gospel was to take root.

In the royal household were two great groups of pages, attached either to the private apartments or to the great audience hall, all of them potential chiefs. Among their number at this time were *Mukasa Balikuddembe*, a young Muganda of about seventeen, who was doing so well in his work in the private quarters that he was shortly to be appointed as Mutesa's personal valet and nurse. Another favourite of the King's was Kaddu Nannungi, as was also Mukasa, called Omuzigiti because he was in charge of the mosque-hut which had been erected in the palace yard, but which was now the place where Dallington Muftaa read Christian prayers. His brother, Kibega, was attached to the Queen Mother's palace. *Kadoko*, one of the older pages, was soon to be given a chieftainship in Kyagwe; his brother, *Serunkuma*, and his friend *Ngondwe* had just reached the age when they could be appointed to the royal bodyguard. Among the younger boys, under sixteen years of age, were *Muzeyi, Ngonzabato, Lwanga Lugajju*, who was already winning the royal attention as a wrestler, *Badzekuketta*, and little Mukasa Naganafa.

Within the palace compound lived Kolugi the store-keeper, and in his group of retainers were *Munyagabyanjo*, soon to be made the gate-keeper, *Kifamunyanja* and Kagwa Kalibala Gulemye, who was one day to be the great Christian leader and Prime Minister of his country.

There were other households closely linked with the palace. On the slopes of Natete Hill, two miles to the north-east, was the main Moslem quarter, where lived Toli, the Malagasy who had been to France and was now Mutesa's factotum with the special task of training a band of European drums and cymbals Living in his charge were another *Kaggwa*, a slave captured from Bunyoro twelve years before, and now about twenty-seven years old; and a little slave, also from the west, called *Mukasa Ludigo*. On the same hill lived Kisule, the king's gunsmith, and possibly in his household already was young Nyonyintono, who was later to be appointed head of the king's mechanics, and finally, for a short time, the first Christian Prime Minister.

Apart from the palace there were the houses of those great ones who ranked next to the Kabaka: Mukasa, the Katikkiro, who was also county chief of Buddu, with whom were closely associated two of his sub-chiefs, Mwira and Sebwato; Tebukoza Kyambalango, once invested with a leopard-skin as the king's wrestling trainer, and now the Kimbugwe, keeper of the royal umbilical cord (the second minister in importance in those days); Muganzirwaza, the Namasole or Queen Mother, in whose household were two pages, Sematimba and Kibega; and Nkinzi Nawati, the Lubuga or Royal Sister, who was to become a keen Christian, exhorting her whole household in the faith. Of lesser degree were the various princesses, daughters of Mutesa, of whom Magali, Nalumansi (with her refined, scholarly looking servant, Semfuma) and the twins, Nakabirye and Nakato, were to play an important part in the early days of the church.

C

Around the palace were also the town houses of the great *batongole* and the country chiefs, whose complete retinue might sometimes be found at the capital, sometimes away in the country at the chief's administrative seat. One of the most important of these 'clusters' was that which surrounded young Kabunga, the Mukwenda, the chief of Singo county. He himself was to become a regular 'reader' with the first Christians, and among his servants were a young man, Mukasa, who had recently married Nakima, a chief's daughter, and his friend Dutamaguzi. All three were to become outstanding Christians. Close to the Mukwenda was the Mulumba, his right-hand man, a man of about thirty-five, called *Kalemba*. In his establishment were another sub-chief, *Banabakintu* the Muwanga, and an older man, *Mawaggali*, a skilled potter, with his sister, Munaku. Another sub-chief of the Mukwenda was his steward Balamaze, in whose house were two small boys, *Kibuka* and *Kiwanuka*, who within nine years were to be martyrs of Christ. The whole of this remarkable assembly, when it was not at the capital, was settled at Mityana, the county headquarters of Singo.

At Kasengeji, near Rubaga, was the home of a large, jovial chief, Mayanja the Munakulya, who was the official keeper of the shrine-tomb of Mutesa's grandfather, Kabaka Kamanya. With him at this time was his sixteen-year-old son *Buzabaliawo*, who was a relative of one of Mutesa's wives. Also in the household was a Musoga slave, Sembera Kamumbo, through whom Christianity was to be introduced into this group. A near neighbour of the Munakulya was *Walukaga*, the royal blacksmith, who had a considerable household including a boy called *Mukasa*, later baptized as Musa.

A lesser *mutongole* was Sembuzi, the man whom Stanley had chosen as his guide and envoy when he set out to explore Lake Albert. He was now known as the Mutambuza, and had a country seat in the county of Gomba. Living in his town household was a servant called Muta-kirambule, and some time later, *Badzekuketta*, whose name has been mentioned among the royal pages, was transferred to his group.

So, in the palace of the Kabaka and in the great households of the nobility, were already gathered together the groups of men and women and young boys who were soon to be the living cells of the Body of Christ. Here were almost all the leaders of the future; here were the martyrs[23]; the very form and structure of the church had been prepared in advance.

NOTES

1. The *Mugema*, keeper of the Masiro (royal tombs) and chief of Busiro, was of the Monkey clan till Mutesa's reign. The *Kangawo*, chief of Bulemezi, was of the Lung-fish clan, and the *Kago*, chief of Kyadondo, was always of the Colobus or Grasshopper clans until Mawanda's reign. The chieftainship of Busuju belonged to the Grasshopper clan till the reign of Mutabi, who gave it to the Ant-eater clan. From their inception the chieftainships of Gomba and Butambala were given to the Blue Duiker and the Sheep clans respectively.

2. In the case of the royal household these men ranked as important officers of state.

3. R. F. Burton, *The Lake Regions of Central Africa* (1860), vol. ii, p. 190.

4. J. H. Speke, *The Discovery of the Source of the Nile* (1863), p. 252.

5. C. W. Pearson, Letter in *Church Missionary Intelligencer*, 1880, p. 418.

6. Burton, op. cit., vol. ii, pp. 190-1.

7. J. P. Thoonen, *Black Martyrs* (Sheed and Ward, 1942), p. 50.

8. Article by Apolo Kagwa and H. W. Duta (*Uganda Notes*, 1902) reprinted in *Uganda Journal*, vol. 11 (1947), p. 110.

9. Speke, op cit., pp. 284, 308, 421, 444.

10. Speke, ibid., p. 313.

11. S. W. Baker, *Ismailia* (1874), vol. i, pp. 3-4; vol. ii, pp. 98-9.

12. Sir John Kirk, Letter to Royal Geographical Society, 13 Oct. 1871, in *Proc. R.G.S.* (1871-2), p. 186.

13. Colonel Gordon, Letter to Sir Henry Rawlinson, 22 Aug. 1875, in *Proc.R.G.S.* (1876), p. 53.

14. H. M. Stanley, *Through the Dark Continent* (1878), vol. i, p. 193.

15. Speke, op. cit., pp. 283, 294.

16. Stanley, op. cit., vol. i, p. 321.

17. A. M. Mackay's journal, 23 Dec. 1879, in *Mackay of Uganda* by his sister (1890), p. 164.

18. This assessment would receive further support if it could be finally established that Mutesa's violent persecution of those of his subjects who had become Moslems did in fact take place in 1874. It could then be shown that, in spite of his decision to make terms with Moslem Egypt, as represented by Chaillé-Long, as soon as he felt that Islam had intruded on the divinity of the monarchy, he had tried to stamp it out. However, though Mackay says this persecution took place before Stanley's arrival, Apolo Kagwa and Henry Wright Duta place it later, and link it with Mutesa's period of enthusiasm for Christianity, shortly before the arrival of the first two missionaries. Even they, however, give 'disobedience' as the real grounds for the persecution (*Mackay of Uganda*, p. 183. Article by Apolo Kagwa and H.W. Duta in *Uganda Journal*, vol. 11 (1947), p. 110).

19. Thoonen, op. cit., p. 50.

20. *Mackay of Uganda*, pp. 217-18.

21. *C.M.I.* 1878, p. 154.

22. Sir John Gray, 'Sir John Kirk and Mutesa,' *Uganda Journal*, vol. 15 (1951), p. 1.

23. In the preceding paragraphs the names of the future martyrs have been printed in italics to show what a large proportion of them were already gathered together in these groups.

2

Response and Responsibility

IT was Sembuzi, Stanley's guide to Lake Albert, who was sent to bring the two missionaries up to the palace on that last day of June 1877. The full court was in session in the audience hall. The Kabaka came down from his throne, and, practising the piece of Western etiquette he had learned from his previous visitors, shook hands with them and motioned them to the seats which had been placed in readiness for them. 'Then', writes Wilson, 'we sat for some time looking at one another.' And in the long silence, one hundred chiefs and pages watched the newcomers and wondered. Overhead flew Mutesa's flag, 'a nondescript sort of thing, consisting of pieces of red, blue and white calico sewn together'—but it was the symbol of Buganda's allegiance to the Christian faith which Stanley had taught, and was flown in defiance of the Moslems. When the official letter of the Church Missionary Society was translated, a special salute of drums greeted the name of Jesus. The missionaries then presented a second letter, from the Foreign Office.

The following morning they had another interview with Mutesa, again in full court. Wilson says, 'He wanted us to make guns and gunpowder and seemed rather disappointed when we told him we had not come to teach such things; but afterwards he seemed satisfied and said what he wanted most was to be taught, he and his people, to read and write.' Then and there a site was pointed out for a mission house and a school.

The people in the capital were soon to realize, however, that the new teaching was not available to all comers. The Kabaka had no intention of allowing all and sundry to enjoy the benefits of the white man's wisdom, so classes were only permitted at the palace and in his presence. The missionaries were declared to be his personal guests and no one might sell food to them, so that they became completely dependent on him.

After one month Shergold Smith returned to the south of the lake to bring up the main caravan, and Wilson, the young Anglican priest, was left alone. He was granted frequent access to the palace to teach the Kabaka to read in Roman script, and as he was never allowed any interview in private, these lessons always reached a large number of retainers. 'I always take up my Bible with me,' Wilson writes of these visits, 'and am nearly always able to read and speak to the King and his people. They listen with attention and he often asks questions, many of them decidedly intelligent ones.'

The main opportunity for proclaiming the Gospel came, however, at the services which he was allowed to conduct almost every Sunday, in the royal chapel which Mukasa, keeper of the mosque, had to maintain for his use. Then, before a congregation of a hundred or more, he would take a chapter of the Old Testament, reading a few verses at a time in English, which Dallington Muftaa then translated into Swahili, and Mutesa himself into Luganda. With frequent interruptions for questions and explanation, a chapter must have taken some time to read. It was then followed by a chapter from the New Testament, treated in the same way. After this Wilson would give a short expository sermon based on the two chapters. He notes that it is the parables of our Lord which evoke the greatest response in his hearers, but he appears to rely mainly on mission preaching of the sort that was commonly heard in the evangelical churches of Britain. His first sermon at the palace was on the Fall of Man. On a later occasion, 'after speaking of our Lord's power and willingness to save all who come to Him, I urged them to come to Christ at once while there was time'. And again we find him 'speaking pretty fully of our need of a Saviour and of our Lord's atonement for us'.

What such sermons meant to those who heard them at that time it is impossible to say. But what is of the greatest significance for the growth of the church is the fact that before the end of the year a small number of the King's entourage have reached the point of making an independent decision and have become Wilson's pupils in spite of the Kabaka's ban. By this time the Arabs had sown suspicion in Mutesa's mind, and spies were constantly watching Wilson's movements. He was miserably housed and kept short of food, while the King renewed his bullying demands for guns and gunpowder. Yet the desire for the new learning was sufficiently strong to draw a few people to the side of the stranger, even against the tide of popular disfavour. It was not, on the face of it, a religious choice at this stage, yet it was immensely significant in terms of spiritual history.

On 15 December 1877 Wilson wrote: 'I have four pupils, two men and two boys, whom I am teaching to read and write, and I expect to have more before long. I should have begun teaching here long ago, but the King would not let us have anybody to teach. My present pupils have come *of their own accord*, and asked me to teach them.'[1] His expectations were justified. Unfortunately he had to leave Buganda for eleven weeks early in the new year owing to the killing of Shergold Smith and O'Neill, who, having purchased the dhow which Songoro had at last completed, were unwittingly involved in his quarrels with the King of Ukerewe. Yet on Wilson's return the classes started again, and at the beginnning of May he was writing: 'There seems to be a great desire among the younger chiefs and the King's servants to learn to read and write, and I am frequently asked for paper that they may learn. They are shy of letting me teach them, though I have a few pupils.'

According to African chroniclers these first pupils came almost entirely from two of the 'clusters' mentioned in the previous chapter. There was young Kabunga, the Mukwenda of Singo, which his sub-chief Kalemba, the Mulumba, his servant Mukasa and Mukasa's friend Dutamaguzi, called Duta for short, the nephew of Namalere the Kangawo. Then there was Mayanja Kamanya, the Munakulya and his son Buzabaliawo, and their Musoga slave, Sembera Kamumbo. One other chief is mentioned, the great Tebukoza Kyambalongo, the Kimbugwe; and also Mukasa Omuzigiti, the keeper of the royal chapel, and young Kaya who was shortly to be made Gabunga, or admiral of the fleet, while still only a boy.

Unfortunately, Wilson's contact with these people suffered a second and longer interruption, when, in June 1878, he went to meet Mackay at the south of the lake and the shipwreck of the Mission boat delayed their return until the beginning of November. However, the two men were able, apparently, to pick up the threads where they had been dropped, with a growing influence both at the court and in the small circle of visiting pupils. Within a month Mackay can report that 'the King and I are great friends and the chiefs also have confidence in me'. The interdict on pupils going to the missionaries to be taught was withdrawn. 'We daily have some or other of the chiefs calling on us,' wrote Mackay. 'More than one chief has told me that the Baganda want to be followers of Isa (Jesus) because Englishmen are so.'

This was, however, definitely not the sole reason for wanting to adopt the new faith. It is quite clear that, even at this early date, the life and person of Jesus Christ made a deep impact upon the Baganda, which was probably not fully realized by the missionaries themselves, and has certainly not been taken sufficiently into account in subsequent mission-ary teaching. During December 1878 Mackay, in his instructions at the palace, was going through the reading of the Sermon on the Mount, and tried to emphasize the poverty and the manual labour which character-ized the earthly life of Jesus. Early in January he is able to report: 'I believe the reading of the life of our Lord is not without effect. Today the King remarked to his people, "Isa—was there ever anyone like him?" ' The sub-chief Kalemba, who earlier had embraced Islam, has recorded his own reactions to this Christ-centred preaching. 'I asked myself whether I had not made a mistake, and whether, perhaps, the newcomers were not the true messengers of God. I often went to visit them and attended their instructions. It seemed to me that their teaching was an improvement on that of my first masters. I therefore abandoned Islam, without, however, asking for baptism.'[2] Others went further and several of the chiefs began to discard their charms and fetishes.

One reason for this greater response was that the missionaries had begun to assimilate themselves to the social structure and to look less foreign. Wilson, on returning from his first absence, had begun this process by replacing the Wanguana servants he had brought from the coast with several Baganda boys. His household at once began to look more like that of a Muganda chief, and shortly afterwards he was invited to sit with the other chiefs in council. When the garden was planted and Mackay's first workshop erected, even though it was strange to find the heads of a household engaged in manual work, at least they were doing something that could be recognized and fitted into the pattern of society, something that could be watched for hours and in which others might perhaps take a hand. The visitors had started to belong.

The first half of 1879, however, must have brought extraordinary confusion to the minds of the Baganda. In January only Mackay was there. During February Wilson returned with three young missionaries whom he had gone to meet at the end of their journey up the Nile. These were Pearson, a merchant marine officer, Felkin the surgeon, and the newly ordained Anglican priest, Litchfield. A week later Père Lourdel and Brother Amans, the pioneers of the White Fathers' Mission, landed at Entebbe. There were now seven missionaries in the country, and in April this number was again increased by the arrival of two more Anglican missionaries, Stokes and Copplestone. Severe tensions whicharose among the C.M.S. missionaries, and doubts about their *bona fides* and authority, added further to the misgivings and perplexity of Mutesa and his court.

Then there were fresh comings and goings. In May Felkin, after only three months, started north on his return to England, taking with him three rather bogus envoys from the Kabaka. In June Wilson left to go with them, and Stokes and Copplestone went south across the lake. Within three days of their departure three more White Fathers, Pères Livinhac (the leader), Girault and Barbot, reached Entebbe.

But worse than the confusion produced by this fluctuation of personnel was that which resulted from the conflicting teaching of the two missions. In a society which appeared to take its cue from one man only, it was impossible for the two missions to agree to a partition of the field; it was rivalry, blatant and bitter, however much this might be mitigated by genuine friendship and respect on the personal level. Never again were the Baganda to be confronted by the single choice of refusing or accepting Christ. The currency of that supreme exchange was henceforth debased to an option between the three 'religions'—Moslem, Roman or Protestant—which at that time was also a choice between the three powers, Arab, French or British.

Mutesa's first reaction was to make the choice on behalf of his kingdom. He became a regular member of Lourdel's catechism class and, in spite of having sent envoys to Queen Victoria, sounded the French fathers about the possibility of placing his country under the protection of France. Meeting in them a natural hesitation, he decided for the Protestants, and on 7 September asked Mackay for baptism. This was refused him until he could demonstrate a change of heart by giving up witchcraft, polygamy and other practices. The following month he made the same request of Lourdel and was given virtually the same reply. So the voice of the church proclaimed that Christianity was not a man-made religion but one which laid its absolute demands on all, even on the Kabaka of Buganda. This was the word which above all Mutesa needed to hear; but it is a word which cannot be spoken unequivocally by a divided church. For there is an obvious reply when partisan Christians talk of a divine imperative: 'When one saith, I am of Paul, and another, I am of Apollos, are ye not men?' And, being men, Mutesa knew how to deal with them; for he was a past master at playing one faction against another. For him the spiritual crisis was over; but for us the question remains, whether a divided witness must not always produce a Corinthian church.

In the meantime the two missions had settled down into a regular routine, with fairly constant personnel, which was to continue unchanged, as far as the Protestants were concerned, for the next five years. For most of that time their staff consisted of Mackay and two others; first Pearson and Litchfield, and later the two clergymen, Philip O'Flaherty and Robert Ashe.

The daily programme at the Protestant mission, which had now moved into two large houses at Natete, some way from the palace, has been described by Mackay as follows. They rise at dawn and have prayers for the whole household, which consists of the paid Wanguana and a growing number of pupil-servants, mostly boys who sleep and feed with the missionaries, together with a few young men living in the compound with their wives. Mackay then starts work with the Wanguana, mostly building and carpentry, while one of the others takes the boys and women to cultivate the *lusuku*, or plantain garden. At 9 a.m. they break off for a breakfast of porridge. After this, one of the clergy goes up to the palace to take what opportunity is offered there, or assists the other in teaching various classes until 1 o'clock. Meanwhile, Mackay takes the meteorological readings, deals with the cooks, and works with the builders, or in his forge or printing-press, until noon, and then has one hour of Luganda translation before lunch. At lunch they have an open table for visitors. Afterwards there are more classes in both houses until 3 or 4 p.m., when all the pupils go again to the plantation to cultivate food. By 6 o'clock all visitors have gone and the whole household has supper together. After this the missionaries enjoy some privacy, smoking, talking or reading aloud until bedtime.

O'Flaherty described the afternoon classes more fully in December 1881. 'Mackay teaches in the afternoons the Senior Bible class. There are some young men of some promise in this class. I teach several—the Alphabet class, four spelling classes, a grammar and a translation class, and the Junior Bible class—the room is full several times a day.' What is surprising is that all this teaching was carried on, not in Luganda, but in Swahili. To be a pupil at the Anglican Mission was to be a member of an intellectual and courtly *élite*. Swahili continued to be the medium of instruction until the end of 1893.[3]

The White Fathers, who until 1882 were rather more *personae gratae* at the palace, had their establishment closer to Rubaga. In the end this may have been to their disadvantage, for not only was the process of 'detachment', which we shall describe shortly, less marked, but their ascendancy incurred the more vicious jealousy of the pagan and Moslem chiefs, which, suddenly coming to a head, resulted in the Fathers' decision to withdraw from Buganda in the autumn of 1882.

It was the policy of the Roman Catholics to create a rather more enclosed mission community such as was the pattern common to other denominations elsewhere in East and Central Africa. Philip O'Flaherty, who enjoyed a deep personal friendship with Père Livinhac,[4] writes:

'Their system is good in its present stage. They have purchased thirty slaves of different nationalities whom they teach during a certain time and cause to work in various ways in order to raise their own food and be self-supporting.' He goes on: 'Our system is different. We teach the people how to build and cultivate, etc. Of course the people fluctuate; they ever come and go, but then they ever talk. We have but two of us and therefore we aim for future more than present good. We have in our eye a wider field of usefulness in the reformation of the people.'

Father Thoonen, of the Mill Hill Mission, gives a more theological explanation of the different objectives of the two missions.

'Mackay's method, somewhat puzzling to Catholics,' he says, 'is in accordance with the strictly Protestant idea of conversion, the essence of which is a psychological act of trust, or even an emotional crisis, on the part of the candidate. Conversion in the Catholic, missiological sense, consists in the incorporation of the candidate in the visible Church. On the part of the neophyte this requires the desire and the essential dispositions; on the part of the Church and its minister it demands the active acceptance, the "reception", with the necessary sacraments. If this missiological conversion has also to be accompanied by a moral conversion, that is, a change of morals by the turning away from culpable practices, then this is but an accidental element, a preliminary, the necessity of which depends on circumstances.'[5]

In practice, however, there was far less difference between the two missions than their exponents supposed. Though Lourdel certainly started by pressing forward towards early baptisms, and eight had been baptized within fifteen months of their arrival, yet he was soon restrained by an order from Archbishop Lavigerie to the effect that all adult enquirers must undergo four years of training before being admitted to baptism. And the following quotations, one from a Roman and one from an Anglican priest, reveal fundamentally the same concern:

'Among those who have been baptized this morning, there is one in whom the action of grace has been truly apparent.'[6]
'Among my baptism candidates are two of my boys, one of whom I believe to have been really converted. His fruits certainly point to a change of heart.'[7]

But whatever principles may have been in the minds of the missionaries, the actual experience of those Baganda who were becoming

Christians took very little account of the differences between the two missions. Quite often the same men are to be found among the cate-chumens of both missions at the same time, and this in perfectly good faith. This should not surprise us when it was possible for one of Robert Ashe's pupils, writing many years later, to confess: 'At that time I never knew that the religion of Jesus Christ and the Mohammedans was not all one. Of course I found it out afterwards, but it was after many years.'[8]

The fact is that this thing that was taking place, the church dormant waking into response and becoming the church militant, was happening at a deeper and more subtle level than most missionaries were aware of. The Spirit was blowing where it listed, bringing into its mysterious operation many factors which are often omitted from the categories of our theology.

The process by which, in this situation, people were becoming Christians, and that by which the new church was becoming more holy and more effective, seem to have been one and continuous. By analysis it can be seen to consist of four consecutive components which we might call, Congruence, Detachment, Demand and Crisis.

There was in the first instance a congruence, or fitting together, of the new community and the new ideas, with the old structure and the emergent aspirations which already existed. We have already seen the way in which Wilson's household was partly assimilated to the patterns that were familiar and how this produced a new degree of response in the attitude of the chiefs. During the next few years the process was carried much further, though often the missionaries seem to have been unconscious of what they were doing. Gradually they came to resemble the great chiefs in the pattern of their homes and in their relationship to the Kabaka. He treated them as special *batongole* whose skill was at his disposal; he rewarded them with gifts of land, 'up to five times the original size', as Mackay records in March 1882. He went further and offered them wives and chieftainships. 'The King', wrote O'Flaherty in the same month, 'has again offered me one of his daughters, or if I preferred it, the handsome Naswa, his niece. He also offered me a first-class chieftainship and a large tract of country. He said, it will give you a larger sphere for your energy and influence. You will then be revered and heard. I refused with thanks.' They did, however, accept the pages who were occasionally given to them. The Katikkiro complained bitterly that they were receiving gifts of boys as if they were chiefs, though a short time afterwards he himself gave them his slave Ndongole, who was later baptized as Timoteo. The mission household soon became a 'cluster' of retainers in the familiar pattern, and boys like Kakumba and Mukasa Naganafa, who had now been baptized Yusufu and Samwili, began to *senga*, or transfer their services to the mission households, when their previous master died.

The missionaries themselves were by no means unaware of this need for congruence. Mackay, writing to Robert Ashe in 1887, said:

> 'I believe we shall gain a great point when Christianity ceases to be called the white man's religion. The foolish phrase, "Kusoma Kizungu" (to read the English thing) creates needless suspicion. I am ever battling with it among our own people and trying to get them to use "Soma Luganda" instead. When will they learn that Christianity is cosmopolitan and not Anglican? But there is so much in our ways and methods that strengthens the idea of foreign rule—English *men*, English *church*, English *formularies*, English *bishop*.'

It is easy, being wise after the event, to see where a real fitting and belonging was achieved, and where it was lacking. It is desperately difficult to discern these things within one's own contemporary context. Yet the history of these years seems to demonstrate that without such a congruence there may be imitation, but there is very little authentic and lasting growth.

The second element in the process of making and sanctifying this church was what we have called 'detachment', the loosening of the ties which bound men to the old way and the old pattern, gradually bringing them to an independence sufficient to set them free to make the choices which the Gospel was demanding. This part of the process seemed to begin almost as soon as any real congruence had taken place. But for the most part it was a hidden and unconscious process, issuing from no deliberate human policy, and a multitude of unpremeditated factors contributed to it.

We have already seen that there was a general air of disillusionment with the old customs and an expectation of something new, in which the Kabaka himself had led the way. Then his ban against pupils going privately to Wilson's classes called forth the first independent decision of those few who were determined to learn to read in spite of the Kabaka's displeasure. During 1879 the changeable reactions of Mutesa towards the rival religions stimulated many of the Baganda to make up their minds for themselves, without waiting to cast in their lot with the royal decision. This was nothing less than a revolution of thought in Buganda.

It is, however, important to understand that detachment, in the sense we are considering, does not mean attachment to the missionaries. In the experience of the Baganda converts their contact with the missionaries counted far less than the missionaries supposed; their contact with other African 'readers', and their attachment to the Christian community-groups that were beginning to appear, had a more decisive influence. In those 'clusters' of the new faith a sense of solidarity was being created by their observance of Sunday, grace before meals and hymn singing. The Swahili hymn, *Killa siku tuusifu* (Daily, daily sing the praises), was becoming a sort of theme song and was to be heard in the banana gardens and on the roads wherever Christians met. Moreover, it is significant that the three years' absence of the Roman missionaries was the time when the detachment and responsibility of their adherents showed the most conspicuous development.

As the years passed, the intensified waves of antagonism turned the process of the detachment of the Christians into much more conscious response, and the persecutions of Kabaka Mwanga succeeded in transforming the church into an underground movement, organized for self-preservation and, ultimately, for revolution. Finally, the expulsion of all the remaining missionaries in 1888 left the refugee Church to work out its own salvation in fear and trembling, taking its own decisions and making its own responsible answers to the God who was working in it, both to will and to work for his good pleasure.

The third factor in the birth and growth of the church in Buganda was the demand which people felt the Gospel laid upon them. This was something inherent in the Gospel itself, which appealed directly to the conscience and to which the conscience gave assent. To obey this demand always meant to become in some respect different from the rest of society. The terms in which this element of demand expressed itself differed not only from one individual to another but also from one stage in the growth of the church to another, so that it is possible to trace, albeit very dimly, the outline of a definite progression of spiritual awareness.

At a very early stage, for example, those who were beginning to be drawn to the new teaching felt an inherent demand to abandon the charms and fetishes which played a large part in their normal lives. Towards the end of 1879, for example, Mackay reported that 'the other day, when Mukwenda was in, he of his own accord cut off two charms he was wearing on his arms, and gave them to me. He did so as a sign that he has no faith in the *lubare*.'[9]

The next form in which the demand of the Gospel seemed to present itself is surprising because it is not something which would have been given prior emphasis in the ethical teaching of the missionaries, though it probably derived from their example. It was the call to humility, and it is a startling thing to find in Kiganda society at that time. It began as a recognition that Christianity was not the prerogative of the chiefs and their families only, but that the prince and the herdboy met as equals at the font. The acceptance of this spiritual truth may have been facilitated by the hard pedagogic fact that peasants might learn the new art of reading more quickly than the chiefs. Within a few weeks of his arrival, Mackay recorded that 'I find the slaves generally twice as quick as their masters'. By the beginning of 1880 the mission is already incurring the derision of some of the chiefs for taking on mere peasants as pupils. 'Will the poor people (*bakopi*) learn about God Almighty and we follow our *Lubari*?'[10] Some time after this we find some of the aristocratic converts demeaning themselves by doing manual labour side by side with peasant workers. One young man called Byekwola, according to O'Flaherty, 'left aside his native pride, and has come with his two boys to dig by my side in our plantation'.[11] Of Matthias Kalemba the Mulumba it has been said:

> 'The practice of humility entered into the smallest details of his daily life. For example, agricultural work was done exclusively by women, and a free man felt disgraced if he was seen working in a plantain garden or potato plot, but Matthias, bent on imitating Christ's example, was not ashamed of manual labour and was often seen handling the hoe and helping his wife, Kikuvwa.'[12]

Later O'Flaherty tells how Sara Nakima, the proud daughter of a chief, who came to live with her husband Firipo Mukasa at the mission, at last unbent and agreed to dig with the other women in the communal plantation.

Later we see a greater depth and variety in the demand which men felt the Gospel laid upon them. For example, in the summer of 1883 Edward Mukasa, one of the first five to be baptized, was persecuted by a sub-chief for refusing to carry timber for repairing the shrine of a *lubaale*. Later that year O'Flaherty records how Yokana Mwira had told him 'that the inmates of three houses at his place all cease labour on the Sabiti, as it is called, because it is the Lord's day'. Ashe also tells of a young chief, Mutegomba, lately baptized, who at the end of 1885 needed a supply of cloth and was about to take the usual course of selling a girl slave in order to raise the necessary cash, until Mwira pointed out that Christians could not sell 'their children'.[13]

During the months leading up to the great persecution the Christian demand focused upon the actual witness of continuing to be numbered among the 'readers', and, for those who were pages, upon the refusal to participate in the homosexual practices which had become common at Mwanga's court. Here is an example of the Christian demand coinciding with the ethics of the old pagan society, which equally condemned such practices, but superseding it by insisting on uncompromising obedience to the known standards, even in defiance of the Kabaka himself.

After years of persecution and exile, during which the demand had been so clear-cut, and at the same time so limited, there was inevitably a slackening of tension. For many it became possible, for the first time, to give allegiance to the Christian faith without any sense of its demand. But for others there was the discovery that the demand persisted, and was reaching down into the more hidden levels of personal thought and behaviour. As an example of this a few extracts from the autobiography of a young Christian of those days, Ham Mukasa, may serve to demonstrate the deeper responses that the Gospel was then calling for.

As a page at Mutesa's court he had attended, rather spasmodically, the classes at the Anglican mission. He had a boy's typical attitude to his tutors. 'Our friend Kidza,' he says, 'used to talk over with us every day what we heard, and he used to make fun of Mr O'Flaherty and this we thought very funny, and it made us laugh.' Early in Mwanga's reign he went to live in the household of Nuwa Walukaga, the blacksmith at Kasengeji, where Musa Mukasa, the household servant, taught him to read. When the persecution of 1886 broke out he was accused as a reader, but Yusufu Waswa, the Christian chief of Bulemezi, sent him into hiding at his country seat. Later he was pardoned by Mwanga and put in charge of the pages at the palace.

Now for the first time his conscience was troubled, through reading with a fellow-Christian the story of the destruction of Sodom—an apt text—and he began to study more seriously under the guidance of Waswa, his protector, and four others who were attached to the palace, He says, 'I used to go by stealth to Natete to hear about religion, but I never understood what they taught me.' However, he learned by heart the correct answers in the baptismal catechism and was eventually baptized by four African leaders. Tomasi Semfuma, the servant of the Princess Nalumansi, who knew the young Ham Mukasa well, disapproved of this baptism, but arrived too late to stop it. So the young man joined the growing ranks of those who accepted the name of Christian but resisted the demand that he felt was inherent in it. He says, 'I knew that many of the so-called readers still kept on many of their old sinful habits.'

He was next caught up into a most adventurous participation in the rebellion against Mwanga, the exile in Ankole, and the battles by which the Christian party fought its way back to power. Following a bullet wound in his knee, he became seriously ill and listened with a new attention to the teaching of four African friends who were concerned for his life. Gradually, fighting step by step his old temptations, he began painfully to win through to moral victory and to a complete committal of himself to Christ. This kind of prolonged struggle was something new in the experience of the young church of Buganda, and it won a new kind of spirituality, less naively innocent than that of the first generation, but more battle-scarred and mature. The contrast can best be seen by comparing him with Samwili Mukasa Naganafa, also a page at Mutesa's court. Each of them is very conscious that he bears the name of Mukasa, the great *Lubaale*. Soon after his baptism in December 1883 Samwili had exclaimed to one of the missionaries: 'Do not call me Mukasa; Mukasa is dead.' But this other Mukasa, only a few years his junior, described his experience in words that are significantly different.

> 'This war that I have in my heart', he says, 'is a fight between Mukasa, the name I had before I was baptized, and Ham, the new name I took on being baptized. So I find that Mukasa is daily annoyed that I will not follow the natural inclinations of my body. But the new man, Ham, whom God sent to drive out Mukasa, will not allow Mukasa to come back and reign in my body, for God wants Ham to be there by himself.'

So a new generation discovered on quite new levels what was the demand of the Gospel; and so it has gone on ever since.

But there is another kind of demand which appears in the story. It was not inherent, but, rather, extraneous; that is to say, it was a demand laid upon the would-be converts by missionary pronouncement and did not appear to arise directly out of the challenge of the Gospel itself to the conscience of the Baganda. When, for example, Wilson, within two months of his arrival, proposed that the dancers and musicians of the palace should cease operations while he was teaching there, he was making a demand to which there was no response in the conscience of those who heard it, and which appeared to have no logical basis in the Gospel he preached. Sometimes a demand of this kind was extraneous merely because it was premature; we might say it was being made by men sooner than it was made by the Holy Spirit. It is debatable (but impossible to determine conclusively) whether the demand to abandon polygamy was of this kind. For example, in December 1883, a *mutongole* called Kizito Kisingiri was baptized Zakaliya, of whom Ashe wrote: 'This was the young man whom we had to refuse to baptize unless he would promise to give up his wives and to marry one with Christian rites. This finally he consented to do.' However, the discussion of this question must be reserved for another chapter. It seems clear that in the religious debates at the court Mackay, 'the Anti-Mukasa' as his colleagues called him, over-reached himself in the demands he made so that there was a reaction even among his would-be followers which the leaders of the *Lubaale* party were quick to exploit. Mutesa had to bow to this reaction, though he was careful not to get rid of the missionaries entirely.

Finally, the fourth element in the process of the upbuilding of the church is that which we have called Crisis. Quietly and unobtrusively the other three elements of Congruence and Detachment and Demand have been at work. Gradually individuals and groups have found themselves beginning to belong to the new thing; almost unnoticed they have been eased away from their homogeneity with the old, and have grown independent; steadily their conscience has been made aware of something demanding some specific change of attitude or behaviour. But none can tell how real a response, or how permanent a transfer has been made, until suddenly some development precipitates a crisis, for a moment the old and the new ways fly apart and people are either found adhering to the new, or they spring back to the old. This very clarification itself introduces a new situation, a fresh chapter, as it were. Then the moment of revelation passes and the continuing process starts up again out of sight.

This can best be demonstrated by a short résumé of the story of the first fifteen years.

We have already mentioned by name the first pupils who attached themselves to Wilson in 1878, and have seen how they mostly belonged to two household 'clusters'—that of the Mukwenda of Singo and that of the Munakulya. There was also Mukasa, the keeper of the royal chapel, and the great Kimbugwe, Kyambalango. Mackay's early influence drew a number of the other great chiefs into the Christian orbit, and several of them began to respond to the demand of the Gospel by abandoning their charms. Then at the end of 1879 came the first crisis. Kabaka Mutesa turned his back on all three of the alien religions and called in the priests of the three chief *balubaale* to heal his sickness. The

D

county chiefs of Kyadondo and Gomba were the main advocates of the *balubaale*, but it is clear that Mackay regarded many of the other chiefs as his pupils and hoped to hold them. For several days he went desperately from house to house, pleading in turn with Mukasa the Katikkiro, with Wilson's old pupils, Tebukoza Kyambalongo, Kabunga the young Mukwenda and Mayanja the Munakulya, with Kolugi the store-keeper, Sembuzi, Stanley's old guide, and Wakibi another of the chiefs. But all of them failed him. Kolugi, whom Mackay called 'a *mutongole* who had always been a great friend of mine', was obviously shamefaced and abashed; and Kabunga was a sort of Nicodemus, of whom Pearson wrote: 'One chief has been our friend, Mukwenda; he is young and was forced to acquiesce in the decision, but he has sent us information of what has transpired at court since.'

The greatest disappointment was Mayanja, the Munakulya, a man who years afterwards was described as 'a great, jolly giant, but one would like to see more of the true mettle about him'. Litchfield, who had been his regular teacher, described in his diary how he visited his home on 10 August 1879:

'I tried to explain the death, resurrection and love of Christ to him in my broken, stammering language. After a while he went outside and sent a slave to fetch me. I went to him, and found him in a very small hut on his knees and he asked me to pray. I said I did not know Swahili, but he said "Pray in English; God understand you". Five days later he had built near his house a little hut which he called the house of God.'

And yet, when the crisis came, Pearson wrote:

'Munakulya, who used to be at our place constantly, and who professed to believe the message of salvation, was also against us. He had received many benefits from us and we thought the good seed had taken root in his heart. Indeed, all those chiefs with whom we had been most friendly, were the worst against us.'

The first crisis had come, and almost all had reverted to their old allegiance.

Now began a longer period of quiet growing together. The White Fathers completed a chapel on their mission and opened a first catechism class. Mackay completed in December 1879 the first book of Swahili hymns and began, in January, to translate St Matthew's Gospel into Luganda. During the first half of 1880 four men were baptized by the White Fathers, one of whom, Matthew Kisule, the Kabaka's gunsmith, became at once a leader whose home at Natete was the centre of a

Christian 'cluster'. From time to time the royal command to carry out a wholesale slaughter of sacrificial victims came as a fresh test, but none of the greater chiefs was found, as yet, to resist the Kabaka in this matter. However, among the pages, and the lesser *batongole*, there were signs of a new steadiness. In November Mukasa, the Mukwenda's servant, and his friend Duta, were bound and taken off to an island in Lake Wamala for refusing to go to Moslem prayers (which the Kabaka had again tried to make compulsory), and for saying that the religion of Jesus is the only true religion. In the middle of June 1881 Mackay wrote: 'Converts we have not yet found but half-believers many.' His regular afternoon classes include several who were also attending the classes at the Roman mission: Kalemba, the Mukwenda's sub-chief, and his retainers, old Mawaggali and Banabakintu; Mukasa Balikuddembe, the Kabaka's valet, and Kaggwa the drummer. The Katikkiro, the Kimbugwe and Kolugi the store-keeper were back in Mackay's class. So also, at this time were: Mukasa, the keeper of the royal chapel, Mukasa the servant of the Mukwenda, Mukasa Naganafa, one of the royal pages, who continued coming in spite of the fact that his fellow-pages laughed at him, and a young man called Damulira. The following month Sembera Kamumbo, the slave of Mayanja the Munakulya who had been such a disappointment (it may have been he who was sent to fetch Litchfield to pray with his master before his defection), began attending the class after a long absence. With joy Mackay wrote in his diary in October 1881: 'My old faithful pupil and assistant, Sembera Kamumbo, has turned up again several times.' A little later his truant pupil, who had during his absence been teaching Mayanja, his master, to read, handed to Mackay a note written in Luganda: 'Bwana Mackay, Sembera has come with compliments and to give you great news. Will you baptize him because he believes the words of Jesus Christ?'

But Sembera was not the first to be baptized among the Protestant readers. That honour was reserved for Damulira, about whom little is known except that about this time he fell ill and asked a pagan friend to fetch one of the missionaries. On being refused, he contented himself with reading laboriously in the Swahili Gospel of St Mark which he possessed. He grew much worse and, in his loneliness, he persuaded the pagan boy to sprinkle water on him in the name of the Father and the Son and the Holy Ghost. Shortly afterwards he died. And then his friend plucked up courage to go and tell the missionaries what he had done.

That solitary baptism seemed, in a strange way, to unlock the doors and usher in a new phase of courageous confession. On 18 March 1882 the first five were baptized by the C.M.S. Mission. They were Sembera Kamumbo, who took the name Mackay; Mukasa, keeper of the chapel, who was baptized Edward; Mukasa, the servant of the Mukwenda, named Firipo after Philip O'Flaherty; Buzabaliawo, the son of Mayanja the Munakulya, whom Sembera had taught, and who was now called Henry Wright[14]; and Mutakirambule, a servant of Sembuzi, who took the name Yakobo.

During the next two months the White Fathers also baptized eight more of their catechumens, including Mukasa Balikuddembe, the king's valet, who took the name Joseph; Kaggwa the drummer, who was called Andrew; Kalemba the Mulumba, who was baptized Matthias; his retainer, Banabakintu, who was called Luke; and Kamya, another of that group, who became Cyprian.

It was these men, and the 150 or so other adherents of the Roman Catholic Church, who were plunged into the next crisis. In the autumn, for a variety of reasons which to this day remain somewhat confused, the White Fathers decided to leave Buganda. There were rumours that the Arabs, stirred by news of the Mahdi's successes in the Sudan, were plotting to kill all the priests, directing their enmity against the Roman mission because of its greater influence at the court. There were also rumours that the Kabaka was preparing for a wholesale massacre of the Christians, which the departure of the priests might possibly avert. Whatever their reasons may have been, the missionaries did withdraw and the young community of their followers was left to fend for itself. The recently baptized leaders rose magnificently to the occasion and under their guidance the Church continued to grow in numbers and in spiritual understanding.

Meanwhile the Anglican community was still exempt from any such crises, though it remained under such royal disfavour as to discourage any easy discipleship. Just after the baptism of the first five, Kabunga the young Mukwenda was deposed and moved from the capital, and his going reduced the classes to about half their size. However, they were soon joined by a new member who was to prove a tower of strength. Mackay had been ordered to make a huge copper coffin for the Queen Mother, who had died that March, and his fellow-worker was Walukukaga, the king's blacksmith. He now came and asked to be instructed. During the summer of 1883 Duta returned from Zanzibar, where he had gone to accompany Pearson on his way home and where he had been baptized Henry Wright by a missionary of the U.M.C.A. He at once joined Firipo Mukasa, his friend, as one of the permanent staff of the mission in teaching and translation work, since Dallington Muftaa had given up all Christian pretensions and taken a chieftainship in Buddu.

From the autumn of 1882 people began responding with greater courage and decisiveness. Sebwato, an important sub-chief from Buddu, had been deeply impressed by a discussion between O'Flaherty and the Arab teachers at the palace, and came to ask for teaching. O'Flaherty began visiting him at his town residence and on one notable occasion found him teaching the women of his household. His account continues:

'His *Mandwa* (priest),[15] who had his eyes fixed on me during my instruction, came forward, knelt at my feet, and said "I will cast off these charms of Lubari whom I will never again serve. He is a liar and a cheat. I will follow Jesus, and learn his ways"; so saying, he cut off his valuables, and cast them into the fire. The women and the mutongoli were astonished.'

On Christmas Eve Sebwato came to say that he was being sent away to Buddu country, but that he was determined to follow Jesus. The women and the *mmandwa* stayed behind to join in the Christmas celebrations, then they too went away to Buddu.[16] A few months later O'Flaherty received an urgent message from Sebwato asking him to visit him at his country home in order that he might be baptized, but this he was unable to do.

Another sub-chief from Buddu who started responding to the new teaching about the same time as Sebwato was Mwira, who early in 1883 asked to be allowed to join the Anglican establishment. He was a slow reader, but steadily worked his way through the Swahili gospels of St Matthew and St Mark and other books of instruction. What this meant to him he described one day to O'Flaherty, and even the good Irishman's rather extravagant translation cannot conceal the reality of this man's experience.

'I am like a man travelling in a mountainous country. He climbs and passes ridge after ridge with pleasure. But as he surmounts he looks before him to the heights beyond and he becomes impatient, and wonders if he will ever surmount the last. . . . Not so I. When I climb I like to lie on the top and rest and enjoy the others before me. Yes, I like to rest and drink of the fountains that gush forth as I climb. Oh, the pleasure of reading and of thinking upon those delightful books, and of meditating on the wonders of the Son of God becoming man to save me from Lubari!'[17]

Then he also disappeared into the country, but returned after a few months with his wife and a baby of a year old. When Mackay and O'Flaherty examined the woman, they were amazed to find her reading without a mistake. After some time they were baptized Yokana and Malyamu.

During the second half of 1883 Mackay, who always advocated extreme caution in administering baptism, was away building a new boat at the south of the lake. R. P. Ashe had joined O'Flaherty in May 1883 and the two clergy baptized nearly sixty new adherents before the end of the year. Sara Nakima was baptized and married to Firipo Mukasa by Christian rites. Edward Mukasa brought his brother Kibega, who was baptized Albert, and married Doti, 'a young, sprightly creature' who had arrived, no one quite knew from whence, and had been taken into the home of an older woman living on the compound. A number of women began at this time to make an independent decision to attach themselves to the new way. The first of these was Mubulire, later baptized as Fanny, and in quite a short time she was teaching her household servants. She afterwards married Freddy Kidza Lubeli, the young guide to Bugala, the captain of the guard. Several of the princesses began reading in earnest, and one of these, called Nalumansi, was baptized. Sematimba, one of the Queen Mother's pages who had been a spasmodic reader for a long time, was baptized Mika during this year, and was the first of a great number of younger boys from the palace who began to associate themselves openly with one or other of the Christian groups.

In the early autumn, 1883, O'Flaherty was elated by the steady flow of converts. 'While', he exclaimed, 'we have such specimens here as Yokana and Malyamu, Firipo and Sara, Yakobo Kitati and Albert Kibega and Henry Wright Duta and Henry Wright Buza and Edward Mukasa and Fanny and Sembera Mackay and many others, I am as sure of the regeneration of Buganda as that I am writing this letter.' Then, with an awareness that this growing Church was as yet untried, he added: 'But signs, and very intelligent signs, are cropping up showing themselves that the seeds in process of growth shall be watered with tears, if not with blood.'

The crisis, when it came, was not a very important affair, but it served most effectively to sift the wheat from the chaff. Mackay returned just before Christmas with a consignment of goods concerning which very exaggerated accounts had preceded him to Mutesa's palace. On Christmas Eve two minor officials had arrived, intoxicated, at the Anglican mission and tried to get hold of some of these goods, but were driven off somewhat violently by O'Flaherty. On Christmas Day there were fifteen baptisms and a celebration of the Holy Communion, followed by a great feast with several hundred guests. The two officials, Musisi and Namukadde, then complained at the court that they had been beaten, that the missionaries were enticing hundreds of people to be disloyal to the Kabaka and were harbouring many women who had escaped to them from the royal harem. Hoping to force the missionaries to give him more lavish presents, the Kabaka permitted the two officials to attack the mission, which they did, burning several outhouses and trying to round up all the mission retainers. Almost to a man the Christians stampeded, and did not show up again for about two months. One reason for this total collapse was probably their knowledge that over the matter of the Kabaka's women the missionaries were, albeit unwittingly, in the wrong, for it turned out that young Doti and another girl had in fact run away from the royal harem. But whatever the immediate causes, the sense of judgment was upon them. Of the five who had been first baptized two years before, it was now evident that two or three had fallen away, and Duta, the trusted translator, was found to have been systematically stealing, and, in Mackay's words, 'proved to be a scheming rogue of a loose character'. O'Flaherty expressed the deep disappointment of the missionaries when he wrote: 'Even Sembera Mackay, whom we thought a rock, fled. So did Henry Wright Duta. Firipo Mukasa and Sara Nakima alone stood their ground and braved Musisi and Namukadde.' Even in Firipo's case courageous loyalty did not mean perfection, for he was often unfaithful to his wife, Sara. Yet, when he fell as the first victim in the outbreak of smallpox at the end of the next year, she tended him with devotion until his death.[18]

However, by March the Anglican adherents began shamefacedly to return, and as a result of their experience they appear to have achieved a deeper level of commitment, which the new catechumens immediately shared. On 16 March a second princess, Rebecca Magali, was baptized, together with Sajja, the young, consumptive goatherd. The next week Sebwato, the sub-chief from Buddu who had returned to the capital, was baptized Nikodemo. In honour of the event he presented to the Mission his little Muhima captive, the eleven-year-old Lugalama. Of Sebwato Ashe wrote that he 'professed a willingness to give up all his wives but one and said that he truly wished to follow Jesus. He has been very regular in coming and keeps the Sabiti (Sunday).' His *mmandwa* was baptized later in the year, as were also Robert Munyaga, the king's gate-keeper, Nuwa Walukaga, the faithful blacksmith, and 'the great jolly giant', Isaya Mayanja, Sembera's master, who had for so long been undecided. In June Ashe wrote: 'I am glad to say Duta has returned. I hope that he may be kept.'

The process was still going on, but the detachment of the converts was more complete, and they were responding to more radical demands in their discipleship. When the next crisis came they were not found wanting.

The rest of the story is so well known that there is no need to repeat here more than the barest outline. After Mutesa's death on 9 October 1884, the chiefs were restrained from the usual outbreak of slaughter and pillage, but early in the new year they gave vent to their animosity in an attempt to terrorize the young boys who were attached to the mission. Yusufu Kakumba,[19] Nuwa Serwanga and little Yusufu Lugalama were seized, together with the faithful Sara Nakima and her baby, and led to the execution ground on the edge of Mpimerebera Swamp. There Sara was reprieved, and Freddy Kidza, who accompanied the captain of the guard and made a bold confession, escaped only through the tolerance of his master. But the three boys were mutilated and burned to death. As to whether they sang the popular hymn, *Killa siku tuusifu*, on their way to execution the evidence of the witnesses was doubtful, but Ashe says that Serwanga was the kind of young man who might have done so. At the same time Mwanga sought to arrest Henry Duta, as the leading Christian teacher, but he escaped and hid himself on his family estate, changing his name for concealment from Dutamaguzi to Kitakule.

This event produced an immediate increase in the number of those seeking baptism in both churches. The Anglican Church was now well organized for emergency, making inspired use of the natural structure of 'clusters' which was already there, and appointing twelve, who were the heads of such households, to be the church council. The first members were Nikodemo Sebwato, Zakaliya Kizito Kisingiri and Paulo Nsubuga Bakunga, who had the establishments of considerable chiefs; Sembera Mackay and the grave-faced Tomasi Semfuma, who led the very numerous congregation in the home of Isaya Mayanja at Kasengeji; Nuwa Walukaga and Shem Bekokoto, who together led another large cluster at Natete; Freddy Kidza, Henry Wright Duta and Samwili Mukasa, who had households quite close to the mission; Mika Sematimba and Robert Munyaga, each of whom had a considerable group of pages to look after in the palace itself.

In October 1885 Bishop Hannington, approaching by the direct eastern route, was murdered in Busoga, and, for protesting against this crime, Joseph Mukasa Balikuddembe, who had for so long been the leader of the Roman Catholic Church, was beheaded and his body burned. The missionaries were in grave danger and were saved only by a timely warning from Princess Nalumansi. All 'readers' were now forbidden to go to the mission, but continued to do so by night. At the end of May 1886, persecution broke out afresh. Between 25 May and 3 June at least thirty-two Christians were martyred, most of them on a great pyre at Namugongo. Probably much greater numbers were killed in the country districts. Besides the martyrs, many Christians were cruelly punished. Honorat Nyonyintono, now the major-domo at the palace, was shamefully mutilated; Apolo Kagwa, the assistant store-keeper, was severely gashed and beaten by the Kabaka Mwanga; and Nikodemo Sebwato was publicly flogged by his old master the Katik-kiro. Tomasi Semfuma was only saved from death because Mackay redeemed him with two tusks of ivory. Yet in the next few months the rate of baptisms increased as never before. The places of the three members of the Council who had been martyred were filled by others, and the church carried on. They soon had to learn to stand alone and make their own responsible decisions; for within twelve months O'Flaherty, Ashe and Mackay had all left the country, and Cyril Gordon and Robert Walker who replaced them remained only a year before they too were expelled.

As a result of the persecutions the church had become a well-organ-ized underground movement, with a system of secret communications and escape routes; and any underground movement is an incipient political party. The men who were responsible for its leadership and preservation were sub-chiefs or palace *batongole*, which is to say they were candidates for senior chieftainships. This meant that they were, potentially, military commanders, and the two churches between them were capable of putting two thousand armed men into the field. Revolu-tion against the Kabaka was always difficult in Buganda, and went against the grain, but it was possible, at least in the early years of a new reign. Meanwhile the Arabs throughout East Africa were organizing themselves for a desperate bid to win domination and expel the European powers, and in Buganda they prepared for a *coup d'état*.[20] On his side, Mwanga had an implacable determination to be absolute master in his kingdom,[21] and he now set about a monstrous attempt to rid the country at one stroke of all the Christian and Moslem leaders. Events were moving rapidly towards a show down. The church leaders decided to act responsibly; and in that context responsible action meant force of arms. A coalition of Moslem and Christian parties drove Mwanga from his throne.

It is not easy, after this span of time, to perceive, beyond the mere facts, the feeling of these events. But Captain Macdonald, Acting Commissioner for Sir Gerald Portal, describing something occurring five years later, has given a glimpse of one of the chiefs in action which well conveys the quality of these Christian leaders. Writing of Nikodemo Sebwato, then the Sekibobo, who had been regarded as the senior member of the church council since its formation in 1885, he wrote:

> 'With this stern old Waganda chief, it was like a return to the ancient Covenanting days in Scotland: for, every evening, the day's work closed with a prayer-meeting conducted by the Sekibobo in person, and always largely attended by his followers. The discipline he maintained in his contingent was particularly good and he carried out my orders in the spirit, not merely in the letter'.[22]

The next round, however, was won by the Arabs. Kiwewa, the new Kabaka, was replaced by their candidate, Kalema; the last of the missionaries were driven from Buganda; and the Christian refugees fled across the border into the kingdom of Ankole.

They were soon planning to regain control of Buganda. In order to legitimize their campaign they sent Ham Mukasa and others to Mwanga offering to restore him to the throne. The messengers went on to visit Mackay, who urged them not to go to war in coalition with the Roman Catholics, but this advice only annoyed them. When Stanley, returning from the Emin Pasha relief expedition, passed through Ankole, Samwili Mukasa and Zakaliya Kizito approached him to ask for help, but he refused to be embroiled in a civil war. So, once again, they made their own responsible decision, and, calling in the help of Stokes, the old missionary now turned trader, they fought their way back in a series of engagements and by March 1890 had won the political control of Buganda, with Mwanga as their puppet on the throne. It was after this victory that the Anglicans obtained the commanding site on Namirembe Hill as their headquarters.

But the coalition between the Roman and the Anglican parties began to break up, their natural disunity aggravated by the rivalry of the European powers that were then scrambling for Africa. Lugard's inflexible determination to succeed in securing the control of Uganda for the Imperial British East Africa Company, introduced new and higher stakes into the gamble, and in January 1892 the 'French' and 'English' parties, as they called themselves, were at war. In the battle of Mengo,

Sembera Mackay was killed and Tomasi Semfuma seriously wounded, but the Anglicans won the day. After two months' confused negotiation a settlement was reached whereby the Anglican leaders were established in the greater part of Buganda, the Roman Catholics in Buddu, and the Moslem minority sandwiched between them in Gomba, Busuju and Butambala.

The great chieftainships were all in the hands of well-known Christian leaders. Apolo Kagwa was Katikkiro and Stanislas Mugwanya, the Roman Catholic, was Kimbugwe. Other Anglican county chiefs were: Paulo Nsubuga Bakunga, county chief of Kyadondo; Yona Waswa, county chief of Singo; Nikodemo Sebwato, of Kyagwe county; Zakaliya Kizito Kisingiri, of Bulemezi county; Yoswa Kate Damulira, of Busiro county. Alexis Sebbowa, the Roman Catholic, was county chief of Buddu. These same men were the leaders and counsellors of their church. They have been criticized by a later generation for such un-spiritual use of temporal power; British administrators, even of those early days, deplored this gross confusion of church and state. Certainly such a beginning leaves a heritage of grave problems for any church. Yet perhaps these words of Dietrich Bonhoeffer are the truest comment that can be made on their decisions:

'Some seek refuge from the rough-and-tumble of public life in the sanctuary of their own private virtue. . . . Only at the cost of self-deception can they keep themselves pure from the defilement incurred by responsible action. . . . Who stands his ground? Only the man whose ultimate criterion is not in his reason, his principles, his con-science, his freedom or his virtue, but who is ready to sacrifice all these things when he is called to obedient and responsible action in faith and exclusive allegiance to God. The responsible man seeks to make his whole life a response to the question and call of God.'

If that is true, then the Buganda Church was beginning to become responsible.

NOTES

1. C. T. Wilson, Letter to Headquarters, *C.M.I.* 1878, p. 484. (The *italics* are mine.)
2. Thoonen, *Black Martyrs*, p. 50.
3. Ernest Millar, Article in *Uganda Notes*, Jan. 1913, p. 20.
4. 'Livinhac I love. He and I have many long walks, talking of the deep things of God—those delightful things that refresh the spirit. And O, the spirit needs to be refreshed in this dry parched land. We take a mutual pleasure in each other's company.' Letter from O'Flaherty, 25 Dec. 1881.
5. Thoonen, op. cit., p. 57 note.

6. Thoonen, ibid., p. 61.

7. MS. Diary of George K. Baskerville, 26 Mar. 1893.

8. 'Autobiography of Ham Mukasa', published in 1st (1904) edition of *The Wonderful Story of Uganda* by J. D. Mullins.

9. *Mackay of Uganda*, p. 154.

10. C. W. Pearson, Letter, 7 Jan. 1880, in *C.M.I.* 1880, p. 418.

11. *C.M.I.* 1883, pp. 546, 551; 1884, p. 219.

12. Thoonen, op. cit., p. 72.

13. *C.M.I.* 1886, p. 637.

14. Not to be confused with Henry Wright Duta Kitakule, who was at that time in Zanzibar.

15. The word *mmandwa* is better translated 'spirit-medium'.

16. P. O'Flaherty, Letter in *C.M.I.* 1883, pp. 551-2.

17. P. O'Flaherty, Letter, 1 June 1883, in *C.M.I.* 1884, p. 220.

18. R. P. Ashe, *Two Kings of Uganda* (1889), p. 132.

19. It is strange that later accounts, and the official memorial of their death in Namirembe Cathedral, give Kakumba's Christian name as Ma·ko (*Uganda J.*, vol. 15 (1951), p. 88). Yet both Ashe and Mackay, writing at the time, called him Yusufu, Mackay actually remarking on the strange fact that two boys had the same name (*C.M.I.* 1885, p. 715; Ashe, *Two Kings*, p. 127). Sir Apolo Kagwa also agrees in one place that there were two called Yusufu but is confused over the name Ma·ko (*C.M.I.* 1903, p. 525; cp. *Ebika* 1949 ed., p. 125).

20. Roland Oliver, *The Missionary Factor in East Africa* (1952), pp. 101-8.

21. The Baganda gave Mwanga the cognomen *Kitatta*, from the proverb, *Ekitatta Mwima tekimumalako nte*—'Short of killing a Muhima you'll never get his cattle': meaning that Mwanga's attitude to every party that tried to control Buganda was, 'Over my dead body.'

22. J. R. L. Macdonald, *Soldiering and Surveying in British East Africa* (1897), p. 266.

3

The Church in Leading Strings

FOURTEEN years is a short time in the life of a church. And yet within so brief a span the Buganda Church had reached, if not maturity, at least a real responsibility towards God and society. Bishop Tucker, describing the strength of the church at the beginning of 1893, wrote:

'There were those moving in and out daily amongst us whose faith in Christ had been tested and tried in times of fierce persecution, and whose lives had for years past been given up to the service of their Master. . . . They had given full proof of their ministry—they knew their Bibles. They knew something of their Prayer Book—something of Church order and history. . . . A further indication of progress which pressed itself upon my notice immediately on my arrival in Uganda was the deepened sense of responsibility evidently entertained by the members of the Church Council with regard to their office and work.'[1]

After such a beginning, what might not happen in the second fourteen years? In 1904, Victor Buxton, the first member of the Home Committee of the Church Missionary Society to visit Uganda, was present at a conference of missionaries in Mengo and reported their discussion on the strength of the church.

'A good deal was said on the one hand on their unfitness on the whole for bearing responsibility; they were "still mere children", as one leading missionary remarked. Another drew attention to the prevailing lack of truthfulness, and to the fact that comparatively few could be thoroughly trusted in financial matters. . . . Of those sent out and scattered over the country a considerable number—including some, even, of the ordained men—had become listless and inactive in the work committed to them. And it was urged on these grounds that higher education and a period of further training were needed before the Christians of the country could be entrusted with the management of their own church affairs.'[2]

Whether things were really as bad as the missionaries supposed is a matter for our further investigation. They had perhaps forgotten, as missionaries often do, that Christ builds his Church on very shaky saints; that, for example, the convert who had once 'proved to be a scheming rogue of a loose character' had become Henry Duta, the pillar of the church and Pilkington's right-hand man in the translation of the Bible; and that Firipo Mukasa, who was often unfaithful to his wife, had, with her, stood alone, in 1884, when all other converts fled. Yet the very fact that such things could be said about the same church shows that, within the second fourteen years, some impulse of retro-action had been introduced into the situation. Was it simply the natural decline of a second-generation church which had outgrown its spiritual strength, or was there some new factor setting in motion a tide that flowed counter to the movement towards responsibility which had so far been unimpeded?

Of course, the political triumph of Christianity brought its train of nominal adherents. The church was contending with temptation in that new dimension of moral choice which we have illustrated from the testimony of Ham Mukasa. With an eye on the spiritual casualties rather than on the victories the Rev. George Baskerville, one of the new missionaries who arrived with Bishop Tucker at the end of 1890, wrote two years later:

> 'I am hoping that another year will see great spiritual advances in the church here. It sadly needs cleansing, especially with regard to drunkenness and immorality; many of our people get drunk at times, and many make a regular practice of it each evening. . . . There is another thing, too, which is not as it should be, and that is that no one seems to *know* that they are saved; they hope so; they do not seem ever to have realized that it is possible to know.'[3]

Towards the end of 1893 several of the missionaries were burdened by a similar dissatisfaction, and their thoughts were clearly turning towards the hope of some spiritual revival of the sort that was already familiar in the evangelical churches of Europe and America, and was at that time specially associated with the missions of Moody and Sankey. In December 1893 Baskerville was reading *What hath God wrought?*, a book describing an evangelistic tour undertaken by George Grubb, the special missioner of the Keswick Convention, in Ceylon, South India and Australasia. At the same time his friend George Pilkington, after months of deep disillusionment, was taking a holiday on Kome Island and reading a revival tract by David, the Tamil evangelist from Colombo, who had received the 'baptism of the Holy Ghost' through contact with the Salvation Army in 1887. He returned to Mengo with the testimony of his own spiritual renewal, and this stirred the small group of missionaries at the capital to launch a ten days' 'mission', at which they spoke to the daily congregations on the fulness of the Spirit and invited their hearers to 'accept life'. A sense of shame and failure had been crystallized by the incident of one, Musa Gyabuganda, who had publicly announced that 'this religion of yours is no good. I sin as much as ever I did. I want you to give out my name in church as one going back to heathenism.' During the next few days hundreds confessed a like failure and accepted the gift of spiritual power. The movement then spread to the outstations. Baskerville wrote from Ziba, in Kyagwe county, on the last day of 1893:

'Praise God, the blessing has come on here. Last Sunday Crabtree had a solemn time at the prayer meeting. Timoteo, the local chief, came to him to ask what this holding up of hands meant; he professed to have life, but begged not to be urged to make a public profession. However, today he was one of the first to stand up.'

The immediate result, and the most lasting, of this revival was the impulse it gave to ordinary Christians to offer themselves as teachers and evangelists. This was no new thing, but the stirring up of an old gift. It had been the constant refrain of the heads of the Christian groups in the early days that their pupils and followers must be witnesses of the Gospel. Cyril Gordon records how he learned from Mika Sematimba and others what was the heart of the teaching that had been given them by Nuwa Walukaga and Robert Munyaga during the last months before their martyrdom.

'They showed the young men whom they taught the words in Luke xix. 20. "And another came, saying, Lord, behold thy pound, which I have kept laid up in a napkin." They made their comments on the words thus:—"Here was a man who had work given him to do and did not do it; we who teach you give you work to do. Teach and tell others about God, and Jesus Christ his Son. Do this work constantly and do not neglect it." '[4]

Bishop Tucker had noted the same spontaneous propagation in the church on his first arrival in 1890.

'No sooner was a reading sheet mastered than at once the learner became a teacher. It was the same with the Gospels; every fact noted, every truth mastered, was at once repeated to groups of eager enquirers. It was a most touching sight to see little groups scattered about here and there in the church, each of which had in its centre a native teacher who was himself at other times in the day an eager learner.'

The decision to move out from the capital into the country districts came not from the missionaries but from the African church-leaders. In the early months of 1892 thirty-seven of the chiefs were asking that missionaries might live with them on their country estates in order to help them to build up local churches.[5] Towards the end of that year Baskerville wrote in his journal, 'Personally I have no wish to leave Mengo.' But Nikodemo Sabwato had decided that work should be opened up in Kyagwe county, over which he had just been appointed county chief, or *Sekibobo*; he persuaded the council to invite the missionaries to undertake it, and Baskerville was one of those chosen.[6]

The revival, therefore, only fanned a flame that was already burning, and renewed in ordinary Christians the impulse to offer themselves as evangelists. On the following Easter Sunday thirteen young men were sent out to the islands of the lake by the church council, which undertook to support them. Every month 'missionary meetings' were organized by the council at which some evangelists reported on their work and called for fresh recruits. Within one year of the beginning of the revival, 260 new evangelists were at work, occupying 85 stations, of which twenty were beyond the borders of Buganda. The number of catechumens in the Anglican Church had risen from 170 to 1500.

The outreach of the Buganda Church during the next twelve years was an amazing demonstration of responsibility, which the members of that missionary conference in 1904 had perhaps forgotten when they passed their strictures on the church. It needs to be remembered and set over against the account of spiritual decline, which is also a part of the whole story. But it is always hard for the assessors of missions to realize that a church can be so strong and so weak at the same time.

The islands were the first fields to be occupied, but as early as 1894 the king of Koki, a small principality lying between Buganda and Ankole, appealed to the church council for teachers, and four evangelists were sent under the leadership of a lame man called Mikaeri. At about the same time Busoga in the east was entered by Nuwa Kikwabanga and Yoswa Kiwavu, while Petero Nsubuga and Sedulaka Makwata went westwards to the kingdom of Toro. In 1895, when these two returned to appeal for more men, Apolo Kivebulaya went back with them, and a year later he and Sedulaka expanded work already begun by Petero at Mboga in the Congo.

Two Baganda evangelists had been planted by A. B. Fisher in Bunyoro as early as 1896, but it was not till 1898 that Tomasi Semfuma,

1. One of the *Masiro*, or shrines of the dead kings

2. The dwelling-place of the *lubaale* of one of the clans

3. A pastorate church

4. The pastor and catechists of one pastorate

who had previously been in Koki, was sent to lead the work at Masindi. He was that servant of the princess whom Mackay had redeemed from Mwanga's clutches twelve years before.

The older generation of Christians had always felt indebted to the kingdom of Ankole which had given them sanctuary during their years of exile, and in 1898 Apolo Kagwa, the Katikkiro, applied to the church council, and two evangelists were sent there. After a few months they came back to report failure. Then Yoswa Kate Damulira, county chief of Busiro, sent two of his own men as evangelists; but they also were beaten back by the champions of the *balubaale*. In 1899, however, two more Baganda, called Firipo and Andereya, were sent, and this time they stayed.

In 1900 Semei Kakunguru, one of the most notable Christian chiefs of his day, who had since 1895 attained a remarkable influence on the northern marches of Buganda, and had helped to capture the fugitive Kabaka Mwanga in April 1899, was authorized to open up and administer the Bukedi country between the Nile and Mount Elgon, and at once set about the evangelization of that people with the assistance of Andereya Batulabadde, a lay-reader. At the same time Benyamini, another lay-reader, began his long ministry at Budaka, where Kakunguru had made his headquarters. In 1906 six Baganda evangelists reached out to Gondokoro in the Sudan, fulfilling in strange reverse the dream of evangelization which General Gordon had dreamed in that outpost thirty years before.

The spirit of passionate service which inspired these African missionaries is one of the marvels in the annals of the younger churches. Though members of the dominant tribe, which was at that time providing the chiefs and agents through whom the Protectorate government was administering the outlying areas of Uganda, these men lived in poverty, housed like the lowliest peasants, in order to demonstrate the ways of Christ. Often they endured bitter persecution. In 1902 all but one of the eighteen evangelists in Bunyoro had been killed by sleeping sickness. At a great missionary meeting in Mengo, Henry Wright Duta explained that it was unthinkable that the church council should send anyone into such danger, so they were appealing for volunteers. He reminded his hearers that, in the past, Buganda had often raided Bunyoro, killing men and carrying off slaves. 'Now', he said, 'we go to take them the Gospel which makes them free, and we should not forget that we owe them many lives.' More than three times the number required volunteered to go. From the diary of Apolo Kivebulaya, who

E

was to spend nearly forty years in Toro and in the Congo forests, comes this prayer which expresses the spirit of many of these men.

'O God our Father and his Son Jesus Christ and Holy Spirit bless men in the land, in the forests, the lakes and the mountains, where You have enabled me to pass to do your work for You among your people. Grant me to be loved by You and to be loved by your people. Amen.'

Such a story of expansion springing from revival does not, on the face of it, suggest a church in decline. It is not, however, the whole story, for expansion breeds its own problems. If we are to discover the factors which were working counter to the development of responsibility in the church we must select one area for more detailed examination in order to see what was taking place below the surface.

In response to the request from Nikodemo Sebwato and the church council, George Baskerville and W. A. Crabtree opened the first of the outstations in Kyagwe on 15 February 1893, on Kikusa hill at Ziba, on the main road from Mengo to the Nile crossing, the place where Stanley had camped just before his second encounter with Mutesa only eighteen years before. Hitherto the Gospel had been preached in a cosmopolitan environment where people were comparatively unrooted and accustomed to change. Now it was going to the deep country where men lived on their clan lands according to the traditional patterns of rural life, and the over-riding realities were food and the family and the ancestral spirits.

Every area has its own peculiar problems, and south Kyagwe was marked by idiosyncrasies which are operative even to the present day. Kyagwe was not part of the original Buganda and its population has always contained a mingling of tribes. Heavily forested and fertile, it attracted Banyoro and Bakedi from the north, Basoga from the east, and in the south both customs and language had been heavily influenced by the Bavuma islanders. This mixed population had a reputation for insubordination against their chiefs, and at the time when the mission was opened at Ziba, the wide Mabira Forest had for a year been the haunt of the *Futabangi*, or 'hemp-smokers', a considerable rebel movement intent on restoring the old religion.

There were already several factors that were bound to make a deep rooting of the church in that soil difficult. It has always been a somewhat disrupted society, crossed by the trade paths between the lake-shore harbours and the capital. Fishermen and fish-traders do not settle long in one place. Markets along the deeply indented southern shore accustomed the people to movement and change, and the population developed a high proportion of roving hawkers and fair-ground types. Simple agriculture was almost everywhere supplemented by fishing, hunting and trading, and these three occupations have greater hazards than agriculture, in a country with a regular rainfall, and are, therefore, more deeply associated with magic and the old religion. It was not surprising that the missionaries met more resistance in south Kyagwe than in many other places, nor that the people there were a prey to those suspicions of Christianity which have recurred throughout the centuries, even repeating the rumour that Christians meet together to eat human flesh.

And yet, eleven days after their first arrival, Baskerville recorded that they had a congregation of two hundred at their Sunday service and five received Communion. This surprising fact is a reminder that the missionaries were not, in the strict sense, pioneers. The church was already there before them in the persons of a large number of Christian chiefs. These men were mostly new arrivals, for under the recent settlement by which Buddu county was allotted to the Roman Catholics, the Anglican, Nikodemo Sebwato, who had been county chief of Buddu, had now changed places with Alexis Sebbowa, the Roman Catholic chief of Kyagwe, and most of the sub-chieftainships had undergone a similar exchange.

Under Sebwato there were at that time six district chiefs, known by the official titles of *Namutwe, Namfumbambi, Katenda, Mulondo, Omunywa* and *Mutoro*.[7]

When Baskerville started work in Kyagwe, the *Katenda*, who lived at Ziba, was Timoteo Nkangi, who had helped Cyril Gordon in his translation work before the exile in Ankole. The *Namfumbambi*, at Mpumu, ten miles to the west, had long ago been Alexander Kadoko, one of the martyrs. Now the office was given to Eli Njiri, a lay-reader of the diocese. The *Mulondo*, whose headquarters at Bulondoganyi was forty miles to the north, was none other than Samwili Mukasa Naganafa, who had succeeded Semei Kakunguru in that office.

Under each of these district chiefs were from six to eight *Muluka*, or parish chiefs, though in those days, before the administration had been tidied up into a neat, hierarchical pattern, it was not unusual to find that a *muluka* chief who lived in one district was answerable to the chief in charge of another district. A glance at Baskerville's sketch-map will show how many of the *muluka* chiefs in south Kyagwe had Christian names.

The missionaries worked, at first, entirely through these chiefs, regarding them as the natural leaders of the church, as indeed they were. They had the same functions as had been exercised by the heads of the cluster-households in the capital. Bishop Tucker recognized and set his seal on this state of affairs when he ordained the first six deacons in the Buganda Church a few months after Baskerville went into Kyagwe. Of the six, four had some sort of chieftainship. Nikodemo Sebwato was the Sekibobo of Kyagwe, and Zakaliya Kizito Kisingiri the Kangawo of Bulemezi; and Bishop Tucker wrote of the appointment of Yonasani Kaidzi and Yairo Mutakyala that they 'have the country within the limits of their respective chieftainships in which their work of teaching will be carried on.'[8]

Almost at once, Baskerville arranged for Timoteo Nkangi, the *Katenda*, to be the regular preacher at Ziba on Sunday afternoons. Then, three weeks after his arrival there, he wrote in his journal:

> 'Last Sunday I went out in the afternoon to a small neighbouring chief to hold a service at his place. We had 23 people present. The place is about half an hour off from here. He talks of building a small church so that all his people can meet regularly each week. One of us will go over as often as possible. We wish to do the same with other neighbouring chiefs.'

This plan was soon put into operation and every afternoon of the week was spent in visiting a different chief who was expected to call his people together for a service. Nor did their responsibility end there, for if they were at all established in the faith, the chiefs would undertake the regular teaching of their people. On 18 July 1893, Baskerville wrote:

> 'We had a nice little gathering at Nansambu's (at Bulaji) this afternoon and the people gave us a warm greeting. The Nansambu (Yokana Gabili) must be an energetic teacher for the bulk of our catechumens come from his place. Nearly all the others come from Semu (Kiwanuka), the Mulwanyi.'

A week later, on the way home from a longer journey to Nkakya, near the lake, Baskerville called at Nampanyi hill where the chief was called Misaka.

> 'I was very encouraged by what I saw at this place. Misaka had only been there about two months, and before he came scarcely anyone could read at all; now I saw about 200 or 300 gathered together, one batch learning letters, another the Commandments and others the Gospel, and I was particularly sorry not to be well enough to speak to them. Today I have just heard of 130 readers at a place to

which I hope to go next Monday. It is some 2½ hours off to the north-east. The name of the chief is Seruti and his place is called Buikwe.'

It is clear from these and many other references that the missionaries did not instigate these activities but used what was already there. It was the church itself which was in action, and its spiritual leaders were the chiefs. As soon as he was ordained deacon, Nikodemo Sebwato transferred his headquarters from its usual place at Mukono, near the county boundary closest to the capital, to a new site at Ngogwe, two miles from Ziba, and the following spring the mission itself moved there to be with him. From that time onwards the Sekibobo was a constant help, not only in regular preaching, but in many practical ways. Baskerville's journals are full of references to him.

'Nikodemo and I were from morning to night in the church, superintending final touches, and not only so, but carpentering ourselves, making seats, etc.'

'The Sekibobo is opening a market tomorrow which, if it succeeds, will be a great boon to me and save much expense in the way of meat.'

'Last year the collection in church amounted to Rs. 455 odd, but it is only fair to say that the great bulk of this was derived from a tusk of ivory brought by the Sekibobo.'

In February 1895 Nikodemo went off to the war against Bunyoro, but contracted pleurisy and came home to die. Baskerville's account of his end reveals the deep personal friendship which existed between them.

'The dear old man is gone from us to the Higher Service. It was so unexpected. I can hardly hold my pen, and feel worn out. We did all we knew but the trouble settled down on the lungs and at the last he could scarcely speak. On Tuesday the 26th I went down about 3.0 p.m. and found him in the garden behind his sleeping house; he seemed so glad to see me and fondled my hand. He tried for a long time to make himself understood; he had something on his mind. At last he was understood—he wanted, while I was there, to hand over a tusk of ivory for the Church expenses. He had sent off, some time before, men to hunt as our funds were low. News came that the hunters had been successful just a few days before his death, and he told me with such glee, but grieved over the coldness of his brother chiefs in the matter of giving. We took him back to bed and put on a mustard poultice, and then Blackledge went back and cooked him some arrowroot, of which he took a little. I came away about 7.0 and at 10.30 we heard wailing—we knew he had gone.'

His loss was a most serious blow to the church in south Kyagwe. Later the work in north Kyagwe suffered a similar setback; when

Samwili Mukasa Naganafa went to take up his appointment as Kangawo of Bulemezi, the people said, 'The Church at Nakanyonyi is dead.' For a church so dependent on the chiefs is very vulnerable, as is Ganda society in general. Even at the present time, in spite of a highly developed administration, it is remarkable how much the functioning of the social services and the vigour of local society still depend upon the mere presence of the chief. But in those days the chiefs were frequently called away, and the whole of society disrupted, by the succession of wars which followed one after the other.

Baskerville's arrival in Kyagwe coincided with the ending of the war against Buvuma Island, when for the second time a European had indulged his taste for adventure by helping the Baganda to defeat these islanders. Four months later the Moslems, exasperated because Sir Gerald Portal's new land settlement had awarded additional counties to the Roman Catholics but none to them, threatened revolt and implicated Selim Bey, the faithful commander of Emin Pasha's force of Nubian veterans, whom Lugard had enlisted in the service of the I.B.E.A. Company. Baskerville wrote then, 'Nearly everyone is away just now', and two months later he was still complaining:

> 'No one comes to work on my house these days. It is provoking, for very little remains to be done and a few men could finish it off in a week. This proves that as yet we are very far from getting hold of the lower classes. The chief being away, no one works.'

There followed a series of expeditions against Bunyoro in 1894 and 1895; Kabaka Mwanga's final revolt in Buddu in 1897; and, soon after, the very serious Sudanese mutiny centred at Luba's fort in Busoga, in the attack on which George Pilkington was killed. In 1900 there was an expedition against the Nandi in Kenya, in which Samwili Mukasa Naganafa distinguished himself; and that year there was a resurgence of the old *Futabangi* insurrection in the forests of Kyagwe, with fighting in several places. In every one of these wars Kyagwe was disrupted by the continual marching of chiefs and their levies to and from the front.

In 1894 Samwili Mukasa Naganafa gave up his chieftainship as Mulondo in order to be trained for ordination (though the Katikkiro later persuaded him to take up office again). Others began to make the same choice, and the significance of their decision is that it represents the first growing apart of church and state in Buganda. The earliest hint of such a separation had appeared when the Christians fought their way back from Ankole in 1889, and there was tension between Nikodemo

Sebwato, as head of the church, and Apolo Kagwa, the new Katikkiro. This had not prevented Nikodemo and other members of the church council from holding major chieftainships, nor even from combining a chief's duties with ordination. From now on, however, the two callings are to diverge.

Both the African church and the mission recognized that this was necessary; but it is important to realize that their grounds for doing so were different. For the African church it was a purely pragmatic adjustment. There were evident difficulties in the way of a man being both a chief and a pastor or evangelist. They, therefore, accepted the fact that clergy, teachers and catechists had a ministry that ought to be separated from the affairs of state. They did not, however, identify *ministry* with church *leadership*, nor suppose that guidance and authority must necessarily rest in clerical hands. Even now there was no feeling that the leaders in the state should not also be the leaders of the church. On the other hand the new generation of missionaries, and Bishop Tucker in particular, came with thoroughgoing Anglican assumptions about the separation of ecclesiastical and secular leadership. Many of them shared also the impoverished conceptions of those days regarding the position of the laity in the church.

For the first fourteen years of the church's life there had never been more than a handful of missionaries in Buganda, with virtually no power to impose their will. The destiny of the church lay, humanly speaking, in the hands of the church council and other Christians in positions of secular leadership. But by 1904 there were 79 missionaries of the C.M.S. in Uganda, 83 of the White Fathers' Mission and 35 of the Mill Hill Fathers[9]; and, though they might make no overt use of it, they were supported by the authority of the Colonial Government. They enjoyed an almost limitless freedom to make, and carry out, their own schemes. The tension that such missionaries must find in their relationships with tried African leaders was evident quite early. Baskerville, writing in November 1892, described how he discovered that the church council had, on their own account, been debarring offenders from the Holy Communion without consulting the missionaries. After explaining to them the gravity of this, he wrote: 'Our meeting with the elders on Saturday did a lot of good, and I think they will not be so independent in future.' The old type of African church-leadership could not for long be maintained in partnership with this new missionary assertiveness, and it was steadily replaced by a new leadership that was both more clerical and more filial.

Bishop Tucker himself it is true, tried in vain to persuade his fellow-missionaries to accept a constitution by which they would have become equal fellow-workers with their African colleagues under the same legislative body. Yet even he took it for granted that the responsible leadership of the church must be largely identical with its clerical ministry, and that in setting aside men to be catechists, lay-readers and pastors in the church, he was building up the real hierarchy of authority by which the church was to be led and governed. It has often been pointed out that one reason for the phenomenal growth of the Uganda Church has been the exact parallelism of the ministerial hierarchy of the Anglican and Roman Churches to the political structure which had evolved in the country. But the point that has generally been missed is that the very idea of separate hierarchies of church and state was a foreign conception, and implied a dualism which Ganda thought has only accepted with the greatest reluctance.

The change from the old to the new church-leadership was, however, made more gradual by the quality of the first generation of African clergy. This remarkable group of men, in their social status, their experience and their relationship to the Europeans, stood nearer to the old, chieftainly church-leaders than to the new, catechist type that was to succeed them. At first, as we have seen, four out of the six were in fact chiefs; both the others were sons of chiefs. The next group, ordained in 1896, included Samwili Mukasa, another of the 'perpetual deacons', who was later to be the Kangawo; Batolomayo Musoke Zimbe, who had been a district chief; and Nuwa Kikwabanga, who had been chosen from among the Christians in exile to travel with Stanley from Ankole to the coast, and on his return journey had been Pilkington's Luganda teacher. Among the men ordained in 1899 was Tomasi Semfuma, who had been page to the princess Magali, and had been chosen, with the leading Roman and Anglican chiefs, to sign the agreement between the two factions on 3 February 1890. Though the other ordinands were distinct from the potential chiefs in that they had never been royal pages, and some of them had a poor reputation as warriors, neverthelss they belonged to the Christian *élite* whose qualification was that they had been among the refugees in Ankole in 1888.

The quality of these men is well illustrated in Yonasani Kaidzi, who, as much as Baskerville himself, *was* the church in south Kyagwe. As soon as he was ordained, he and his wife, Ketula, joined the mission at Ziba, and he emerges from Baskerville's diaries as an equal colleague and brother in the work. This is the more remarkable in view of the

paternalism of the missionary's relationship with all his boys and
catechists; but it is typical of a partnership which existed at that period
between the missionaries, the African clergy and the Christian chiefs,
and then disappeared from the story.[10] Itineration, preaching, Biblical
exposition, training of the catechists, these and other tasks were taken
by Kaidzi and Baskerville, a week each in turn. Only the baptism of
infants, who seem invariably to have been provokingly unmanageable
in Baskerville's hands, he relinquished entirely to Yonasani! There are
many references to the vitality and beauty of his sermons. The most
impressive testimony was given by Nikodemo Sebwato when Yonasani
was still comparatively young, and he, a man of over fifty, had been
virtually the head of the church. Preaching to a packed church at
Ngogwe, the old man had said, 'It was Kaidzi who broke me in and
taught me, coming to my house daily; and now, though older than he
and a bigger man, if he says a thing is not right or seemly, I listen—his
word is enough.'

But after the chiefs and Kaidzi, the main agents of the Gospel in
Kyagwe were the pupil-servants of Baskerville's household. At least six
boys accompanied the two missionaries on their first move to Ziba.
They included Firipo, who had been Baskerville's cook for two years,
and Nasanaeri Mulira, a lad of sixteen, whom he had recently begged
from his previous master who had since fallen in the Buvuma war.
There was another Mulira, Yakobo, and Aloni Muyinda and Silrasi
Aliwonya. Their duties could not have been arduous, but to each was
allotted his own particular tasks. Nasanaeri Mulira has recorded how
he was expected to sweep the yard in front of the house, and help
Firipo, the older boy, with the cooking, to wash his master's feet every
evening, and to carry his books when they went to church. He and the
other Mulira were enrolled in the baptism class immediately after their
arrival at Ziba, and baptized three months later. They were soon
encouraged to take their share in simple teaching in the daily classes
at the mission or in the enclosures of one of the neighbouring chiefs.

New members were soon added to the household. There was little
James Soka, who came voluntarily to live and work with them, and was
soon teaching others to read in the church every morning, and acting as
guide in their afternoon visits. There was Balunaba Kibate, who built
his hut near by and later became 'almost Salvation Army-ish in his ways
and methods', and Yusito Bakisula and Kironde, who were both
baptized on New Year's Day, 1895. Every day, after lunch, the 'family'
was collected for informal worship. Baskerville wrote: 'I have prayers

with the boys: hymn, reading round with exposition, and prayer. On Sundays we all choose hymns and have no reading.'

His affection for them was very strong. He notes in his diary, 'It is 7 years today since Firipo came to be my boy.' When another Firipo was killed in the Sudanese revolt at Luba's in 1897, he grieved over the loss almost as deeply as he did over his friend George Pilkington. When two of them were married, though they set up their homes near by, he writes: 'I feel a blank in my house without the boys, though they are still with me and working for me—but when one has been accustomed to see their beds occupied by them, now occupied by others, it is a miss [sic]'. 'Basika', as they called him, was like a father to them, and whatever he sent them to do they accepted as the call of God. Almost all of them were eventually put in charge of various village churches in south Kyagwe.

Nasanaeri Mulira records how, after his confirmation, he began teaching younger boys in the church at Kikusa, near Ziba. Then in September 1894 he was sent for three months to take charge of the church at Gulama, seventeen miles to the north-east, beyond Buikwe.

Aloni Muyinda was sent with a companion to a church close to one of the big shore markets where the Buvuma islanders come to sell fish and pottery. In a letter to Baskerville he says:

'Yesterday we went to the market to preach the words of God, and we implored the headman of the market (a man who levies a tax on all articles bought and sold for benefit of the lord of the soil) to seat the people, and he seated them all, about 500. The Bavuma sat in one company by themselves, and one of us preached to them, and the other to those of these parts. The Bavuma sat very well, and further, they said, "These words we accept," and they excel the Baganda to answer well.'

At another time this Aloni was sent to relieve James Soka, who was due to come in for a rest and further training. They were two Sundays together before James left. Next Sunday no one came at all; at last he got them together and said,

'Those who come here just for a walk, or because James was your friend, you come to see him, hear him—please do not come any more. But those who come to hear of Christ, come. I have the same book as James had, I preach the same Gospel. We do not want, "I am of James and I Aloni". James has gone, and I shall go, but James' Jesus has not gone, and he is also my Jesus.'

Next Sunday the church was full again.

Meanwhile, in the county of Singo, A. B. Fisher had, towards the end of 1893, devised a system of teaching centres, which he called 'synagogues'. Within a radius of twenty miles he had found as many sub-chiefs who undertook to build and maintain a reading-house in their precincts, to sell books, to collect their people for daily classes, and to come in with as many of them as possible to the central Sunday services at Mityana. The actual teaching in the synagogues, however, was undertaken by young men trained and sent out from Mityana. It was a combined operation by the Christian chiefs, as heads of local clusters, and the new young catechists.

After the impetus of the revival the same pattern was adopted elsewhere. On 20 March 1894 Baskerville wrote:

'After Easter I am to go itinerating for three or four months during which time Gordon will be here. I shall not, though, be much on the move, being a month in each place founding "synagogues" or reading rooms, at each of which are to be placed two teachers—one old and one young. The readers are to be changed every six months and they will teach six months and then be taught for six months in Mengo. Pilkington is going to do a similar work in the Islands and in Kyadondo, and Leakey in Bulemezi.'

That April the central church council at the capital inaugurated for the first time a fund for the maintenance of the teachers and catechists who were being sent out. At first each cost the church twenty-five rupees—less than £2 per year. This was raised mainly through gifts from the chiefs, but the revival had brought great enthusiasm and the congregations accepted their responsibility willingly. Baskerville, who was in the capital that Easter, described what took place.

'On Easter Sunday the people brought to the church a great amount of shells, cloth, bark-cloths, mats, and some 15 to 20 have gone out entirely supported by the Native Church. Many, in fact, are boys from sixteen to twenty, but generally speaking they have gone in pairs, one of each two being an older man.'

Later on, similar services of commission were a normal feature of the central churches in the outlying counties. Baskerville's diary for 3 September 1897 has this entry:

'We had a solemn service this morning to say farewell to 21 teachers going out to our outstations. . . . After the collection I read out the stations to which we were sending teachers, with the names of the teachers; as each name was read out the teacher stood up during a brief pause for silent prayer. I then spoke on the passage I had read. Then I asked all the congregation to stand up in prayer, while our brethren knelt; the native pastor commended them, and I followed, and then, sentence by sentence, we pronounced on them the Benediction, the whole congregation standing, repeating each sentence after us. Then all kneeling, we had one of Pilkington's beautiful (Luganda) hymns, a prayer for the Holy Spirit and for cleansing. May God bless each one.'

Within two years of his first arrival at Ziba, Baskerville had fifty teachers supported entirely by the Kyagwe church. He soon realized that the regular return to the centre to communicate and report was essential to the success of the method, and he called them in once a month. Nasanaeri Mulira recorded how gladly they 'returned to our own home at Ngogwe, bringing a great crowd of baptism candidates with us'. Each received his tiny salary, and there was a week-end of conference before they were sent out again. This consisted of:

'a prayer meeting on Saturday, the Sunday services, Conference on Monday morning, and devotional meeting in the afternoon; then some stay for the Missionary Meeting on Tuesday morning, when they tell us about their work.'

In order that these catechists might be prepared for taking greater responsibility, there quickly grew up a ladder of professional training. Robert Walker, now Archdeacon of the Anglican diocese, ran a training centre at the capital to which men were sent, successively, to qualify for the Certificate of Junior Catechist, Senior Catechist and Lay-reader— commonly known as the first, second and third letters. In 1901 numbers had grown so great that all Junior Catechists were trained in the district centres.

This professional ladder became, henceforth, the main, and almost exclusive, recruiting ground for the supply of ordained clergy. Undoubtedly most of them were tried and faithful men. But inevitably their standing, toward their own society and toward the missionaries, was different from that of the earlier African leaders. Towards the chiefs their relationship was that of protégés, not of equals, yet they were expected to be their ecclesiastical counterparts. Their relationship to the missionaries was still fundamentally the same as when they had been their boys and pupils. Baskerville treated Kaidzi as an equal and a colleague; but Aloni Muyinda, who was ordained in 1900, was always his 'boy', and the delightful but dangerous paternalism of that household was extended into the relations between the missionary and the African clergy. They were 'still mere children'.

To match this ordered hierarchy of ministry there was a corresponding organization of the body of the church itself into a pyramid pattern. At the end of 1894 the whole country was divided into thirteen missionary districts; Kyagwe was divided into two districts, north and south, with centres at Nakanyonyi and Ngogwe respectively. Every little congregation in the district was to send one representative for every ten baptized adults (it later became every fifty communicants) to sit on the district church council; and every district was to send one representative for every hundred baptized adults to sit on the Mengo church council. In this way the members of the councils became primarily delegates, and any pastoral or paternal care over the Christians they represented became incidental. The democratic, representative principle had been fully introduced into the church, and was to prepare the way for its acceptance, many years later, in the state. But at the same time the principle of 'presbyterian' responsibility, which had been a truly indigenous insight from the earliest days, was lost.

It was, however, retained in a small degree, on the local level, by a resolution that every congregation of ten or more baptized adults was to choose six church-wardens, or *bakebezi*, whose duties were to clean and repair the church, to collect and administer the people's offerings, to teach, visit and preach the Gospel, to examine and select candidates for baptism, and to help the catechist who was sent out from the centre. They were to meet in council every Saturday after the daily service under the presidency of the catechist.

As the church in south Kyagwe expanded, Baskerville delegated more responsibility to the senior catechists who were appointed to such places as Ntenga, Buikwe, Gulama, Si and Mukono, where important sub-chiefs had their headquarters. He and Kaidzi attempted to celebrate Holy Communion at a different sub-centre every Sunday. In 1899 he wrote:

> 'We are getting some really good superintendents for our sub-districts now—two of them we feel can do all the preparation for baptism and from those districts we shall not in future call in the candidates here.'

In 1903 the number of clergy in south Kyagwe increased to four when Aloni Muyinda, who went to Toro, was replaced by Andereya Batulabadde, just recalled from Bukedi, while Yoeri Nakumanyanga, one of Baskerville's early catechists, who had succeeded Mulira at Gulama, was ordained deacon and posted to Mukono. This enabled Baskerville to delegate some of the central responsibilities of Ngogwe to two or three other 'pastorates'.

Within a few more years the pattern had hardened into the structure which has remained until the present day. There were the large missionary districts, later to be called Rural Deaneries, which were mainly coterminous with the political counties. These were subdivided into pastorates in the charge of African clergy, which generally coincided with the *gombolola* or sub-counties. Each pastorate contained from six to ten *miruka* (singular—*muluka*), which are best described as parishes, partly because the word gives English readers a true impression of their size, and partly because a parish, like a *muluka*, is a civil administrative district. It must be remembered, however, that in Buganda there have never yet been enough clergy for the parish to have its own parson. Finally, within each parish there were a number of small village churches coinciding roughly with the hamlets supervised by the *batongole* of the local landowners. Today, however, the parallelism between the ecclesiastical and civil administration is less exact, since the latter has grown and subdivided more rapidly than the church, so that now a pastorate will contain several *gombolola*, and so on.

So the process of building an entirely independent ecclesiastical organization was completed. Perhaps it was inevitable. It may only be the naivety of first-generation Christians to believe that their religious community and leadership can coincide with the secular. In the second generation of any church the sacred and profane worlds tend to part company. And yet, as the story unfolds, one cannot escape from the suspicion that the institution which emerged was not the authentic answer to the needs of the time made by a responsible church, but a pattern of preconceptions built up by architects from Europe.

To continue for a moment the architectural metaphor, the structure they created was a pyramid, or a series of arches, supporting one great arch. But a pyramid directs the eye always to the apex; and an arch leans upon its keystone. It was this absolute dependence upon the centre which was the mark, and the weakness, of the church of Buganda from the beginning of this century.

We have already seen that Baskerville soon realized, at Ngogwe, that the strength of the catechists depended upon their regular return to the centre for spiritual refuelling and maintenance. It was at the centre that the problems of the church must be faced and discussed by the delegates to the council. It was at the centre that the needs must be made known and new recruits enlisted for the work. And at the centre was the missionary. It was a very dependent church which had to face the many different factors which were combining to bring about decline. What were these factors?

In the first place some of the chiefs began to fall away from Christian living and support of the church. This was to be expected in men who were only nominally Christian. They usually started by transferring their allegiance from the Anglican to the Roman Church, or *vice versa*, but ended by drifting away from all Christian participation. This has a serious effect on their people. In June 1898 Baskerville wrote:

'We had a service this morning at Gulama, but only a very few people came. A lukewarm chief, a bit of a drunkard, and then a long *interregnum* before a new one was appointed, the old one having been placed elsewhere, then the new chief being a mere boy—all these things have combined to produce an empty church.'

Many of these lapses were bound to happen. But probably some of the chiefs fell away simply because they no longer carried the same responsibility for the life of the church as had once rested upon them.

The Europeanization of the church, also, antagonized those who were already affected by the crescendo of anti-white feeling which rose to a climax with the flight of Mwanga into Buddu in 1897. All the people round Nakanyonyi were in revolt at that time; in south Kyagwe the number of catechists dropped from sixty to twelve. Pilkington estimated that '90% of people in the country and 50% of people in the capital detested and disliked Europeans'; and Dr Albert Cook reported that the Katikkiro wrote 'rather a gloomy letter to Walker, saying he does not realize how serious a matter it is, and that the people hate and destest the Europeans. . . . The chiefs hate us because a Christian is expected only to have one wife and because no slaves are allowed, and the people hate us because they are obliged to carry loads and to make roads (Government levies) and because the old heathen customs are dying away.'[11] The combination of anti-colonial with anti-Christian sentiment is no new problem to the Buganda Church.

Lack of enthusiasm in the chiefs certainly made life much harder for the catechists. In the early days they went with 'neither purse nor scrip', taking simply what was offered them and accepting their hardships with humour. Baskerville mentions one who 'said to his companions, after a foodless day, "What is death like, because this is remarkably like it?"' But now they were established as a permanent ministry and they expected greater security. Their tiny salary, calculated on the assumption that they would be virtually the protégés of some chief, compared unfavourably with what was being offered elsewhere. In 1898 Baskerville says: 'The Government having found it necessary to employ Baganda in transport work, many, I am sorry to say, finding the pay much larger, have left their teaching work.'

A year later he had found some solution to the problem: 'At most places we are getting gardens given us and these we give to the teachers who can thus take their wives and families and settle down.'

In 1900 the Buganda African Government gave a small piece of ground to every teacher and church official, but obviously this could not be repeated perpetually. So, soon after, there was a serious lack of catechists and a falling away of quality in the men who offered themselves. In 1902 more than half the small churches in south Kyagwe had no catechists, and in 1905 the catechists in seven districts were on strike for double pay. Their grievance, however, was not only financial; it was a laymen's protest against the special prerogatives of the clerics—missionary and African. They objected to a collection for the British and Foreign Bible Society, which they thought was going to the missionaries, and also to the African clergy getting the Easter offerings. 'We understand now', they said, 'that this is the work of the clergy; *our* work is despised.'

Lapses of the chiefs and the falling off of catechists inevitably led to a serious decline among the ordinary adherents. For them the Christian life meant perpetually holding at bay the three constant temptations of drink, sexual laxity and magic, and the growth of material prosperity in the country enhanced the strength of these. With regard to all these temptations, the missionaries seemed always too ready to believe that evil had been vanquished, so that they were frequently being dismayed by the discovery that it was still there. In 1904 Baskerville reported with deep grief that the congregation at Katente, near Mpumu, was living in open immorality and opposition, refusing to come to Holy Communion, and two shrines of *balubaale* were still in full operation in south Kyagwe.

The church had also to contend with the tremendous social disruption caused by two other events. The first of these was the land settlement brought into force by the Agreement of 1900. Apart from the large estates allowed to royalty and the great chiefs, 8,000 square miles was divided among some 3,000 to 4,000 new landowners, most of whom were anxious to stake out their allotment in the vicinity of the *butaka* of their particular clan. Bishop Tucker described what happened in these words:

'Thus the game of "general post" went on merrily until the whole population was in movement. Streams of men, women, and children going east with all their household goods, cattle, sheep, goats, and

5. The interior of Makindu parish church

fowls, met similar streams going west. Evicted tenants from the north were able to greet their friends in a similar condition from the south.'[12]

But a far more devastating depopulation was on its way. In 1901 Dr Cook first identified the appearance of sleeping sickness in Uganda, for which there was at that time no cure, and in the next few years great areas were ravaged, especially in the islands and along the lake shore. In Kyagwe 14,000 died during 1902, and the island of Kome, which at one time was said to have a population of 10,000, was left with barely 500. Eventually the Government removed the entire population from the infected areas in order to stem the advance of the disease, and certain areas of south Kyagwe remained empty until about 1917. The effect upon the life of the church was very serious. In the Mugomba parish a man appeared, possessed by a spirit, who claimed to have a 'medicine' to cure the sickness. Many people gave up Christianity, saying, 'If Katonda (God) is powerful he will remove this plague, and then we will come back and read.'

And yet the terrible challenge found the living church ready to respond with heroism. Rachel Sebulimba and three other women of the Ngogwe congregation offered themselves in 1903 as evangelists to the condemned population of some of the islands. After a year all four returned and told of a great response to their preaching. Rachel went back for a second spell, contracted the sickness, and returned to the mainland to die. To an enquirer at Ngogwe she is reported to have said, 'My body hurts me very much but my spirit rejoices.' Bishop Tucker writes movingly of his first meeting with her, when she had been taken to Mengo Hospital to spend her last months under medical care.

'Some few months ago I was officiating in the Cathedral at Mengo. . . . The last communicants had returned to their places, and I was about to close the service, when from the extreme end of the building —a corner of the south aisle in which she had been sitting by herself —a woman advanced slowly up the nave. I waited wonderingly. As

---

6. George Baskerville and his household at Ziba, 1894

Back Row (right to left): Yusito Gwavu, valet and laundryman; Nasanaeri Mulira, assistant cook, later promoted steward; Yakobo Mulira; Yusito Bakisula, the new herdman; Musa Kabusemere, herdman; Kezekiya Disasi; Ibulayimu Kyagulanyi.
Centre Row: Esiteri Bakyerabidde, daughter of Tebuta, later wife of Gwavu; the Rev. George Baskerville; Aloni Muyinda, the head-boy.
Front Row: Enoka Kinywa, head cook; Zipola Tebuta, assistant cook; Agiri, wife of Disasi; Enoka Kategere; Musa Tabula, herdman.

she took her place, kneeling alone at the rail, Harry Wright Duta, who was assisting me, whispered in my ear, "It is Rakeri." . . . With a voice ill controlled through the emotion that welled within, I administered to her the emblems of the dying love of Our Lord and Saviour Jesus Christ. Slowly, and with dragging footsteps, she returned to her place, and with the Gloria in Excelsis and the Benediction the service came to an end.'[13]

It seems, perhaps, strange to us that in the year of Rachel Sebulimba's death the Missionary Conference, which Mr Buxton attended, should have accepted unchallenged the assertion by a 'missionary of wide experience' that 'the spirit of the Baganda had entirely changed and their qualities had gone down'.

We should recollect that it is easy, from the ring-side seat of a later generation, to see weakness and strength, decline and advance, existing side by side in one church, as they so often do in one Christian; but it is very hard, while standing in the dusty arena of the immediate struggle, to see more than one side of the truth; and that will probably be its most menacing aspect. Yet, however justly we excuse it, it is a very dangerous form of blindness. Failure to see where the strength of the Buganda Church lay and to believe in the responsibility of its leadership had gone a long way towards sapping that strength and fatally undermining that responsibility.

The most frightening fact of all is that this damage to the church was being done by as remarkable a group of missionaries as can be found in the annals of any mission field. The men who served the church in Uganda during the second fourteen years included leaders like Robert Walker, Cyril Gordon and Ernest Millar, quiet and humble men of heart whose greatness was none the less acknowledged by African chiefs and British administrators alike; pioneers of extraordinary initiative and strength such as A. B. Fisher, G. K. Baskerville, Clayton, Leakey and Lloyd; scholars such as John Roscoe the anthropologist, George Pilkington the Bible translator, and the other great linguists, Blackledge, Crabtree, Rowling and Maddox. There were Sir Albert and Lady Cook, who were to win world renown in the field of tropical medicine; Purvis and Borup, founders of the industrial mission; the pioneer educationists, Miss J. E. Chadwick, H. W. Weatherhead and C. W. Hattersley; and those other early women, Miss Furley, Miss Pilgrim, Miss Thomsett and Miss Browne. These are but a few of the names that should be remembered. It ill becomes a missionary of these latter days to find fault with predecessors of such calibre, or to condemn what was, essentially, a form of love. Many older Christians in Buganda say that they have not met so much love in later generations of missionaries. Yet theirs was a love which could not bear to take the same risks with the church that God had taken in 1886. It was protective and possessive; and so, like all possessive love, it damaged where it meant to bless. Having listened to the whole of that Missionary Conference of 1904 and seen a good deal of the church in Buganda, this was Victor Buxton's assessment:

> 'It is difficult to balance rightly the various causes to which this saddening change may be due, but at least it seemed evident that a policy of leading-strings had not been wholly successful and might easily be carried too far. A higher standard of diligence and faithfulness among catechists, teachers and pastors might perhaps be promoted if all were directly responsible to some central authority, whose right to supervise and direct they would recognize without question.'

In the next few years the missionaries made sincere attempts to carry this advice into effect. But the problems could no longer be eradicated by a few changes of organization or constitution. From now on two contrary factors were at work within the Buganda Church—the freely responding and inherent life, and the principle of tutelage, the 'policy of leading-strings'. The latter is seen most obviously in the continuation of missionary control, in one form or another, but it is not limited to that. The principle of tutelage in a church is revealed by any clericalism which cannot trust the laity with spiritual responsibility; by any bureaucracy in which every official is supervised by the man above him; by a centralization which only recognizes as part of the church's life those things that are initiated, supported and controlled from a central office; and by the imposition of 'extraneous' demands which do not touch the conscience of the local Christians. Above all, it expresses itself in attitudes of watchfulness, anxiety and pessimism. On the other hand, in spite of the demoralizing and inhibiting effect of this principle, the Buganda Church continued to exhibit also the marks of responsibility. African leaders were making important decisions, in affairs of state as well as of religion, by reference to the Word of God. The Cathedral built on Namirembe hill in 1901 was the symbol of a protracted effort and sacrifice undertaken by the whole church and maintained for two years. When that building was burnt in 1910, and £20,000 was needed for a new one, each Anglican chief undertook to contribute a third of his income for three years, and some continued to do so when that time was over. Sir Apolo Kagwa, the Katikkiro, and several other leading chiefs, continued to regard the church as their responsibility, drawing the Bishop's attention to any reduction in the number of adherents which their census returns revealed. And, however much the church might be beset by bewilderment or relapse, there were at all times great numbers of ordinary people in quite humble walks of life, able and willing to respond as Christians to the demands of their immediate situation.

The greatest service which Bishop Tucker rendered the Uganda Church was to believe in it; and this faith of his was often in conflict with the rest of the missionary body during the years when the leading strings were being woven. Today, in the continuing dialectic between free responsibility and the spirit of watchful tutelage, his courageous example points the way ahead.

NOTES

1. A. R. Tucker, *Eighteen Years in Uganda and East Africa* (1908), vol. i, pp. 235, 238.

2. *C.M.I.* 1905, p. 174.

3. Journal of G. K. Baskerville. MS. held by the present Bishop of Uganda, from which most of the quotations in this chapter are taken.

4. *C.M.I.* 1893, p. 511.

5. Bishop Tucker, Letter, 19 Apr. 1892, in C.M.S. archives.

6. Tucker, op. cit., vol. i, p. 255.

7. Besides its own individual title, every chieftainship may also be called by a name describing its relationship to the immediate overlord. So the *Namutwe* is the Sekibobo's *Mumyuka*, or second-in-command; the *Namfumbambi* is his *Sabaddu*, the head of the servants and chaplain in the old religion; the *Katenda* is his *Sabagabo*, and the *Mulondo* is his *Sabawali*. On the same system the different county chiefs are known as the *Sabaddu* or *Sabagabo*, etc., of the Kabaka; and at the other end of the scale each district chief has sub-chiefs under him who are his *Sabaddu*, *Sabagabo*, etc.

8. Bishop Tucker, Letter, 27 Jan. 1893, *C.M.I.* 1893, p. 508.

9. To counteract the impression, made in the time of the 'religious' war of 1892, that the Roman Catholics were all French, the Mill Hill Mission, representing St Joseph's Society for Foreign Missions founded in England by Cardinal Vaughan in 1866, was invited into Buganda. It opened its first station at Nsambya in 1895, and took responsibility for all work east of Kampala, while the White Fathers continued to work on the west.

10. R. H. Walker records that in the early 1890s the leaders of the African Church commonly addressed their missionary colleagues as *mwana watu*, literally 'my darling child', *Proceedings of the C.M.S.* 1897, p. 113.

11. Sir Albert Cook, *Uganda Memories* (1945), p. 67; and Journal Letter in *C.M.I.* 1897, p. 815.

12. Tucker, op. cit., vol. ii, pp. 260-1.

13. Tucker, ibid., vol. ii, p. 308.

4

The Period of Disengagement: 1905-1955

THE church in south Kyagwe, as we have seen, had some extraordinary setbacks to overcome. A naturally unstable society,
further disrupted by wars and the resettlement of land, and then
drastically reduced by sleeping sickness; a church weakened by the lapse
of Christian chiefs and the defection of catechists—these had already
caused many adherents to fall back into the old religion or to turn
towards Islam. As early as 1903 Baskerville noted that in many places
the Sunday congregation did not greatly exceed the number of the
baptized; in other words, the church was not expanding. Indeed, in the
statistics for that year, the total of baptized Christians in south Kyagwe
showed a serious drop. And then, without warning, the missionaries,
with Yonosani Kaidzi and the new Sekibobo, Ham Mukasa, left Ngogwe
for good. One reason for the move was the sleeping sickness, though
Ngogwe was never one of the evacuated areas. A more important reason
for the removal of the mission station was the decision to unite north
and south Kyagwe into a single, enormous missionary district with its
centre at Mukono. But the blow to the church in south Kyagwe was a
staggering one, from which it has never recovered to this day. In the
next year the total of communicants in the area dropped from 476 to
291; only 122 adults were baptized that year instead of 279 the year
before. The catechists in the Buikwe-Bukunja area, who had been
taught to rely so much on their contact with the mission, now found
that they began to lose touch with a centre that was twenty-five miles
further away; in the next two years their numbers dropped from 116
to 31.

The same thing was happening, to a greater or lesser degree, throughout the diocese. The reason for it is given in the Church Missionary
Annual Report, 1906,[1] which says:

'With the increase in the numbers of Baganda clergy and teachers
which has since taken place, and the better organization of the work
thus rendered possible, it has become feasible for a European

missionary to superintend a much larger district than in the olden days, when each teacher was directly responsible to him.'

It was the obvious next step in the development of the organization of the church. Undoubtedly it was dictated partly by the shortage of Anglican missionaries, but it was also a genuine attempt to 'hand over' more of the responsibility for the church to Africans. This was a process which has been continuing ever since, so it is well to examine it closely in order to understand better the nature of the church in Buganda today.

The withdrawal of the mission from Ngogwe was devastating because so much had been made to depend upon it. Bishop Tucker had once likened the missionary body to the timber core or pillar upon which an arch is erected. When the arch is completed, the core can be removed without endangering the stability of the arch. But, as we have seen, the mission station had been made the keystone of the arch, and its removal threatened the whole structure.

But, if the keystone position was dangerous, Tucker would certainly not have recommended the complete detachment of the mission from the church as an alternative. If pressed, he would doubtless have withdrawn his metaphor of the timber core, which was based on Henry Venn's principles, for it implied a mission that must never be built into the fabric of the church, but remain an external, temporary structure. Yet this was precisely what Tucker was opposing in his contention with his fellow-missionaries over the church constitution. He was convinced that

'in training native Christians in the art of self-government it is a tremendous mistake to hold aloof from their organization, and this for the simple reason that if the work of the European Missionaries is carried on outside the limits of the native Church, there must be an outside organization. In that case the native Christian will not be slow to realize that the outside organization is the one which really settles whatever questions may be under discussion in the Church and that their own organization is more or less a sham. . . . To my mind, the true attitude and spirit of the missionary towards those to whom he goes is included in the words: "Forget also thine own people and thy father's house." Let him therefore throw in his lot absolutely with the natives, identifying himself as far as possible with their life, work and organization. Let him submit himself to the laws and canons of their Church. Let him not say to his fellow Christians "Go that way or this, do this or that," but rather, "Let *us* go this way or that, let us do this or that"; and the result, in my opinion, will be a real training of the native Church in the art of self-government.'

The same principle led him resolutely to refuse to commission any catechists or clergy who were not wholly supported by the African church, so that the C.M.S. was responsible for nothing but the salaries and maintenance of the missionaries themselves, and the church received no European funds, apart from non-recurrent contribution to exceptional projects such as the building of the Cathedral.

The Uganda Church has reason to be profoundly grateful for the faith and honesty of Bishop Tucker, particularly when it can see in other parts of the Bantu world the tragic weakness of churches wherein the opposite policy has been pursued. It is true that Tucker, like other great exponents of African self-realization, was a more dominating character than he himself realized, and never hesitated to use his episcopal authority to veto the decisions of the church council. Moreover, as the sub-committee appointed by the C.M.S. to examine his draft constitution pointed out in 1898, by including 'all licensed clergy' in the synod and in the district councils, the missionary element was going to preponderate for some years until the number of African clergy had increased. Nevertheless, Bishop Tucker stood unfalteringly for what he called 'the equality of all workers', and for the total integration of the mission into the Uganda Church whereby the missionaries should be at the disposal of the synod.

But Tucker, like many an architectural genius, had to submit to compromises which were a travesty of his original plan. For the other missionaries were united in vigorous opposition to it.

'So long,' wrote one, 'as it is necessary to send *missionaries* to Uganda, so long must they be the teachers, counsellors, directors and leaders of the people. But men and women in such an extraordinary position must surely be responsible to the people who send them, and not to those to whom they are sent.'[2]

Baskerville expressed openly the fundamental fear of them all, when he wrote to the Bishop:

'To me the greatest objection seems to be the proposed equality of European and native workers, thereby in some cases placing Europeans under native control.'[3]

Twice before the turn of the century Bishop Tucker withdrew the whole constitution rather than compromise this principle. In 1904, when Victor Buxton was present, the Missionary conference again discussed, 'with very little practical result, the old threadbare question'. In 1905 the London committee of the C.M.S., who had faithfully supported the Bishop all along, agreed, as a compromise, that the synod should be invited to authorize a board of Europeans only, to deal with the location, transfer and care of missionaries; but this also the Bishop rejected, preferring that the missionaries' Standing Committee, if such an extraneous body were still required, should be honestly appointed from London rather than to lay down any racial conditions for any board appointed by the synod.

There is, however, a limit to any man's power to resist, and in 1909, a year before his final departure from Uganda, Tucker allowed the synod to adopt the constitution, without completely incorporating the Missionary Standing Committee, contenting himself with the fact that whenever the terms 'clergyman' or 'lay-reader' occurred they were to apply to all, irrespective of race. He tried to persuade himself that this was the constitution for which he had been striving for twelve years; but it was not. At least twenty-five years later, Bishop Willis, in his unpublished memoirs, was still able to write, concerning the whole of his own episcopate, that 'although the Bishop thus formed a connecting link between the two, there were clearly two governing bodies within the one diocese.'

By means of this compromise the mission was able to be of the Uganda Church, but never under it; to be included in its constitution, but always in an extraordinary position; to be built into its fabric, but always as the keystone. In order to understand how subtle and unconscious this missionary dominance can be it needs to be stressed again that compared with most mission fields Uganda was blessed with an enlightened policy directed towards the early autonomy of the African church. At the Jerusalem Conference of the International Missionary Council in 1928, when several representatives of the younger churches had been voicing their frustration under too much missionary dominance, Mr S. Kulubya, the Uganda delegate, rose to say that this was not so in his country, where the church had full responsibility. Even today older Ganda politicians say they want to see the Legislative Council fully elected, 'as the Diocesan Council is'.

Nevertheless, it remains true that while missionaries did indeed hand over responsibility into African hands, they always did so by withdrawing into a higher category in the administrative hierarchy. The cooperation of equals which marked Baskerville's partnership with Kaidzi at Ngogwe, or Pilkington's with Duta at Mengo, was hardly ever seen again. Development in Kyagwe did not take the form of partition, giving one mission district to Kaidzi and one to Baskerville, but of amalgamation round a higher centre. North Kyagwe was divided between Yoeri Nakumenyanga at Nakanyonyi, Isaka Lwaki in the Bukoba pastorate, and Eriya Mukasa in Bugerere; Yonasani Kaidzi, after a year at Mukono, was sent back to Ngogwe; and all these pastorates were put under the supervision of Baskerville at Mukono.

Such withdrawal upwards became the stock pattern of development in the church until the present day. One might wonder how it was that there could always be room at the top. But in fact the problem hardly arose, because the number of missionary clergy began to fall off, and the majority of those who came were drafted into specialist, non-parochial jobs. If that had been the whole of the story it might be regarded as a very satisfactory ending in the Henry Venn tradition. But unfortunately a deep change of relationship was insidiously created by this development so that it was also a withdrawal from fellowship. One old catechist in south Kyagwe expressed this to the author by saying of missionaries, 'We call them *Bazungu*, Europeans, now, but "Basika" was not called *Muzungu*.' In 1925 the local mission secretary wrote to a lady missionary, 'I am requested to advise you also that Native classes must not be held in, and Natives must not sleep in, C.M.S. houses without the special permission of the Standing Committee.' That was a far cry from Baskerville grieving over the empty beds of the boys who were no longer in his home.

It was still more serious when the movement of withdrawal upwards 'caught on', like a spoon lifted from a tin of treacle. The more faithful and gifted an African clergyman, the more likely he was to be withdrawn from a pastoral charge into a higher category, in which his time would be absorbed in administration and committee work. The keener the young catechist, the quicker he would be taken away from his flock and given a wider area to supervise. And so that flock, in its unimportant village church, was left with the poorest quality of shepherd, while the men at the top were more and more out of touch with its needs. Looking back, it is a strange story of neglect. The ill-qualified catechist, more than any other of the church's ministers, needed constant refreshment and supervision. But, henceforth, he was no longer called in for monthly renewal, as in Baskerville's early days. The clergy had an annual Refresher Course and Retreat; the catechist was expected to carry on year after year, almost unsupervised. No missionary now went so low down the scale as to visit the village church; even the African vicar rarely went below the Muluka church. These 'first letter' catechists were trained only in deanery centres, where were none of the facilities of the diocesan college at Mukono. And after the Second World War even the 'second letter' catechists were no longer trained alongside the lay-readers and clergy. Yet it was through the medium of the neglected village catechists that 80 per cent. of the Christian population received their spiritual sustenance and instruction in the faith.

The gravity of this problem has been vividly expressed in Bishop Willis's unpublished memoirs. After describing a service at which several hundred candidates had been confirmed in the presence of a congregation which overflowed in great, patient crowds all around the little church, he goes on:

> 'At last the service was over, and I stood on the hillside watching the congregation in little groups as it scattered over the countryside, returning to their distant villages. And the thought came into my mind with irresistible force, What next? Who will look after these immature converts as they go back into their heathen surroundings? With one native clergyman responsible for an impossible area, with no hope for a visit from him, or the possibility of again receiving the Communion, perhaps for months to come, how will they fare? Will they survive? If, in England, with every advantage available, so large a proportion of the confirmed lapse, what hope is there for these in their isolation?'

This gradual disengagement between the higher and lower levels of the church's ministry corresponded with a process of 'stretching' that was taking place in the fabric of Ganda society. This was partly due to education, partly to the great demands which the British policy of Indirect Rule was making upon the higher grade chiefs. The gaps between the rich and poor, between educated and illiterate, between county chief and Gombolola chief grew much wider than they had been in the more integrated society of the nineteenth century. So, too, in the hierarchy of the church the differences in prestige, in wealth and in authority between the higher and lower categories of ministry became more marked. In the phenomenal growth of this church the head had become dangerously remote from the feet.

Meanwhile a process of disengagement was taking place in quite a different way, through the gradual separation from the general life of the church of the specialist functions of the mission stations. In Basker-ville's journals describing his routine work in south Kyagwe it is interesting to see the growing importance attached to the activities at the centre at Ngogwe. At first this was confined to reading and instruc-tion classes, concentrating on the various religious textbooks and catechisms in the vernacular with which the Buganda Church at such an early stage was remarkably well equipped. Then, early in 1897, Miss Bird and Miss Pilgrim joined the staff at Ngogwe, and almost at once a more intense and systematic effort of improvement and instruction began to be manifest, not least in the home life of the mission households. The journals began to speak of 'dining' instead of merely 'having food'! One month after their arrival Miss Bird was superintending a morning school for children, they had a harmonium in the church, and singing practices three days a week. A year later Baskerville records a daily routine that looks remarkably like a school time-table. Miss Pilgrim had also opened a daily dispensary which soon became a considerable undertaking.

In May 1900 Miss Tanner started a class in English for pupils approved by the Ngogwe church council, 'as we do not want to be teaching disreputable people English'. After a few months this class was very large, and, in addition, 96 men were learning writing and arithmetic. Women were taught various domestic skills also. At the same time the children's school had grown, and Baskerville was appealing for 'fifty good, genuine slates', and some footballs. On 3 June 1902, 125 children assembled for the first school prize-giving in Uganda. A training class for school-teachers was already operating at Mengo, and that spring one of its pupils had been posted to Ngogwe to help train pupil-teachers for the district. The number of buildings on the mission station increased, and most of them were connected with medical work, the training of teachers, and the supervision of schools.

Anyone reading through the records and reports of the Uganda mission cannot fail to be struck by a change which quite suddenly comes over them about the year 1904. Up to that time there is a regular yearly account from each mission district of the missionaries' itinerations, the work of the catechists, and the successes and failures in the outreach of the church. But in later reports almost all the space is devoted to the educational and medical work of the mission as a whole. They are paragraphed not according to districts but by institutions, and the catechist ceases once and for all to have any news value. This, in a rather startling way, reveals what was certainly a gradual, and largely unconscious, change of interest in the mission as a whole. The mission stations first took on a dual function—both as the administrative hub of the church in the district and also as the premises of the specialist activities of the missionaries. Then, gradually, in the Anglican mission, the specialist function took precedence, while the pastoral oversight of the district was maintained by a diminishing number of men. At

Mukono, for example, when the mission first was moved there from Ngogwe, it was planned that two men should share between them the itineration in the district and the training of the catechists. But soon the responsibility for the churches in Kyagwe was left entirely to one man, while several others were engaged in running the new 'Bishop's School' for the sons of chiefs, the diocesan training centre for clergy and teachers, and the maternity centre and dispensary. The 1920s saw the withdrawal of nearly all the missionaries from any commitment to the life and struggles of the Buganda Church in its pastoral and evangelistic aspects.

The effects of this withdrawal can be clearly seen from a comparison of the present alignment of missionary work in the Anglican and Roman Catholic Churches in Buganda. For purposes of comparison the Roman Church's organizational structure has been taken as the pattern; it is in fact almost coterminous in its planning of deaneries and dioceses with the Anglican Church, but two of the Anglican deaneries which are properly included in Eastern Buganda are for this purpose counted in the Rubaga diocese.

	No. of pastorates	Pastorates with European priests on the staff	European priests available	European lay-workers	African clergy	Paid catechists
Archdiocese of Rubaga:						
Roman Catholic	27	17	48	14	34	586
Anglican . .	37	0	1	17	44	187
Diocese of Kampala:						
Roman Catholic	27	20	49	66	21	255
Anglican . .	36	1	13	50	54	175
Diocese of Masaka:						
Roman Catholic	16	0	0	4	59	312
Anglican . .	11	0	0	1	13	42
TOTALS:						
Roman Catholic	70	37	97	84	114	1153
Anglican . .	84	1	14	68	111	404

N.B.—In the Archdiocese of Rubaga figures are not available of the number of European Sisters in the Roman Catholic Church. If these were added, they would bring up the total of European lay-workers by at least another 50. The figures for Anglican lay-workers include the wives of missionaries.

It can be seen from this table not only that the Roman Catholic missionary force vastly outnumbers the Anglican, but that they have adhered to a policy of maintaining a high proportion of their clerical staff as participants within the parochial system of the church, and with responsibility for the work of the pastorates. In Kampala Diocese, for example 30 out of 49 European priests are on pastorate staffs. This does not, however, at the present time, mean that the Roman Catholic Church is greatly behind the Anglican in the number of its African clergy, though it is certainly true that, outside the Masaka diocese, African clergy have a very much smaller degree of real leadership and responsibility in the church than their Anglican brethren enjoy.

The change of concern (represented by this withdrawal from the pastoral responsibilities of the church) was not peculiar to the C.M.S. in Uganda. It was a corollary, in the realm of missions, to the popularization of theological liberalism and the social gospel which had taken place in the west. It also reflected the rise of American leadership in the field of missions after the First World War, with its emphasis on huge institutions and welfare projects which put to shame the meagre achievements of European missionaries of an earlier generation. That sense of shame was to a great extent responsible for the disengagement of the educational system of Uganda from the life of the church in which it had grown up.

For the schools had in the beginning been completely integrated with the life of the local congregations. It began with the church's rule, made as a test of sincerity rather than for any educational motive, that none might be baptized unless he could read the Gospels in the vernacular. The proceeds from the sale of books and writing material in the Anglican Church in 1898 amount to more than six million, or ten tons of cowrie shells It was in that year that C. W. Hattersley was invited by the Bishop to organize a system of children's primary schools and the training of school-teachers for them.

He was in some ways a strange choice, though it certainly is no discredit to him that his own education had never proceeded beyond that of an elementary Board School in England and training as a pupil teacher. With immense energy he set about providing for Baganda children in their thousands the same kind of schooling that he had experienced himself, and if that was educationally hide-bound, Hattersley himself is not to blame. The curriculum was entirely academic and there was no attempt to relate school to life by any inclusion of agricultural, industrial or health training. The little village schools were, as the Phelps-Stokes Commission saw in 1924, 'educationally futile'.

There were, it is true, a small number of schools, in which the richer experience and imagination of men like A. G. Fraser and H. W. Weatherhead were brought to bear on the creation of a more relevant pattern of education. And there was for a few years only, *pace* Mackay, a very promising technical school which, through a mistaken policy, was then handed over to a commercial undertaking. But these were all the products of the specialist activities of the mission, and lay beyond the competence and control of the church.

For the ironical fact was that the village schools, in spite of their blithe unconcern for 'relevance', were completely integrated with the life of the Christian community and belonged to the people in a way that has never been equalled since. They were the extension of the local congregation with regard to its children. The catechist, called *omusomesa*, the one who helps people to read, and the school-teacher, called *omusizi*, the sower of the seed, were trained in the same centre at Mukono and worked as a team of two, using, very often, one building as school and church. However remote and tiny, the school had its own uniform, often no more than a sash of coloured cotton, and, in many places, its own band of drums and bugles. The parents watched with stern and jealous pride over every change, every success or failure, in their school. It was, in fact, the school of initiation into the local Christian community. This was its function, and if the 'inspectorate' was concerned mainly with the quality of the preparation for baptism and confirmation, that was because these were the visible culmination of the initiation process. Nevertheless, a certain number of the brighter pupils did graduate to the 'Central' schools, as the lower elementary schools at the main centres were called, or to the 'High Schools', an ambitious title for the boarding-schools (one for boys and one for girls in each province) which gave elementary education to those who could afford the higher fees. Some even reached the 'Intermediate', or junior secondary, school at Budo for the sons of chiefs. A surprising number of the older leaders in church and state in Buganda today recall with embarrassed pride the village school in which their education began.

Several times the Anglican bishop had made representations to the Government asking for greater financial assistance in the educational field. But it was not until after the First World War that most of the Government departments had had a chance to develop beyond the stage of preliminary organization. Communication had been arduous—

it took twelve days to travel from Kampala to Hoima and over-expendi-
ture of even £10 by a Department was likely, in those days, to provoke
a reproof from Whitehall. The 1920s were the great period of administrative outreach, and it was in keeping with this development that,
besides the visit of the Phelps-Stokes Commission, the Governor
invited Eric Hussey, the Director of Education in the Sudan, to visit
Uganda and advise on the establishment of an Education Department
there. In both reports the village schools, those 'little nothings' in the
care of 'blind leaders of the blind', came in for undisguised con-
demnation.

The reaction had very far-reaching effects upon the life of the church.
The mission began to show a new sensitiveness to criticism and an
anxiety to put up a good show educationally in the eyes of the secular
world. This was admirable in its results as far as the more advanced
schools and the teacher training-centres were concerned; but the sense
of shame towards the village schools did them grave damage. The
Phelps-Stokes report recommended the formation of an inspectorate
which should embrace and raise up all the village schools. But in fact
the greater part of Government grants went into the development of the
more advanced schools rather than into the provision of an inspectorate
large enough to work patiently for the improvement of the sub-grade
schools. Moreover, by drawing the line between grant-aided and non-
aided schools, a large number of these village schools were made to feel
immediately discredited and disowned. Parents lost confidence in them
and, naturally, tried to send their children away to a recognized and
aided school. The educational system, like the church hierarchy, began
to be 'stretched' upwards, and the village school, like the village church,
tended to sink down into neglect.

As time went on education became more than ever a specialist
activity. Missionary educationists, supported by government grants,
had necessarily and rightly to concentrate on their professional task and
could not be expected to participate in any of the concerns of the parish
or deanery in which they worked. The principle of self-support which
Tucker had insisted on for the church was no longer applied to the
schools, and this emphasized the difference between them. Government
officials in the Department of Education naturally continued to think
of their dealings with the schools as being a relationship with European
educationists, in spite of many formal reminders that they were dealing
with an African church. Young African school-teachers, aware of the
new distinctness of their profession, began to be resentful when the

local vicar continued to assume that he had the right to expect them to preach or lead Sunday services, and they protested loudly that they were civil servants, not church workers. The churches were still represented in strength on the local Education Authorities, but the schools were no longer the agencies of the local congregation for the initiation of its children into its own community life. The link between the schools and the church was only at the top, institutionally, not at the bottom, organically. It is very easy to understand what African clergy and laity mean, though it is a misconception, when they repeat constantly the question: 'Why has the mission given away our schools to the government?' It is the integrated life of a society without specialization that they cry for.

The Conference of Missionaries which in 1905 had reiterated the weakness and unreliability of the Baganda Christians decided that the only way of dealing with the problems of such a church was through some solemn spiritual recall. They resolved that 'a series of special services should from time to time be held throughout the country, with the object of deepening the spiritual life of the church through the setting forth of the salvation from the power of sin which there is in Christ Jesus our Saviour'.

The phrase 'from time to time' is significant, for it became an accepted pattern in the Anglican Church in Uganda to meet the recurring doldrums of moral and religious decline with an organized mission for renewing afresh the Wind of the Spirit. There are obvious dangers in looking for a revival to solve the problems which may be due to mistaken policy or some other unrecognized factor. Nostalgic attempts to recover the simplicities of a first-generation church may prove to be only an evasion of responsibility towards new demands facing the third or fourth generation. Nevertheless, although the periodic missions in Uganda have generally left most of the problems unsolved, they have held up the drift and brought thousands of individuals to personal conversion and moral victory.

The 'mission' of 1906 began with special services in Koki, and then in other districts. The most striking response was in the cathedral at Mengo during March, when between three and four thousand people attended each service for eight days. Apart from one address by Henry Wright Duta, all the preaching was undertaken by Europeans. Just as the revival of 1893 was strongly coloured by the longing of the missionary leaders to reproduce in Buganda the features of the Moody and

Sankey 'missions', so in 1906 the model was the evangelistic campaigns of Torrey and Alexander, whose 'Glory Song' was translated into Luganda and became the theme song of the 'mission'.

These periodic evangelistic 'missions' gave expression to the need in a church which had been created, to a great extent, communally, for that element of individual decision which is essential to Christianity. They also gave voice to the divine impatience and the longing for a pure church, which is found wherever the Gospel is being preached and the Bible studied. Normally these needs lead to the appearance of separatist, 'holiness' sects, and one of the most remarkable features of the story of the church in Uganda is the comparative absence of these.

The quietly influential Yoswa Kate Damulira, the Mugema of Busiro, had for a long time considered that the spiritual weakness of the church was due to its admission of doctors and medicine which, owing to an unfortunate translation of Deut. 18. 11 and similar texts, he believed to be forbidden by the Word of God. In 1891, when Basker-ville and Pilkington tried to persuade him to have an ulcerated leg treated by Dr Gaskoin Wright, who had just joined the mission, he refused. He seems to have nursed this grievance privately, however, until after the retirement of Bishop Tucker. Bishop Willis, newly consecrated, began to receive letters from him pointing out that the weakness of the church was due to failure to observe the Law of the Lord, particularly as given in the Old Testament. In 1914 a very different man, Malaki Musajjakawa, extrovert and hungry for a follow-ing, joined himself to the gentle Yoswa Kate and began wholesale baptisms for entry into the 'Church of the One Almighty God'. Another powerful leader who joined the new church was Semei Kakunguru, who after a remarkable career—as chief administrator over the Bakedi he had by 1902 made himself virtually their king, and was later President of the Busoga Lukiiko—had lately returned to his estates at Mbale, still influential but ripe for dissent. The offer of baptism without previous instruction, the attraction of a fresh 'gospel' which claimed to explain and put right the evident weakness of the established churches, and above all the appeal to existing prejudice against government quarantine and inoculation orders, drew many followers, and the census of 1921 showed over 91,000 'people of Malaki', in Buganda alone, as they were called. In 1929 an attempt to enforce medical regulations in Bulemezi country led to a fracas in which government officials were seriously wounded. Yoswa and Malaki were exiled to the Northern Province. Kakunguru had died a few months earlier. Almost at once

G

there was a widespread return to the Anglican and Roman folds, and, although the sect still exists, they are quite unmilitant and seem anxious to assert that the bar on medical treatment, 'the strange god', is the only point of difference between them and the other churches. 'God is King; all people are his tribes; he does not make distinctions.'

In 1929 a separatist church was founded which had many more of the features of a breakaway, nationalist church. This was the African Orthodox Church, significantly described as 'a church established for all right-thinking Africans, men who wish to be free in their own house, not always being thought of as boys'. The leader, Reuben Spartas, had come under the influence of the African Orthodox Church in South Africa, which combined a delight in the worship forms of the eastern churches with Marcus Garvey's mystique of a world-wide black nationalism. His activities focused mainly on a large independent school, but he attracted a considerable following of dissatisfied members of the Anglican and Roman Churches. So far his sect was running true to type and closely resembled other 'Orthodox' groups in East and Central Africa. But then the strong Kiganda instinct for coherence and order began to assert itself, and Spartas sought recognition, and the validity of his orders, from the Greek Patriarch of Alexandria. This was granted in 1946, and his church, now numbering about 10,000, is formally linked with the Greek Orthodox Church. The Greek Liturgy has been translated into Luganda and services are attended by some of the Greek residents in Kampala. No doubt deviations from strict Orthodoxy are to be found in many of their twelve centres, but when the Baganda who are being trained in Alexandria and Athens return to their country these may be corrected. Spartas has been gaoled for alleged implication in the riots of 1949, and we may say that his church arose out of a protest against European domination rather than against spiritual lukewarmness in the more established churches. Yet to draw such a line between spiritual condition and racial attitudes is, perhaps, to beg a major question. It is, in any case, important to understand the appeal of the Eastern Orthodox Churches as offering to Africans the status and catholicity of one of the great churches without the disadvantages of involvement with any of the colonial powers.

The Baganda's deep aversion to schism is strikingly illustrated by the failure of a C.M.S. missionary, Mabel Ensor, who had resigned from the mission in 1928, to found a permanent 'Gospel Church' in the country. One of her devoted African followers, who had made great sacrifices to support her, wrote:

'As she was equipped with all these wonderful gifts I am sure she would have revolutionized the whole Church of Uganda. . . . I and many others broke away (from her) because she had introduced such things as re-baptism of her followers, and the celebration of the Holy Communion by anybody at any place, and intended to form a new church other than the Native Anglican Church.'[4]

It is interesting to consider what are the reasons why there have been so few separatist movements in Buganda, and why those that have appeared have so quickly gravitated back to one or other of the well-established churches. One reason must be the strongly unified structure of Kiganda society. A second is surely the small number of Christian missions in the field; the rivalry of the Roman and Anglican Churches has been sad and disruptive enough, but they present a far simpler confessional picture than in almost any other part of the world. Thirdly these churches themselves, each in its own way, have at least to some extent satisfied those needs which so often are only met by schism. In the Anglican Church the perennial cry for a greater moral purity and consistency in the church has been met by the evangelical tradition within the church itself, expressed particularly in special 'missions', and continually in the preaching of individual decision in conversion and sanctification. In the Roman Catholic Church, on the other hand, the use of sacramental confession and penance has been the main stay of an emphatically pastoral ministry, which, while it is no guarantee against sin, does provide, for the genuine upward-striving Christian, a steady access to that grace of renewal which many Anglicans were finding only spasmodically, and therefore more noticeably and subjectively, in special 'experiences'.

The revival movement which spread from Uganda throughout East Africa has been described in a number of books.[5] There are several unusual features in the story. First, revivals are commonly found in the early years of the second generation of a church, and the revival of 1893 is typical in this respect; but it is much less usual to find revival in the third generation of a church. Again it is remarkable that a movement which has continued to spread with renewed vigour for more than twenty years should not have become a separate sect, and this not merely in Buganda, where, as we have seen, there is a strong tendency against separation, but also in several areas of Kenya and Tanganyika where sects are numerous.

The actual break-out of the revival was preceded, as always, by a long period in which many widely separated individuals were deeply troubled by their own spiritual powerlessness and that of the church. For the first time, however, in Uganda, this seems to have been felt even more acutely by Africans than by missionaries. The son of an important sub-chief under Yoswa Kate Damulira in Busiro, who would have inherited his father's office, was personally converted as far back as 1922, and realizing, as he said, the unconverted state of many of the clergy and catechists, gave up his political career in order to preach and recall the church to more uncompromising obedience to God's demands. For several years he was disregarded and lonely, but his young brother was converted through his influence. This young man, Blasio Kigozi, was sent as a school-master into Ruanda, which, though it is mandated territory of the Belgian Congo, was included in the Anglican diocese of Uganda. There, in 1935, the same sense of failure and disillusionment as had burdened Pilkington long before overwhelmed him, and he retired to meditate and pray for a week. Like Pilkington he returned 'in the power of the Spirit', and from his witness at that time there came the first large-scale response, first in Ruanda and Ankole, and then, as a result of an address he had prepared to give before the synod, in Kampala. He died of tick fever before he could deliver it, and his written words were read with a special sense of solemnity.

He was not the only one to sound the note of recall. Another of the periodic 'missions' was being planned, this time to celebrate the diamond jubilee of the arrival of the first missionaries, and everywhere sermons were being preached on Joel 2. 25—'I will restore to you the years that the locust hath eaten.'

This revival, like the earlier 'missions', showed the signs of European initiative. Just as in 1893 the missionaries were reflecting the influence of Moody and Sankey, and in 1906 consciously reproducing some of the features of the Torrey and Alexander campaigns, so in the 1930s some of the Europeans who played a leading part in the movement were debtors both to the Oxford Group and the Keswick Conventions. From the start there was an emphasis upon 'sharing' frankly, in mutual confession of sin and failure, as the basis of a more sincere fellowship—'walking in the Light', as it later came to be called. Huge conventions, numbering up to 15,000, have been a regular feature of the revival; and European influence was clearly at work on what might be called the 'ethics' of the revival, in the formulation of those things which were condemned under the terms 'worldly' or 'modernist' or 'high church'.

In spite of this, however, the movement has developed certain strongly African characteristics which make it more deeply indigenous than any 'mission' that went before it in the history of the Uganda Church. In the first decade of the revival dreams played an important part, and were generally treated in a truly African way, as being the direct impact of the Spirit of God. At present the official attitude of the revival is to treat dreams with suspicion and discouragement, and this is in keeping with a general tendency towards respectable normality. The same is true of ecstatic phenomena such as trembling. On the other hand, the repetition of a theme song, reminiscent of the early genera-tion's use of *Killa siku tuusifu*, has become a conspicuous outward sign of the movement. The chorus of a gospel hymn, of which the first word in Luganda is *Tukutendereza*, 'We praise thee', is used as a signal of recognition and greeting between the 'brethren', and as a signature-tune and challenge towards all who are outside. It is sung with syncopated cross-rhythms, with bodies poised on the verge of dancing; it is sung incessantly, until it grows almost hypnotic. It may express the hilarious joy of Africa liberated in Christ, or the hushed adoration of two or three at the close of prayer, or the truculence of a small group challenging the majority.

Confession of sin is common to most revivals. It may be done for release and the joy of honesty at the moment of conversion or renewal; or it may be the 'sharing' that establishes fellowship and frankness at the beginning of a meeting of the brethren; or it may be personal testimony to deliverance used in preaching the Gospel. In all these uses the movement has become steadily more restrained and considerate. There is a further use in the movement, which may be peculiarly African, which might be called 'ordeal by confession', which is de-manded of new converts or renewed Christians as a test of the reality of their salvation and as an initiation into the fellowship. On these occasions it seems as though the element of 'brokenness', humiliation and abandonment to the group, is more important than penitence or faith.

This chapter is not the place for any theological appraisal of these things, nor for a full account of the vast numbers of men and women who have been raised to an entirely new level of Christian living, and, what is more significant, maintained at that level through the group fellowship which the movement offers. What is germane at this point is to draw attention to certain ways in which the revival represents a positive reaction and response in the church to some of those weak-nesses which emerged in the previous chapter; and also to point to other ways in which it appears rather as an extension of the process of disengagement within the church which has been going on for the past fifty years.

In the first place the revival represents a remarkable recovery of the indigenous structure of the church which, as we saw in the first two chapters, consisted primarily of living Christian community groups, or clusters, around some natural head of a household. In many of the places which are regarded as the stronghold of the revival in Buganda it is found that the local leader who is a member of the 'brethren'—it may be a landowner, or civil servant or senior teacher—gathers around him, in his home or in nearby houses, a considerable community of brethren. For example, the man mentioned earlier, whose younger brother Blasio Kigozi was one of the first to fan the flame, has settled on his family estate, within a mile of his own house, almost all the brethren that there are in that parish. If, for example, he meets at one of the great conventions, a recently converted herdman from Ankole, who, having dismissed the casual woman with whom he was living, is looking for a Christian wife, the landowner will very probably offer the young man a place on his estate, or a plot on which to build. There he comes, with the new wife he has found within the fellowship, and settles down. In two years time he is marvelling at the miracle by which he, the degraded flotsam of society, has got such a neat and prosperous little home. So a strongly integrated cluster grows up around the fatherly head. They almost forget the many different clans, or even tribes, from which they originated because of their membership in this new community. When a girl in the community is sought in marriage, they may deny her if her suitor is not approved, particularly if he is not a member of the *balokole*, that is, 'saved ones', as those in the revival are called. If they agree to the marriage, the brethren in the community will undertake the arrangements, provide the feast and the transport, and attend the ceremony in force. Within such a local fellowship there is a security such as no other kinship-group or association in Ganda society today is able to provide.

A corollary of this recovery of the cluster pattern is the reaffirmation of the responsibility of the laity in the church. This may well prove to be the most important emphasis in the whole movement. In the early days of the revival there was undoubtedly an undercurrent of anti-clericalism, the natural response of a living element in the church to the years of underestimation of the laity. Inevitably there was a clash between the great majority of the clergy and the young enthusiasts who sometimes tended to hold the established hierarchy responsible for all the hypocrisy and deadness in the church. This was the point of tension

at which the greatest threat of separation developed. It was overcome
by the deeper underlying unity that existed in the church. Closely
related to this necessary opposition to the entrenched authority of the
clergy was the quiet but persistent calling in question of the spiritual
leadership of Europeans. More than one of the African leaders in the
revival has confessed that, in his unregenerate days, he longed to be able
to tell Europeans 'where they got off'. To say that such a longing was
divinely inspired is not to question his sincerity in 'repenting' of such
feelings. Nonetheless it is true that, though it was certainly a painful
experience for some missionaries, the revival profoundly challenged the
old assumptions of European superiority in the church, and opened the
way for a recovery of African responsibility and leadership. It is not
surprising that we can detect something a little unhealthy, a faint smell
of the guillotine, about the manner in which a missionary was occasionally submitted to the ordeal by confession. The miraculous element in
the revolt—for such it may be called—was the spirit of love and loyalty
with which it was permeated, and the fact that the one issue on which
the *balokole* have produced a Confessing Church, in Uganda, and
supremely in Kikuyuland, was their refusal, in a time of militant
nationalism, to break fellowship with their white brethren.

At the same time, however, as we recognize in the revival this positive
response to the *malaise* in the church, we cannot ignore the element of
withdrawal from the real life of the church which was also present in it.
At a moment when one of the problems of the Uganda Church consisted in its members having to make, as Christians, decisions regarding
questions of politics and social responsibility which had not confronted
an earlier generation, the revival movement was in danger of a wholesale
withdrawal from the encounter with those demands into an other-
worldly pietism.

Again, within the life of the church itself the *balokole* began to show
an introverted tendency to withdraw from full participation and responsibility. Almost everywhere, it is true, they attend their local
church on Sunday mornings, and they have a deeper comprehension of
the significance of the Holy Communion than most other Christians.
But they have generally been reluctant to accept responsibility as
members of the church council, and in the few places where a Sunday
School exists, it is, surprisingly often, someone other than the 'brethren'
who organized it. Even in the field of evangelism where, in the early
days of the movement, their great strength lay, there has been more
recently a withdrawal from responsibility, and Sunday afternoons,

which were once the time for open-air preaching, have been used, increasingly, for large gatherings of the faithful for mutual edification.

The root of the matter lay in the existence within the church of what was, by its very nature, an exclusive group. Revival in a church which contains a great many lukewarm and only nominal Christians must result in a line of demarcation between those who are living below their spiritual privileges in the Gospel and those whose lives reflect the power of Christ to take away sin and give moral victory. Where the conscious experience of that power at the present moment is made the basis of fellowship between members of a group, those who do not qualify are inevitably outside the group. But what a revival movement almost always ignores is the fact that the line of demarcation which it emphas- izes is nothing new, but is inherent in the life of the church. There are always differences between Christians—differences in the degree in which they have experienced and responded to the grace and the power of God in Jesus Christ, and differences in their present moral and spiritual condition. There is more than one toll-gate on the road to sanctification, and the church includes in its fellowship all travellers on that road. But, by the very assurance and eagerness with which they call Christians to realize the highest level of obedience and liberation, the members of revival groups reduce all gradations to one clear-cut line of demarcation which they tend to identify with the stereotyped form of experience which they recognize.

In the church of Uganda it was probably the unshakeable patience of Bishop Stuart, more than any other human factor, which prevented an external breakaway of the revival from the church. More and more those who were in the movement, and those who were not, came to recognize and accept it as belonging to the church for the sake of the church. Nevertheless, the position might be described as separatism without schism. A distinction has been drawn within the body of the church, deeper and of greater consequence than anything that existed before. The disengagement of the church from society, and within its own structure, has been carried a stage further.

This chapter has not attempted to complete the history of the Buganda Church by covering the events of fifty years, but only to indicate a process that was steadily at work throughout this period. There was an inevitability about it which makes mere criticism out of place. A true evaluation must see it, moreover, as a process of gain and growth as well as one of loss and retrogression. History leads one to expect, however, that in the next few decades the forces of life and responsibility within the Christian community, will be those that tend towards re-integration, bringing the church back into closer grips with secular society in all its aspects and at all levels, and binding together, in a more trustful and explicit unity, laity and clergy, rural dean and catechist, African and European, those in ecclesiastical office with those in secular professions, as interdependent fellow-workers in a single Christian enterprise embraced and upheld by the outgoing love of the one Church.

NOTES

1. *Proceedings of the C.M.S.* 1906, p. 78.
2. J. B. Purvis, Letter to Baylis, C.M.S. African Secretary, 18 Oct. 1898, in C.M.S. archives.
3. G. K. Baskerville, Letter to Tucker, quoted by him to Baylis, Sept. 1898, in C.M.S. archives.
4. For this paragraph, and for several facts in the preceding paragraphs, I am indebted to the researches of the Rev. F. B. Welbourn (of Makerere College), whose study in Separatism in East Africa will shortly be published.
5. See Max Warren, *Revival. An Enquiry* (S.C.M. 1954); Anon., *Awake! An African Calling* (Highway Press, 1937); A. C. Stanley Smith, *Road to Revival* (Highway Press, 1947).

II

DESCRIPTIVE

'They have divorced mind from soul, natural revelation from written revelation, and scorn the methods
which science has discovered to be the only means of
ascertaining truth. But truth is one, as mind is one, and
God is one. So, too, there can be but one method of
arriving at spiritual truth; viz. an unbiased examination of *facts*, and a resolve to learn from these as they
are, instead of fanciful supposition as to what ought to
be. As Metaphysics may be called the pure mathe-
matics of Theology, so Missions are its practical
application, and are destined to play as important a
part in correcting the vagaries of theologians, as
practical engineering has done in the domain of theoretical mechanics.' Alexander Mackay, quoted in
Mackay of Uganda, pp. 449-50.

5

The Social Structure of the *Muluka* Parish

THE following chapters are based on an intimate knowledge of one *muluka* parish. There is no such thing as a typical village in Uganda, and the parish of Makindu has its idiosyncrasies. The previous section of this book has suggested reasons why the church in south Kyagwe is not as strong as in some other parts of the country, and some of the effects of social disruption are probably more evident there than in the original counties of Buganda. As far as possible, therefore, enough information has been added from a comparative study in three other parishes to correct and supplement the total picture. The picture, nevertheless, has been drawn unashamedly from the viewpoint of one parish, the details of which fill the foreground while the wider scene appears more faintly in the background. It is a portrait rather than a panorama.

Makindu lies on what used to be the main route from Mengo to the east, passing through Ziba to Kabugoga and the Buvuma Channel. It was here that in 1876 Stanley, on his second visit to Mutesa, was met by the Kabaka's messenger and presented with a walking-stick. Since those days the building of the railway bridge over the Nile, the cutting back of the Mabira Forest and the construction of the Owen Falls Dam have carried the alignment of the main road successively further north, leaving Makindu in a backwater.

As far as the pastoral organization of the church is concerned, the parish of Makindu is bounded by the coast on the east and south, by the road from Kabugoga to Buikwe on the north, and by the river Mubeya and the road to Golomolo on the west. It covers an area of roughly thirty-five square miles and falls under the jurisdiction of three different *muluka* chiefs, for in these days the church parishes are always larger units than the administrative parishes. Makindu itself comes under the *muluka* chief whose headquarters are at Mawota, and it is with him that we shall be mainly concerned; the other two chiefs are centred at Bulere and at Makota. These, with six others, are answerable to the *gombolola*, or sub-county, chief whose headquarters are at Buikwe, and whose title of office is *Mubito*.

The area administered by the *muluka* chief at Mawota contains some 650 taxpayers and a total population of roughly 2,500. These live in the loosely grouped communities which are typical of Buganda, each consisting of from twenty to sixty homesteads scattered over a *kyalo*, or cultivated estate. The most important *byalo* in this *muluka* are: Kigaya, Golomolo, Kabubiro, Makindu, Mawota, Wambogwe, Bufumbe, Sanga and Kitaya. In each of these nine the chief landowner has appointed a *mutongole* to act on his behalf, and these men severally collect the taxes from their areas and form together the weekly council of the *muluka* chief. Though it is only in recent years that the *muluka* chiefs have received a set salary, theirs is an important and exacting task; for through them all the directives from the *gombolola* offices are mediated to the people themselves; through them the schemes of the agricultural, veterinary and other government departments are administered locally; and they have the power to judge certain cases by African law.

The *batongole* are a relic of the days when the clan system was fully operative and the landowner was the natural administrative head of the people on his land. They are appointed by the landowner but are virtually the agents of the *muluka* chief. They may also be charged with the collection of rents for the landowner. The best of them are more than tax-collectors and act as village headmen; but they are everywhere a very mixed bag. In this parish one of them is a successful farmer, owning two cars, while another was a common laughing-stock, drifting from one beer party to the next, until the *muluka* chief had to request the landowner to appoint a more capable person in his place.

At least as important as the *muluka* chief in this society is the landowner. In most parishes there are several of these; but usually there is one principal landowning family, and this is the case at Makindu. Although there are now many owners of freehold land in the area, only this family is referred to as *bataka* or landowners. Andereya Kaddu Nannungi, of the Genet clan, one of the pages to Kabaka Mutesa, who had been amongst the earliest of Mackay's pupils, was, by the agreement of 1900, allotted eight square miles of land by the Regents, covering the *byalo* of Makindu, Wambogwe and Kabubiro. He already had a family estate in Buddu county. He is reputed to have been a leading Christian chief in the time of Baskerville, and to have used his house at Makindu as a church until a proper building was erected. Local legend somewhat enhanced his reputation, and he is claimed to have been one of the first five Christians in Buganda to be baptized—but this is not true. When he died, his brother, Yosuwa Kijoma Nannungi, erected over his grave a small square room, like a shrine, roofed with corrugated iron, and later built a brick church at Makindu, larger than is usual for a parish church, as a memorial to his famous brother.

Yosuwa Nannungi lived to the remarkable age of 117 years, and died in 1952. During his time as principal landowner about half the estate slipped out of his hands. The present generation account for this loss in various ways, more or less sinister according to their personal animosities, but probably he gave most of it away. A large number of the people in the area today own small freeholdings which they received as gifts from Nannungi. The larger of these gifts were generally to members of the Genet clan, but smaller holdings went indiscriminately to friends. A good deal of the land was also sold.

Nannungi's household was maintained in the old style with lavish entertainment for all comers. By his first wife he had eleven children. After her death he married again, but his second wife contracted leprosy after some years and agreed to leave him. She is still living alone at Makindu. As an old man he took a third wife, who bore his youngest son. But though he lived as a fairly strict Christian himself, Nannungi failed to pass on the tradition to his children. Only one son and one daughter of the thirteen children have had a church marriage, and when another daughter became a spirit-diviner he did nothing to prevent her building a shrine for this purpose close to his house. Throughout Buganda, as in any other country, are to be found children of the older pillars of the faith who are a visible reminder that the church has to be converted anew in every generation.

During his lifetime Yosuwa Nannungi gave one hundred acres each to his three eldest sons, forty acres each to his eldest daughter and his fifth son, thirty acres each to his second and third daughter and to the wife of Kaddu's son, and twenty acres each to the last five children. He nominated as his heir his fourth son, Yokana Kirumagenyi, who was invested as principal landowner and entered into possession of the house and the residue of the estate in 1952. Of his three wives, none of whom is a Muganda, Kirumagenyi has had eleven children. This process of fragmentation of freehold estates is common to the whole of Buganda. In the original distribution under the Agreement of 1900 about 3,700 allottees were registered. But by 1952 a rough estimate showed a total of 50,000 landowners in the country.[1]

The main source of revenue for the landowners is derived from the renting of small plots to peasant tenants. In the pre-European days all tenants were expected to give annually one month's labour and certain gifts of produce and beer to the chief on whose land they were settled. These are now commuted into money payments: the *busulu* or ground-rent is fixed at Shs. 10 p.a. for each holding, and the *nvujjo* of from Shs. 4 to Shs. 20 per acre is paid on the cash crops, cotton and coffee, and Shs. 2 for every brew of beer made by the peasant. A premium of anything from Shs. 50 to Shs. 450 may be demanded of a new tenant when he is installed. The tenants have absolute security of tenure; so long as they remain in possession and pay their rents they cannot be evicted, except in rare cases when it can be proved that the landowner himself has not a sufficient area of his land on which to build and settle himself. The right of tenure is passed on in succession to a tenant's heir, and during his lifetime he may leave the whole, or part, of his plot in the possession of a wife or relative. No tenant, however, may sub-let or mortgage any of his holding, though if he allows a temporary resident to build a hut on it, he may charge him a monthly fee. A peasant who wishes to move his home elsewhere may surrender his holding at any time and it reverts to the landowner with all improvements, including the house; compensation may be claimed only for standing crops. In the past, holdings were regularly abandoned in this way as the normal method of resting tired soil and a more fertile plot was sought elsewhere. In these days, however, the increased population and the greater capital value of coffee trees make the peasant very reluctant to give up a holding, and so soil exhaustion is troubling many of them. The difficult choice whether to move or not is a common source of personal anxiety in Makindu.

On their side the landowners also are worried by the question of how to make the most of their dwindling estates. The previous generation could afford a care-free generosity. Not only were considerable gifts of freehold property made to relatives, but Yosuwa Nannungi agreed in many cases to exempt a tenant and his successors from the payment of *busulu* and *nvujjo*. Out of sixty-six tenants in a sample at Makindu and Kabubiro, thirteen had received rent-free holdings from Nannungi. The present generation, however, are not disposed to give away any more of their property. They are anxious to retain as much of the family land as possible and the 'lost square miles' are a topic for endless debate; on the other hand, the temptation to sell in order to raise cash is almost irresistible. This has been done sometimes for school fees, or to buy a motor car, or to indulge the pleasures of the flesh. If a sale is contemplated, then another problem arises—should it be sold to a stranger, or even to a non-Muganda, and the highest possible price extorted, or should it be kept in the family, in which case the closer the relationship the lower the price that could decently be demanded? The probability is that they will sell to strangers. Already a square mile in the parish has been sold to a Moslem from Busamia, and somewhat smaller areas to men from Ruanda and Bunyuli. Besides such sales of estates, a considerable number of peasants, instead of renting their plots, have bought them outright, paying Shs. 600 or more for small-holdings which have never been surveyed and for which no sub-title has been registered. The original landowning family continues to worry over the lands it has sold, and so lost. Sometimes they ask resentfully why the British administration has not imposed a ban on all alienation of land to non-Baganda!

While fragmentation and soil exhaustion proceed slowly and relentlessly the present system militates against any progressive development. The landowner cannot evict tenants in order to turn over a compact area of his estate to mechanized farming, even if he had the skill, capital and initiative to do so. The progressive tenant, on the other hand, finds it very hard to increase the size of his holding by renting adjacent land and is discouraged by the fact that he can expect no compensation for improvement of his holding. The development of tenants' co-operatives may bring about a radical change, but these require a wealth of intelligence and discipline which is often lacking in the rural areas. Meanwhile, in spite of a great deal of cheerful complacency, the tension of personal anxieties and frustrations grows, offering a fertile field for the political quacks.

The presence of immigrants from other tribes has already been mentioned. In every area the factors causing and modifying this movement are slightly different, but everywhere in Buganda their numbers and their effect on society are considerable. The census returns for 1948 show that only 62 per cent. of the African population of the kingdom are Baganda; in the *gombolola* of Buikwe the figure is only 52·5 per cent. In Busiro and Mawokota, where there are many of the original clan estates, the proportion of immigrants is somewhat smaller, but in a sample of 76 householders at Makindu and Kabubiro, only 30 are Baganda, that is just over 39 per cent.

In south Kyagwe the most numerous immigrants are those from the Buvuma islands which lie within sight of the shores of Kyagwe. They have always tended to settle along the mainland shores of the lake, but

H

their numbers increased particularly after the sleeping sickness epidemic. Some of the older inhabitants can remember the enforced evacuation and the firing of the bush over Golomolo, Wambogwe, Bufumbe and the Busagazi peninsula. Within seven years, though the land was not officially opened for resettlement, Bavuma had started to move in. They are already closely assimilated and often describe themselves as Baganda.

The second largest group of immigrants in that parish are Badama. The fertile forest land of Kyagwe has always attracted the impoverished peoples of the dry Bukedi plains. In earlier days, the border hostilities between Buganda and Bunyoro kept them at bay, but the settlement and opening up of the Eastern Province prepared the way for a steady infiltration into Kyagwe from those north-eastern tribes, especially Teso, Bagwere, Badama and Basamia. The distance between Badama and south Kyagwe, however, is considerable, so migration has tended to be in families. For example, in 1915 one of Semei Kakunguru's Baganda officials married a Mudama girl and later brought her to his home in the Ngogwe district. In 1920, a year of drought, one of her brothers came to south Kyagwe to visit her and used this contact to persuade a landowner to rent him a plot, first at Gulama, then at Ziba, and finally at Makindu. He had fifteen children who settled in south Kyagwe, nine daughters marrying Baganda. In 1924 a second brother rented a plot at Makindu. One by one two other brothers and five cousins followed. Their direct descendants in this part of south Kyagwe now number eighty, quite apart from other Badama, connected with them by marriage, who have migrated with them. They are thoroughly rooted in the society of Makindu, Wambogwe and Kabubiro; three members of the family group have made marriage connexions with the Baganda landowners. In this parish there are two other family groups of Badama of a comparable size, which began their migration at a slightly later date, and intermarriage between the three groups has been taking place in the present generation.*

Yet, though the immigrants are so merged into this society as permanent tenants, their integration is not complete, and many inter-tribal tensions exist. Immigrants make it a point of honour not to conceal their tribe and a man who pretends to be a Muganda and is afterwards found out is covered with shame. Badama complain of the laxity of the Baganda, look back regretfully to the more ordered and disciplined society of their homeland, and their youths prefer to look for a bride in

* See Appendix B.

Budama, where they have better hopes of finding an unspoiled girl who will accept discipline. On the other hand, the Baganda blame the immigrants for corrupting manners and introducing undesirable customs. The truth is that the confusion of accepted patterns and the disruption of change which immigration causes, rather than any normal weakness inherent in one or other of the tribes, has brought about the breakdown of standards of which all complain. The Baganda, moreover, whenever occasions of conflict arise, are prone to revert to attitudes of superiority towards the 'less civilized' tribes. While freely accepting immigrant girls as their wives, they are reluctant to allow their daughters to marry non-Baganda. The Badama feel that there is discrimination against them and, at Makindu, they occasionally call tribal meetings to discuss their grievances. The private school at Kabubiro was originally opened especially for Badama children, against strong opposition from some of the leading Baganda in the parish. Sometimes the landowner has refused to rent land to an immigrant and demanded an outright purchase. These tensions, however, are latent rather than evident most of the time, and co-existence is steadily developing into real integration. At celebration dances, for example, Ganda-style dancing is usually interspersed with Dama.

In other parts of Buganda the immigrants have a rather different position and function in society. In a few districts there is a great agglomeration of immigrants as labourers on a sugar or coffee estate; most of them live in labour lines provided by their employers, but a few make contacts with neighbouring villages and eventually rent land and settle down. Elsewhere immigrants, particularly from Ruanda, are employed by Baganda, singly or in small parties, to herd their cattle and work in their cotton and coffee plantations. In country districts within ten miles of Kampala many Baganda professional or business men go daily to their work in the town and employ immigrants to look after their plantations at home. Many of these eventually rent a plot themselves and become tenants. The Banyaruanda in Buganda now number many thousands and have their own well-organized association to look after their interests and make representations on their behalf to the Buganda African government.

Returning to Makindu parish—after the *muluka* chief, the landowners, and their *batongole*, the most influential persons in that society are the traders. There is a store at the cross-roads at Bwoya and another at a road-junction at Makindu; both are fully-stocked village shops specially built for the purpose and both are run by Baganda. Five other shopkeepers, all Badama, run small businesses in their own houses, using one room as a shop and selling through the window; three are in Kabubiro and two in Wambogwe. In these little stores one can buy maize-flour, sugar, cheap packets of tea, coffee and cigarettes, soap, sweets, salt, curry-powder, mineral water and household utensils. Two of them sell bread which is brought out by van every second day. A group of slightly larger shops is to be found at Bulere and at Malongwe. There are licensed bars at Naja and Buikwe which cater for better-class customers, and more disreputable drink-shops at Bulere and Malongwe. These all sell, in addition to gourds of African beer, mineral water of various brands, bottled beer from the brewery at Jinja, and cheap sherry and gin imported from Europe.

Besides these shops, a great deal of business is carried on by mobile traders using bicycles. Most of these carry fish, both fresh and dried, from the market at Golomolo, and elsewhere along the coast, and sell it through all the villages of this area. Others buy eggs, pineapples, skins and peppers from local peasants and carry them for sale in Jinja. A few buy cattle or home-brewed beer and set up beer-shops or butchers' stalls in the various markets. Several local Bavuma are hawkers, selling the pots which their wives make at home. It is interesting that while all the shopkeepers are Protestants, with the exception of one Moslem, two-thirds of the mobile traders are Roman Catholics.

South Kyagwe is rather better provided with markets than many other parts of Buganda. Until recently there was a market within cycling distance of Makindu ever day of the week except Sundays. There is a daily market at Kisala, a large market at Nalubabwe, near Buikwe, every Monday, and another on the lake shore at Golomolo every Tuesday. On Wednesdays there used to be a market at Bulere; on Thursdays one is held near Mawota, and on Saturdays there are large markets at Ngogwe and at Kabugoga. Fish or meat is the primary article of sale, and the smell of dried fish permeates all markets; but traders, arriving by car and lorry, set up their stalls of poles and thatch and display many other goods—bright cotton prints, lengths of bark-cloth, and white and brown *kanzus* (the ankle-length robe, introduced by the Arabs, which has become the common dress for men); saucepans, cutlery and cups, cigarettes and soda-water; ropes, combs, mirrors, soap, knives and little lamps; and African medicines and charms spread out on the salesman's mat. There is always a large space under the trees, or a row of grass shelters, reserved for the sale of beer and, as the day wears on, there is a lot of drunkenness.

Though village crafts have greatly declined with the arrival of imported machine-made goods, there are still a certain number of craftsmen. Those who have the greatest standing are the ones with a modicum of modern technical training. In this parish there are three general carpenters, one of whom has had a course at a technical school; all of them are Moslems. Their business consists mainly of roughly made doors and windows, but they also turn out a regular supply of little folding chairs, small tables, and suit-cases. Linked with these are four or five who, in addition to their own cultivation, make an extra income as wood-cutters and sawyers. There is also at Kabubiro a 'mechanic', brilliantly skilful at repairs to bicycles but not motors. Of the traditional crafts, there are four bark-cloth makers, one of whom is reputed locally to supply bark-cloth to the Kabaka. He also runs a private elementary school and has a considerable practice as a spirit-diviner. There are several potters; those who are Baganda are men, but the Bavuma potters are, traditionally, always women. There is a mat-maker who has followed his father's trade, and a maker of wooden sandals; two blacksmiths who have also been professional hunters; and two professional musicians, one a Mudama who plays the lyre, and the other a Muganda fiddler; each has his own plantation, but is in great demand for dances round the district. Both of these describe themselves as 'a person without religion'.

The majority of the population, including the craftsmen and traders, are ordinary peasant cultivators. Around the hut, or group of huts, which is a man's home stand the plantain trees and the patches of sweet potatoes, maize, millet and vegetables which provide their food. A little further off, in most cases, are the cotton plants or the coffee bushes, the main source of cash.

Those who want to grow cotton can obtain free seed of good quality from the headquarters of the *gombolola* chief. They plant their plots in July or August and harvest the bolls in December and January, separating the long white fibres from the shorter, red-coloured fluff. The peasant cultivators sell their cotton to African buyers at small, corrugated-iron stores at Mawota, Bulere, Mboya or Buikwe, and, provided it has been properly sorted, they receive the price which is fixed annually by the Protectorate government. The long, or 'safi', fibre fetched 52 cents per lb. in 1956. Many growers in these days are members of the Uganda Growers' Association, and receive a dividend of Shs. 1·50 on every 100 lb. sold. The Association has its store at every buying centre and owns a ginnery. The other African buyers outside the

Association sell to the many Indian-owned ginneries scattered over the country.

Even higher reward can be won from coffee growing, but this takes longer to give results. Seedlings can be bought from privately owned beds; one cultivator living at Kabubiro runs a seed-bed for profit. The larger sized seedlings may begin to bear fruit after two or three years. The berries are first harvested in June, a second picking in August, and a third in late November. After sun-drying for one or two weeks, the berries are put into sacks or 4-gallon tins and carried, either to the wholesale stores which are to be found at many cross-roads, or direct to the nearest factory about fifteen miles away. In 1956 a well-filled sack might be sold for Shs. 200. Ten normal trees will produce one such sack in a year, but sometimes as much can be gathered from one really large and prolific tree.

The fishermen are a community on their own. Most of them come from Buvuma and Bugaya islands, or from Buziba on the western shores of Lake Victoria. In all these areas the missions of the Roman Catholic Church predominate and almost all the fishermen are Roman Catholics. A group of about a dozen men from one village will form a team, come to a particular point on the shore of Buganda, build small temporary huts and hire a canoe. The boat is usually the property of a Muganda— a cultivator or trader with money to invest—who pays an expert boat-builder to make a canoe which can be hired to the leader of a fishing team. The fish which the team catches are theirs to sell, but they must pay as harbour dues and market fees one fish in ten to the market steward. The team will spend from four to five years fishing one particular ground, taking turns to spend two or three months on holiday at their home. Eventually they will disband themselves, some to settle down to farming in their own country, others to join up with another team working in quite a different part of the lake. They regard their fishing as a temporary, money-making job to raise enough capital to buy land or pay bride-wealth for a wife. Most of them have a wife, or a girl whom they have bespoken, in their own country, but while they are in Buganda they take local wives, paying two or three hundred shillings in bride-wealth and marrying them by African custom. Sometimes these wives return with them to their homeland, but often they refuse and part from them when they leave.

There are in the community a small number of school-teachers; the headmaster and two others form the staff of the primary school of the Anglican Church at Makindu, where 58 pupils are taught in three classes; and at the private school at Kabubiro, which was founded for the Badama, there is a headmaster and a constantly changing staff of two or three others, with or without qualifications. There is also one very old Anglican clergyman living in retirement on the estate which was given to him by order of Sir Apolo Kagwa at the time when every ordained minister was allotted a portion of land. He is of the same clan as the other landowners. Of him, and of the catechists in the area, more will be said in the next chapter.

To complete this portrait of a parish, something must be said of its links with the outside world, for it is not to be thought that there is any feeling of isolation in such a community. A small number only seem to take one or other of the vernacular newspapers, but there are several homes which have a wireless set. From five until seven every evening this produces an almost unbroken flow of recorded dance music, some traditional, but mostly 'Bantu Jazz'—the haunting, endlessly repetitive swing music of the dance bands of Sophiatown and Kampala. There is also a weekly news commentary in Luganda for which people sometimes walk half a mile to a friend with a radio.

The dissemination of news in a more exciting version is the stock-in-trade of the local representatives of the political parties of Buganda. Until recently the group with most influence over the country people was the Bataka organization, a rather nebulous group with a conservative, 'back to the past', ideology. But, at the time when this survey was being made, the only party in the field, so far as the country villages were concerned, was the Uganda National Congress. The parish had its party office-bearers. On most Sundays excited young men could be seen flying along the rough tracks on their bicycles, wearing shirts, or carrying flags, of the party colours, bound for some gathering. Attempts were made to organize larger rallies at Makota, the *muluka* headquarters, and Buikwe, the *gombolola* headquarters, each month, but these were poorly attended unless a speaker from the central headquarters at Kampala was expected. For one week a concerted effort was made on a nation-wide scale and large meetings were held at every important centre in Kyagwe; these were always accompanied with prayers, and at Buikwe, in deference to the strong Moslem element there, by the sacrifice of a sheep. From time to time a party organizer arrived in his car to consult with the local chairman and secretary. But the political leaders at the capital, a few of whom were men of great ability, were frustrated by the quality of their representatives in the country areas. These have so little grasp of political realities that the majority of the peasants, while always glad of the excitement of wild talk, remained privately sceptical.

Before the end of 1956 local enthusiasm for the Congress was evaporating, and the best of the local leaders had moved elsewhere. Two other parties were gaining ground and all three were becoming more and more concerned with the problems of winning the other tribes outside Buganda. This has become steadily the primary concern, but the issue is confused by the dubious question of the position of the Kabaka in the future African state. Since his return from exile all parties in Buganda have tried to make capital out of the passionate emotions of loyalty which naturally surround him, but the National Congress has represented itself particularly as his champion, and has quite unscrupulously used the charge of disloyalty as a political weapon against its opponents. But naturally it is not easy to reconcile a highly emotional championship of the autonomy of the Kabaka with a Protectorate-wide appeal for united political action to achieve independence as a unitary African state. When some leaders attempted to solve the dilemma by proposing that the Kabaka of Uganda should ultimately be regarded as the head of a federal state of all Uganda, there was naturally an outcry from other kingdoms and districts in the Protectorate. No party, however, has as yet dared to commit itself to a definite policy regarding the African royalty in the various component states, for the matter of the Kabaka's dignity is still too explosive a topic for objective decisions to be taken. Ultimately, however, the various parties will have to seize this nettle and define their positions. At present the issues over which the political leaders are divided are mainly personal or concerned with internal organization. It was overtly on such grounds that a large group of the most intelligent leaders of the National Congress have broken away and formed a new United Congress Party.

These political groupings are essentially ephemeral and may be re-aligned after a few months. The gravest danger is the lack of any important political differences between the parties. All are rightly committed, as a primary objective, to the achievement of self-government, but beyond that none dares to commit itself to one side or the other of any serious political question for fear of antagonizing any group in the community. As a result the electorate, having no genuinely political grounds for choosing one or the other party, tends to be divided along religious lines, as between Anglicans, Roman Catholics and Moslems.

The word 'self-government', which is much on the lips of people during this period of emergence from colonial status, is sometimes

understood in the villages to imply not merely political independence
but complete relaxation of social prohibitions also. So some peasants
have said, 'Of course people are bringing out their other wives, openly,
because now we have self-government.' It is significant that several of
the local enthusiasts of the National Congress are also spirit-diviners
and fetish-practitioners. This is quite definitely not on account of any
deliberate 'back to paganism' policy in the Congress, which has sincerely
disavowed any such movements, but purely the result of the psychological condition of the men concerned. They are frustrated people with
a need to assert themselves, and they find in hare-brained local agitation
the same satisfaction as is provided by their occult activities. Not all,
however, are of that calibre; at least one local politician was a man of
real shrewdness and skill. There was also in the community another man
who had been used from time to time as an informer for the Protectorate
Police. There are few currents from the outer world which do not flow
through Makindu!

Buikwe, which is seven miles distant, and must be reached by bicycle
or on foot, except for the few who have cars, is a considerable centre.
The headquarters of the *gombolola* are there, with a small dispensary of
the Medical Department run by an African doctor. There is a railway
station with daily trains to Kampala and Jinja; the African stationmaster
is also the postmaster. The town consists of, perhaps, two dozen Indian
stores, a few petrol pumps and a dance-hall, where a tiny courtyard is
on Saturday nights the scene of somewhat unskilled jiving and its more
sordid accompaniments, sometimes to a three-piece band from Katwe,
Kampala.

From Buikwe there is transport by bus or train every day to Jinja
or Kampala. The more enterprising may hitch-hike into either place,
though the drivers of cars and lorries almost always charge several times
the price of a bus ticket. Though Jinja is much nearer, the people of
Makindu parish seem (with the exception of the Basoga) to have many
more links with Kampala, forty miles away. There are many ties of
relationship. The landowner has a younger brother who lives in Katwe;
from each of the big Badama groups there is at least one woman married
to a constable in the police lines; the shopkeepers have business con-
nections; the local enthusiasts of the Congress Party have party organizers to call on. It is to the districts of Katwe, Mulago and Wandegeya,
and the African housing-estate of Naguru, that the lines of communication from the country mainly lead; that is where Makindu has its
friends, finds an eating-house for a meal, or a bed for the night. Fairly

well worn, also, are the tracks leading to the Government Hospital at Mulago or to the African government offices at Mengo. A small but significant minority make their way to the Uganda Museum, popularly called 'the house of the fetishes', where they know that magical and cultic objects are preserved. School-teachers, or those who come to gaze at the shops, may foregather at the Anglican diocesan bookshop. But the majority of those who come to the capital do not walk up the hills on which stand the headquarters and the cathedrals of the Anglican and Roman Churches. A considerable number of sick folk and their relatives, certainly, will go to the mission hospitals on Namirembe and Nsambya hills; school-teachers may visit their denominational education office and, occasionally, take a party of school children to see the cathedral; clergy, of course, and some catechists, will have business at the diocesan offices; ordinary laymen attached to the revival movement are likely to find their way to the big meeting on Namirembe hill on Friday evenings. But, for a great number of people, the only occasion for a visit to one of these hills is the wedding of a relative in the cathedral on a Saturday afternoon. The 'church on the hill' has its function as a symbol and a necessary administrative centre; but the responsible church, in its essential being, must be looked for where the people are—in Mulago, Wandegeya, Katwe and Naguru. It does not consist of buildings and institutions, which in these places are conspicuous by their absence; but of persons in the midst of persons; it is in them that the church stands or falls.

NOTE

1. See A. B. Mukwaya, *Land Tenure in Buganda* (East African Studies, No. 1, 1953); H. B. Thomas and A. E. Spencer, *A History of Uganda Land and Surveys* (1938).

[Every home in Makindu village (42), and half of Kabubiro (34)]

1. BY TRIBE

TRIBE	TOTAL	Number born elsewhere	Under 30	30–50	Over 50	Estate owners descended from original landowner	Female head of household	Cultivators	Storekeepers	Mobile Traders	Craftsmen	Teachers	Batongole	Landowner	Spirit-Diviner	No Work	Wives 0	Wives 1	Wives 2	Wives 3	Anglican	Roman Catholic	Moslem	Traditional	None
Muganda	30	4	6	10	14	10	7	12	1	2	6	1	1	1	1	5	7	14	2	–	18	10	1	–	2
Muvuma	17	12	1	8	8	1	2	10	–	3	2	–	1	–	–	1	5	10	–	–	9	7	–	–	–
Mudama	10	10	–	8	2	–	–	6	1	1	1	2	1	–	–	–	1	5	4	–	7	1	1	–	2
Musoga	9	3	1	7	1	–	1	7	–	1	1	–	–	–	–	–	3	4	–	1	2	2	2	2	–
Mukedi	9	9	–	8	1	–	–	7	–	–	–	–	–	–	–	–	3	6	–	–	2	5	–	1	–
Munyaruanda	1	1	–	1	–	–	–	1	–	–	–	–	–	–	–	–	–	1	–	–	–	1	–	–	–
TOTAL	76	39	8	42	26	11	10	43	2	7	10	3	3	1	1	6	19	40	6	1	38	26	4	3	5

2. BY RELIGIOUS AFFILIATION

RELIGIOUS AFFILIATION	TOTAL	Number born elsewhere	Father Same	Father Traditional	Father Another	Estate owners descended from original landowners	Female head of household	Cultivators	Storekeepers	Mobile Traders	Craftsmen	Teachers	Batongole	Landowner	Spirit-Diviner	No Work	Wives 0	Wives 1	Wives 2	Wives 3	African Custom	Abduction	Christian Rite	Moslem Rite
Anglican	38	15	15	23	–	9	7	17	2	3	5	2	2	1	1	5	10	16	5	–	19	4	3	–
Roman Catholic	26	16	7	19	–	2	2	17	–	2	4	1	1	–	–	1	6	17	1	1	8	6	10	–
Moslem	4	3	2	1	1	–	–	3	–	1	–	–	–	–	–	–	1	2	–	–	–	1	–	3
Traditional	3	2	2	–	1	–	–	3	–	–	1	–	–	–	–	–	2	1	–	–	1	1	–	–
None	5	3	–	4	1	–	1	3	–	1	–	–	–	–	–	–	–	4	–	–	3	1	–	–
TOTAL	76	39	26	47	3	11	10	43	2	7	10	3	3	1	1	6	19	40	6	1	31	13	13	3

Note.—All other information regarding land tenure was vitiated by the fact, realized too late, that the word *kibanja* is used by the villagers indiscriminately to describe both leasehold land and small freehold plots bought outright. The word *mailo* is used only of larger estates inherited from the original landowner.

6

The Church Organization of the Local Parish

BUGANDA is nominally a Christian country. In the sample at Makindu and Kabubiro, set out at the end of the previous chapter, it can be seen that 64 of the 76 heads of households, that is 84 per cent., call themselves Christians and have been baptized. Had the sample been taken in Bulere village, where is the main concentration of Moslems in the parish, the percentage would have been lower; so also in Wambogwe, where a larger number of illiterate immigrants from Bukedi, adherents of the old *lubaale* cult, is to be found. In other parishes of the same district the Roman Catholics may outnumber the Anglicans, according to the siting of the *muluka* centres of the two churches, and the denominational allegiance of the landowners and chiefs. By reason of past history Makindu might be called a Protestant *muluka*, whereas Malongwe is a Roman Catholic centre. By the same token Buikwe is strongly Moslem. The same pattern of contrasting spheres of predominance appears on a larger scale at the county level where the effects of the partition after the wars of 1892 are still evident. The latest available figures of religious affiliation for the African population of Buganda are only approximate, being based on the last sample census only. They are liable to a margin of error which has not been accurately determined; they do, however, give a fair picture of the proportions.

Roman Catholic	537,000	equals 41 per cent.
Anglican	311,000	24
Other Christian . . .	1,300	0·1
Moslems	97,700	7·5
Old Religion . . .	350,000	27
Other non-Christian . .	5,200	0·4
	1,302,200	

What these figures do not adequately represent is the numbers that belong to some of the other Christian bodies. The African Greek

Orthodox Church claims a membership of 20,000, though this is almost certainly a great exaggeration. The Seventh Day Adventist Mission, which started work in Uganda in 1903, only moved into Buganda more recently, yet they claim a membership in excess of 3,000. There must be several thousands of followers of the Malaki sect still left. What probably has happened is that most of these, in a census form, called themselves Anglicans, since that was the Church from which they were drawn into their present adherence; a smaller number would be included among those who call themselves Roman Catholics.

What it actually means to the members of the community that such a high proportion of them are Christians is a question that is very hard to determine and must be reserved to a later chapter. For the present it must suffice to observe that of 38 Anglicans in the sample taken in Makindu parish, 6 said that they never go to church and 13 go at festivals only. Not more than 6 are regular in church attendance. The Roman Catholics have a rather better record: of their 26 heads of households, 12 attend regularly at Mass.

Again it may be mentioned that of these 64 Christians all but 4 or 5 consult the spirit-diviner occasionally, and the diviner herself is an Anglican, though one of those who never attend church. In Makindu and Kabubiro villages there are only 7 men and 4 women who do not drink beer; the rest, more or less frequently, get intoxicated. Of the 53 married Christian men, there are only 14 who have homes in which both partners have remained monogamous (8 Roman Catholic and 6 Anglican), and of these only 2 had a church marriage (both Roman Catholic). There are 3 other genuinely monogamous homes, in all of which the man says he has no religion.

These figures represent a state of affairs which, as has been said, is in some respects more acute in south Kyagwe than in many other parts of Buganda. In any case it would be just as superficial to draw conclusions from these outward facts as it is to draw them from the baptism statistics. But it is valuable to mention them in passing, in order to indicate the complexity of that which we are attempting to describe.

As was explained in Chapter 4, the Anglican work in north and south Kyagwe was combined in 1906 into a single missionary district, later called a rural deanery, centred at Mukono. This arrangement continued until 1948, when once again the south-eastern part of Kyagwe was made into a separate deanery with Ngogwe as its centre. The deanery consists of four pastorates, each in the charge of an ordained pastor. Makindu parish, or *muluka*, is one of four in the pastorate of Buikwe.

Buikwe pastorate is a newly formed unit, recently detached from the enormous pastorate of Ngogwe, of which it formed a part. Ngogwe pastorate used to contain two administrative sub-county districts; it is one of these which has now been turned into the new pastorate of Buikwe. Similarly, as was mentioned in Chapter 5, each church parish contains several administrative parishes; in the *muluka* of Makindu church, for example, there are three political *miruka*.

The church which Yosuwa Nannungi built at Makindu in memory of his brother Andereya is the parish church, which is in the charge of a catechist. Under his supervision within the parish there are three tiny village churches—at Lunguju and Nkompe, where two very old catechists live and take services, and at Bulere, which is without a catechist. This is the common pattern, as can be seen from the analysis of another pastorate on page 138.

This structure is supposed to be integrated in two ways. (i) The parish catechist should supervise and draw into a team the village catechists in his charge, and the pastor is supposed to call in the parish catechists monthly to receive their church collections, pay their salaries and hear some report of their work. (ii) At the same time the system of church councils provides a more democratic link-up. Every village church is meant to have its council of ten, chosen by the whole adult congregation. This group chooses four representatives—usually their catechist, their two church-wardens, and one other—to sit on the parish, or *muluka*, council. Every parish council chooses one catechist and one lay representative to sit on the pastorate council; it can also elect a different lay representative for each of the pastorate committees, for schools, lands and finance. In exactly the same way the pastorate councils send a clergyman and lay representatives to the deanery council and committees for schools, lands, finance and marriage guidance; and finally from the deanery councils the members of the diocesan council are elected.

Like all committee structures, this is liable to grow moribund in two ways. At the lower levels the committees may cease to function from sheer futility and lack of interest. None of the village churches in Makindu parish ever has a congregational meeting or a council of ten. The parish council consists only of the three catechists and the two church-wardens of Makindu church.

At the higher levels the committees may devour the time of the best leaders of the church. In some deaneries a whole day is devoted to each committee so that pastorate committees followed by deanery committees occupy nine days, three times a year. A pastor who is also a member of some of the diocesan committees may spend two months out of twelve in committee work.

THE HISTORY OF THE PARISH

The older Christians of Makindu parish look back to the days when there were many village churches all in a flourishing condition. Most of them were founded in George Baskerville's time. At Nkompe, for example, they still remember the day he first visited them, tramping across their hills; it was he who suggested naming the place Nkompe, or Eye-holes, because of some rock fissure he discovered in the forest. Churches were built at Makota, Bulere, Lunguju, Nkompe, Bufumbe and Golomolo, with a trained catechist at each one, and a little school, with its uniform and school flag, in his charge. Sleeping sickness cleared many of the villages, but as the population returned Christians started up their churches again in most places. At Nkompe, for example, re-occupation had begun in 1919. Three men who had known Baskerville, Daudi Waiswa, Danieri Mityana and Jemusi Mayenje, used to meet every Sunday in one of their houses and gradually gathered around themselves a regular congregation. They were natural leaders in the district. Until 1925 Danieri was headmaster of the parish school at Makindu and was followed, for a short time, by Daudi Waiswa. In 1929 they contributed money and built a little church at Nkompe, with half-walls of unplastered mud and wattle, and a grass thatch. In 1935 Stephen Kalungu was sent to be their catechist.

He is typical of the old style of junior catechist that has borne the burden and heat of the day for the past half century. In 1920 he had come to Ngogwe school from Bugaya Island. He recounts how, while he was in the confirmation class, 'God spoke and sowed seed in his heart'. When the pastor asked him what he would do when he left school, he answered, 'I am going to be a shepherd of the sheep.' He went to Mukono in 1929 to study for a school-teacher's certificate under 'Lwekomba', as Daniell, the principal, was called. He was then posted as an assistant teacher at Makindu school; but a year later he was sent as both catechist and teacher to Nkompe, where he remained for twenty years. In 1955 he gave up teaching, and the school ceased to exist, but he still takes the Sunday services. Of the present day, he says, 'The mission does not remember people like me.'

Kalungu's story is of interest also in the light it throws upon the nature of vocation in the experience of many catechists and clergy. Very often a boy has dreamed of himself preaching or teaching children, and the repetition of this dream is taken as a call from God. In many cases the suggestion was made, in the first instance, by a pastor or school-master and the boy recognized in the suggestion the authority of a vocation. The Baganda do not, generally speaking, share the extreme reticence of Western minds in such matters. One of the most able of the clergy in the Uganda diocese has written to the heads of secondary schools in his deanery definitely asking them to bring such a suggestion to likely boys in their care, for, as he said, 'the Apostles did not offer themselves for service, they were called.'

At Makindu itself, soon after Baskerville left Ngogwe, a catechist called Benego was in charge of the parish. He was a strong leader and worked there for many years and finally died in harness. His successor, Katula, was unpopular and soon left. In 1914 Yeremiya Katali was appointed and remained for about five years. He had already been trained at Mukono for his '2nd certificate', and while he was at Makindu he returned to the theological school for a year to obtain his '3rd certi-ficate'. He was supported by Justine and Semu, successive headmasters of the day school, who were keen church workers. In 1920 began the long incumbency of Yobu Waiswa, the son-in-law of Daudi Waiswa, one of the founders of Nkompe church. He was a large and indefatigable young catechist with a 2nd certificate. Every Sunday he called the people to church at 8 a.m. and for half an hour he led them in Bible reading. Then he beat the drum and robed himself for the 9 a.m. service. Most of the congregation used to stay for the afternoon service at 3 o'clock, spending the intervening hours in the compound of Nannungi the landowner. Every Thursday Yobu held a Bible study in his house, at which one of the younger more educated laymen might be asked to give a talk. Baptism and Confirmation classes were strictly disciplined and followed a full curriculum of reading—the gospels of Mark and Luke for the former, Matthew and John for the latter. Yobu was greatly loved and the parish mourned deeply with him when his daughter, who was seduced by a local sub-chief, died in childbirth at the age of fourteen. Yobu himself died in 1938 when he was still comparatively young. He had been succeeded at Makindu in 1933 by Samuel Kasule, another 2nd certificate catechist. He was a humble, hard-working man, very popular in the parish.

It was in Kasule's time, however, that the slight decline in church-going, which has continued gradually ever since, first became noticeable and Christians began openly to 'grow tired' and to 'faint'. The war

7. The caves of Kokkola with the fishermen's property
left in the keeping of the *lubaale*

8. A *Mulaguzi* in a state of possession, shaking the *nsaasi* gourd rattle

9. Great rock sacred to Kungo the Leopard *lubaale*

10. Little shrines built for the *mizimu*

itself was an important occasion of stumbling. Fifteen men from Makindu *muluka* went into the armed forces. Before they left all had been regular church-goers; when they returned not one professed to be still a Christian, for, as they said, they had seen that the white man has no religion. There were many other factors in this decline which we shall attempt to analyse later. But the most important feature was its gradualness. There was no sudden reaction, no marked decrease in numbers. Times of national tension—the riots of 1945 and 1949, above all the deportation of the Kabaka in 1953—accelerated somewhat the process and gave additional excuses to those who were looking for them. A proverb that is often applied in this connexion says: *Analemwa embuzi okutuga nti lintunulidde*: 'A man who fails to kill a goat for the feast says, "It gazed at me."' None of the political events was the cause of the falling away: that has to be sought elsewhere.

The supply of catechists was beginning to dry up at the end of the last war, and after Samuel Kasule had retired to cultivate a plot of land near Ngogwe, there was an interim of eighteen months during which the work of the parish was carried on with only the casual help of school-teachers and occasional visits of clergy from Ngogwe. Then from 1947 to 1952 Christopher Mukasa became catechist in charge.

His career is very typical of the younger catechists who enter the work with the hope of eventually becoming clergy. As epitomized in men like him, it is a pattern of ministry that is still admirably suited to the needs of the parishes; it is still fulfilling an indispensable function; yet economic and social changes in society are pressing it out of existence. Christopher Mukasa was educated at the Bishop's School, Mukono, as far as Primary Standard VI. In 1941 he worked as an uncertificated catechist at Golomolo for one year. Then he joined the deanery training class, obtained his 1st certificate, and for a year assisted the pastorate staff at Ngogwe. In 1944 he had a further year's training for his 2nd certificate, and was posted to a village south of Ngogwe, where he was married. He was soon moved to Makindu, where he remained for six years, the first period of more than one year at any place since his ministry began. He rented a plot of land, built his own house, and became thoroughly rooted in the parish and in the affection of the people. Although the gradual decline continued during his time, there were occasions on which some special effort reversed the process for a year or two, so the actual fall away was very slight. In 1953 he was sent to the theological school at Mukono to obtain his 3rd certificate, but instead of returning to Makindu he was posted to Kasoga, another

I

parish church on the road from Buikwe to the west. His wife and children, however, are still in the house at Makindu, for he cannot afford to
lose the plot, for which he paid a considerable premium and which is
now producing coffee.

After Mukasa left there was no permanent catechist at Makindu for
three years. The old retired clergyman from Namatovu, and a series of
occasional helpers, did what they could; but sometimes there was no
service in the church for several weeks, and practically no visiting or
instruction was undertaken for the whole of that time.

Meanwhile the village churches in the parish were also being left
unshepherded. Since Mukasa left Golomolo in 1942 there has been no
replacement, and the little church there has fallen down. The same thing
has happened at Makota and Bufumbe. At Bulere the man who had
been catechist for twenty years married again after the death of his first
wife; his second wife is a Roman Catholic, so they were, of necessity,
married by an African customary wedding and automatically excommunicated. He is, therefore, no longer allowed to officiate as catechist,
though he remains a stalwart church-warden. It should be added that
this enforced retirement from his ministry was not, perhaps, wholly
unwelcome, for he is now a keen and prosperous shopkeeper. In addition, therefore, to the old catechist at Nkompe, there is only one other
village church which has a worker in charge. At Lunguju is an old man
who came from Buvuma Island to attend school in south Kyagwe, and
became a 1st certificate catechist in 1917. He has lived at Lunguju since
then, continually declaring his decision to retire from church work, but
always persuaded by his tiny congregation to remain. He does nothing,
however, except take the Sunday morning service week by week.

THE CAUSES OF DECLINE

At present there is widespread anxiety in the Anglican Church over the
drop in church attendance on Sundays, which is regarded as indicative
of a general lapse from faith. A survey of 24 pastorates over all parts of
Buganda, with samples from Busoga and Ankole for comparison, shows
the following percentage of baptized adults who attended Sunday
morning service in 1956-1957.

The much lower average in Buganda is due partly to the more
advanced stage of social disruption which that kingdom has reached,
and also to the greater proportion of the population who have been
baptized. A gloomy prognosis might declare that the other areas are
bound to follow the same downward path as Buganda as soon as they

reach the same point of social development. But there is a vitality about the life of the church in Ankole which defies such a verdict. This may be partly due to different historical and sociological factors, partly to the greater strength of the revival there. Whatever the cause, the 65 per cent. attendance in their *muluka* churches is in keeping with many other indications of a remarkable spiritual maturity and responsibility.

Mean average percentage of baptized Adults attending Sunday Morning Service

	In *muluka* churches	In village churches
In 24 Buganda Pastorates . .	20	16·7
In 3 Busoga Pastorates . . .	41	29·6
In 8 Ankole Pastorates . . .	65	57·75

The Sunday afternoon service shows every sign of dying out. In the majority of village churches, even in Ankole, it is not held. Since a midday meal has become almost universal custom, very few are prepared to wait for it until five or six o'clock, and it is quite impracticable in the ordinary village household to cook and serve a meal between the morning and afternoon service, except for those who live on the church compound.

A careful examination of the congregational attendance at two churches over the past eleven years shows that the rise and fall of numbers is definitely related to certain variables in an otherwise static situation. The following figures were culled from the church registers of Makindu parish and of a parish in Busiro county, chosen because of its close resemblance in size and organization to Makindu. The figures included children as well as adults. After they had been computed, a group of Christians in each place were asked to recount the history of their church in the past eleven years, recalling especially any changes or unusual events. After that the figures and the history were placed side by side.

The main impression from these figures is of a slow downward trend, not much accelerated by external events. It can be stemmed, and the tide turned, by any special effort on the part of the catechist; on the other hand, as soon as a church is left without a catechist there is an immediate drop. The disturbances in 1949 had a greater effect, in both parishes, than the deportation of the Kabaka, as far as church attendance is concerned. The deportation had greater effect around the capital than elsewhere.

	MAKINDU PARISH		KABALE PARISH	
	Average congregation Sunday morning	History	Average congregation Sunday morning	History
1945	64	Kasule still catechist	87	Mayanja was cate-
1946	60	Interim, no cate-chist	91	chist to the end of 1949
1947	61	Mukasa started work	84	
1948	68·5	Adult literacy campaign	63	
1949	54	'Bataka' disturb-ances[1]	59	'Bataka' disturb-ances[1]
1950	57	Church choir formed for two years	41	Interim, no cate-chist
1951	60		59	Musoke appointed catechist
1952	52		52	Catechist only part-time, for four
1953	50·5	No catechist for three years	51	years
1954	50	Kabaka in exile	52	Kabaka in exile
1955	52		50	

Two events referred to under Makindu parish need some explanation. In 1948 an adult literacy campaign brought two African welfare workers, and occasionally a European, to Makindu. Local school-teachers and the catechist joined the team, and every house in the administrative parish was systematically visited. Reading classes were held near the church on Sundays after the service. The stimulation of community interest, and the discovery that someone cared about their welfare, had an effect on church attendance which lasted for over a year. Then in 1950 two of the more educated laymen organized a church choir which sang Christmas carols and an occasional anthem on Sundays. This continued for two years and was steadily increasing church attendance; but, unfortunately, in 1952 one of the two leaders decided to devote his energies to the Congress Party in the district, and the other was not ready to carry on alone. It is significant, however, that the application of quite ordinary methods of parochial work—thorough visiting and thoughtful preparation of worship—should evoke such immediate response; for the dead do not respond.

It is quite clear that the lack of this thorough pastoral ministry, more than anything else, is the cause of the steady decline. The occasional missions organized by the diocese certainly have been times of recovery and a spiritual turning-point in the lives of hundreds. But on the continuing life of the church as a whole, taking a longer view, they seem to have acted rather as stimulants, which have slightly less effect each time they are applied.

Everywhere Christians, good and bad, mention the lack of visiting and pastoral care as the reason for the lapse from the church. There is general recognition that, the church having grown in the way in which it did, the local congregations are bound to depend upon the patient supervision and encouragement of some human shepherd. This universal conviction was expressed in various aphorisms: 'Labourers without a foreman soon stop working.' 'Cattle without a herdman wander far.' 'Without the millet how can the beer ferment?'

Where the catechists are still at work many of them appear to their people to be indifferent or censorious. Sick-visiting is no longer customary among the majority of Anglican catechists, who do not seem to see the point of it. Indeed, many catechists never pray in a home unless they are spending the night there. Others restrict their visiting to the regular members of the Sunday congregation, and have been known to refuse to visit the other members of their flock, even for serious illness.

When asked to explain the catechists' failure, most ordinary villagers agreed that, apart from individual laziness, it was due to sheer discouragement and financial necessity. In the old days the church's ministry was thought of primarily as free service. Just as house-servants, whether of the chief or the missionary, never worked for wages, but their master was responsible for feeding, clothing, housing and educating them, so the clergy and catechists were not regarded as salaried workers. They depended on the *omuzigo* (lit. the oil), that is, the goodwill of their congregation and the generosity of chiefs; moreover, their children received free education in the church's schools. The tiny wages were a token of the church council's responsibility for them and authority over them. In 1904 clergy were paid the equivalent of Shs. 40 a year (a labourer working for the Government received Shs. 54); senior catechists got about Shs. 20, and junior catechists Shs. 9 a year. In 1913 the salaries were raised to Shs. 112, Shs. 72 and Shs. 36 respectively. After the First World War clergy salaries went up to £18 a year and in 1927 were again raised to £24. At that point, however, all church ministers began to be regarded as salaried workers, and the laity no longer felt any obligation to support them with gifts in kind. Later they were required to pay a part of the school fees, and other exemptions which they had enjoyed were taken from them. The pastor still enjoys some of the social status which was his when he was the confidant and partner of the chief. But steadily his poverty is lowering the respect with which he is regarded, unless he commands especial admiration for some partly spiritual gifts. One leading Muganda, for example, has been known to rebuke his wife for serving tea to a guest 'in that little clergyman's teapot'. When asked to explain the phrase he said, 'Only a clergyman would serve tea in an enamel teapot all chipped like that'.

The catechists in the villages and parish churches are driven to support their families in the usual ways available to a peasant, by growing all their own food, keeping a few cows and goats, and cultivating cotton and coffee. At first they will use the plot of land, if any, provided for them to live on by the church. But as soon as possible, for their own security, they raise the premium, rent a plot and build a house of their own so that, even if they are moved from place to place, the wife can remain to preserve the right of tenure and to cultivate the cash crop. Inevitably this means that a great part of the catechist's time is absorbed in building or repairing his property, cultivating and marketing his crops. If he is moved, as very frequently happens, his interests are divided between the place where he is working and the home where his wife and family are living; and he constantly faces the temptation to solve his dilemma by marrying a second wife, secretly, in order to maintain the two establishments.

His position, and the quality of his ministry, might be improved by a higher salary. But at the present time a great many catechists are not receiving even the salary that is due to them. Old Stephen Kalungu hopes to receive £10 a year, but has rarely had as much for the past ten years. This arises from the rule made by the Anglican synod in 1913 that the grade of catechist allowed to a local church must depend on the funds raised by that church. In practice this means that the catechist and church workers between them must raise, in the course of the year, enough for the repair and upkeep of their church, for paying the proper quota into the pastorate, deanery, and diocesan funds, and for the catechist's salary. Since in the village churches the church-wardens have almost ceased to function, the catechist is left with the task of raising these funds himself.

CHURCH FINANCES

Since about 1912 the church in Buganda has been anxious about the poor standard of its almsgiving. It seems likely that the trouble started when the 'Pan-Anglican Fund' was used to pay for the Baganda evangelists who were working outside Buganda. It was the first time that foreign funds had been used to support any African workers in the church. However, even earlier than that Baskerville in Kyagwe was complaining of the failure of ordinary Christians to give responsibly since the church relied almost entirely on the liberality of the chiefs. The difficulties really arise from the nature of Ganda gifts and their function in traditional society. The Baganda are anything but mean, but their giving is always personal and always *ad hoc*. Gifts to relatives, to superiors, to guests and visitors are extremely generous and play an important part in social relations. Donations are readily offered for any occasional need such as a journey, or in times of sickness or bereavement. Loans are less willingly granted. But sustained giving, particularly to a fund rather than a person, is very hard indeed to achieve. For this reason, in village and *muluka* churches, thank-offerings from individuals on special occasions very often amount to more than the regular offerings of the congregation.

So it was that in 1912 the regular offerings of the whole church amounted to only £1,908, while special contributions for church buildings and schools were more than £2,200. The synod of the following year took note that in West and South Africa every adult Christian was bound to pay some fixed church dues; no such assessment was imposed in Uganda. They decided that they did not wish to introduce anything that might be interpreted as a religious tax, but proposed the adoption of a scheme of 'Church Builders', in which they hoped that all church members would be enrolled, the senior branch undertaking to pay not less than one rupee per annum to church funds, and the junior branch, for children, not less than 50 cents to the education fund. It was only a matter of time before the *buzimbi*, or Builder's fund, did in fact become a church due which every adult Christian was expected to pay. People who failed to produce up-to-date recepts for *buzimbi* have found that a clergyman would not marry them in church until they could do so; and some who have died without the receipts among their papers have been refused Christian burial. The Roman Catholic equivalent of the *buzimbi* tends to be applied in exactly the same way in their parishes, where it is referred to as *ndobolo*, or a share of the plunder.

The actual amount that most Christians put into the collection on Sundays is very small indeed, but it has been steadily rising over the last ten years. The average gift per head per Sunday rose, at Makindu, from 4 cents in 1947 to 17 cents in 1955, and at Kabale, in Busiro, from 4 cents in 1945 to 13 cents in 1955.

The money which is given to the church is booked under the following heads: Sunday Collections; Baptism and Confirmation 'gifts'; Wedding fees (Shs. 10 each); Thank-offerings; and *buzimbi*. On certain festivals the collection is earmarked for particular objects: Christmas and Harvest for the catechist's salary; Easter and New Year's Day for the Pastor's salary; St Andrew's Day, Epiphany and Ash Wednesday to missions of the Uganda Church (mainly in Belgian Congo); Annunciation Day to the Mothers' Union; Pentecost to the C.M.S.; St Luke's Day to Hospitals; and the 2nd Sunday in Advent to the Bible Society. Unfortunately the week-day festivals raise almost nothing.

The pastor receives these offerings from the parish churches in his pastorate each month and enters them in an analysis book. They are then apportioned according to the following complex system of percentages:

Source of income	To central diocesan fund	To salaries of clergy of the deanery	To travelling expenses of rural dean	To salary of the pastor	To pastorate expenses	To salary of local catechist	Fee to government
Buzimbi . .	10		5	42	10	33	
Collections, Baptism gifts, Thank-offerings	10	20	5		10	55	
Confirmation gifts		50			50		
Wedding fees (Shs. 10.) .		50	25		25		
Harvest . .	10					90	
Christmas . .	10					90	
Easter . .	10			90			
New Year's Day				100			

If the pastorate or deanery funds are in arrears, they are made up by adjustment at the expense of the catechists' salaries.

So, with the total of collections, gifts and thank-offerings at Makindu ranging from £15 to £25 per year, it can be seen that the catechists of the parish will not receive their full salary unless they can round up a large number of *buzimbi* payments. But it is their efforts to do this which arouses the greatest resentment among the majority of Christians. The most frequently heard criticism of the church is in such terms as 'The basket (for collections) is the stumbling-block', or 'The church is a shop'. As one village wag put it, 'They are not looking for the lost sheep, but only for the lost coin.' Since the synod recently decided to raise the amount of *buzimbi*, the resentment is likely to grow stronger. Extra collections and quotas for repairing the Cathedral roof or sending clergy to England add to the impression that the clergy and catechists are concerned only for raising money.

Since, as a result of early gifts and allotments under the Uganda Agreement, 1900, the Native Anglican Church owns more freehold land than almost any other private landowner in the country, its leaders have, naturally, looked towards these estates from time to time as a possible source of income. As far back as 1913 a scheme was actually launched to operate some of this property as coffee and cotton plantations under a European manager, and an attempt was made to float a loan of £2,000 for capital development. However, the difficulties arising from the rights of tenants, which were explained in the previous chapter, have so far proved insurmountable; added to which the large total of church property is made up almost entirely of scores of small areas scattered all over the country. Many times Europeans have proposed that some such attempt be made; but the African leaders of the church, apart from their conservatism and their recognition of the difficulties, seem to have been uneasy about the moral issues involved. They have no wish to see their church guilty of enclosure, or the eviction of tenants of long standing, even if the laws could be circumvented. It certainly would be an adventurous and creative step if those responsible for the church's estates would confer with the African leaders of co-operative movements or of political parties, who are seriously concerned with the need for an agrarian revolution, and, in conjunction with them, offer to pioneer some type of co-operative farming on church lands. But this would depend on winning the goodwill and participation of the majority of the tenants; and any such venture would, by its nature, have to be undertaken out of concern for a problem of society, and as a witness in that field. It could not, at one and the same time, convincingly demonstrate profit-sharing, co-operative development and also earn quick returns for the landowner.

ATTEMPTS AT A SOLUTION

Meanwhile as a result of the poverty which is the prospect for most catechists, the supply of men has virtually come to an end. The training centre for 2nd certificate catechists closed down in 1956; young 1st certificate men are therefore unlikely to remain long in the work. The following record of the actual staffing of the churches in one pastorate in Busiro county in 1956 shows quite clearly that, so far as Buganda is concerned, the age of the catechists is over. Seven pastorates were examined in this way and this one appeared to be most representative in every respect. The Roman numerals represent *muluka* churches, and the small numerals village churches.

I. (Pastorate Centre.) One priest and one 3rd certificate catechist.
   i. Very old 2nd certificate catechist. Has long begged to retire.
   ii. Elderly man awarded honorary 3rd certificate.

II. 3rd certificate catechist, a potential ordinand.
   i. Very old 1st certificate catechist. Already retired on his own plot.

III. Catechist has retired. No services unless the 3rd certificate catechist goes over from Pastorate centre.
   i. Old man with no certificate.
   ii. Clerk in *gombolola* chief's headquarters.
   iii. Young cultivator.

IV. Catechist has retired. No services unless the headmaster takes them.
   i. No catechist.
   ii. Church fell down six years ago.
   iii. Church fell two years ago. Services occasionally held in a private school if a catechist goes over.

V. Young 1st certificate catechist.
   i. New man without certificate.
   ii. Fish-seller. Failed to pass 1st certificate examination.

VI. Munyaruanda cultivator.
   i. Very old 1st certificate catechist.
   ii. Very old ex-Moslem. Retired on his own plot.
   iii. Young Munyankole 1st certificate catechist.

The Roman Catholic Church faces exactly the same difficulty in Buganda. Generally speaking, her catechists are of a very low standard today, and are not being replaced. Her answer to the problem is to rely more and more on the work of vigorous young African priests. It was explained in Chapter 4 that it has been the Roman Catholic policy to retain responsibility for the pastorates in European hands for longer than the Anglicans have done. Her great numerical superiority in missionary personnel enabled her to do this and to take her time over the development of an African ministry, insisting on the full academic training that she requires of her priests in any race. Since the Anglican African ministry no longer outnumbers the Roman, the latter are undoubtedly beginning to occupy an appreciable place in the picture. Masaka Diocese, for example, under Mgr. Kiwanuka, is staffed entirely by African secular priests, fifty-nine in all. In the Makindu area the Roman Catholic pastorate centre, or station, was until recently at Nyenga, where, in addition to the European staff of the boys' seminary, there was a missionary head of the pastorate. It was he who raised foreign money to build, at Naja, Buikwe and Malongwe, three solid brick churches. Two years ago Malongwe was made the centre of a new pastorate with an African priest in charge. At the same time Nyenga pastorate also was placed under an African. The new priest at Malongwe, equipped with a motor cycle, at once made a house-to-house survey of his pastorate, and worked out a plan of campaign in consultation with his brethren at Nyenga. He built a small school at Bufumbe and has installed a young vernacular teacher. Services are held there every Sunday, and as soon as the school qualifies for a Government grant-in-aid, a separate church building will be added. Now a second school is being put up at Bulere. Whenever any concentrated effort is required—for example in the hearing of great numbers of confessions in the weeks preceding Easter—the priests of Nyenga pastorate will be called in to assist, and later this help will be reciprocated. So the Roman Catholic Church is putting into the field a small but compact force of highly trained priests who will use young school-teachers wherever possible in place of the old-style catechists.

The Anglican Church has slowly worked her way towards a partial solution which is very similar. Though there has been a long time-lag between theoretical recognition of the need for a more highly educated ministry and the hard practical steps towards attaining it, the church, while continuing to maintain a reduced supply of the older type of clergy and 3rd certificate catechists, has begun to train in English candidates for the ministry who have had a full secondary education or its equivalent, and to produce also a much younger, higher grade catechist. The necessity for this newer type of ministry, as well as the dangers latent in the attempt to achieve it, have been clearly summarized in Bishop Stephen Neill's report on the training of the ministry, and all that he said in 1950 remains fundamentally true today.[2] It must be said, however, that hitherto this solution of the church's problem has appeared as mainly a European and extraneous policy, mainly because it takes no account of traditional African concepts of leadership and authority. A society which refuses to accept educational qualifications as a substitute for maturity, and a ministerial hierarchy which still rests squarely on the old patterns of authority, have treated very hardly indeed some of the eager young men who have been the 'guinea pigs'

of this missionary experiment. Some of these have made spiritual shipwreck as a result; but slowly the new ideas are gaining ground. Quite
clearly, however, the supply of a greater number of ordained clergy of
both types will not materialize quickly enough to be by itself the answer
to the problem of the unstaffed village churches.

Here, however, appears one of the most striking instances of the
African church itself, out of its own inner life, responding to the call of
God in this situation. Without any directive from the centre, laymen
are coming forward in a number of pastorates to take responsibility for
the village churches. In the pastorate recorded above, for example, this
feature is just beginning to appear. These lay volunteers are of two
kinds: the peasant cultivator who is on a par with the old type of
catechist whom he replaces (see III iii, V ii, VI), and the qualified man
in a salaried profession (see III ii). In another pastorate of Busiro, at
Masulita, rather more than half the parish- and village-churches are
staffed by men of the peasant class. When such responsibility sprang
up there, it blossomed not only by filling the gaps in the ministry but
by taking initiative of many kinds. One farmer who, besides a large
coffee plantation, owns a shop and a lorry and runs a carpentry business,
was moved three years ago to build a church for his village which
previously had none. It is a tiny building, beautifully constructed and
whitewashed, with a corrugated iron roof. He did almost all the work
himself and furnished it with Communion Table, pulpit, lectern and
pews, all of the same yellow wood, which he made after the pattern of a
photograph he had seen. He takes immense pride in keeping the church
clean, and rounds up his friends to fill it on Sundays. He is not eligible
to take the services himself, since he has two wives, but that duty is
undertaken by another cultivator, who also spends much of his time
visiting the homes of the people.

Nearer to Kampala there are several pastorates in which men of the
professional classes are making themselves responsible for the parishes.
In Gayaza pastorate for example, where the pastor has a gift for drawing
out and unobtrusively co-ordinating such voluntary service, different
churches are in the charge of a carpenter, a builder, an agricultural
officer, a P.W.D. clerk and a clerk in the Government hospital. Some
of them are within the revival fellowship, and others are not, but they
work together with mutual respect. This type of leader shows greater
initiative than most of the clergy and catechists in introducing new
pastoral methods. Several have trained choirs; the wives of two of them
have started Sunday Schools. In one church there is a Bible class for

adolescents every Sunday afternoon; in another a trader leads a meeting for married men once a month. Two have formed bands of women for visiting and cleaning the church.

A great deal depends on the sympathy of the pastor and his skill at managing this voluntary work. There are some who are unable to trust their laity spiritually; some who yearn to centralize and clericalize this movement of the Spirit. The people themselves also sometimes fail to appreciate it. Either they despise a man of position who takes on a lowly catechist's task, or they accuse him of presumption in setting himself up above his fellows. In some parishes, as at Makindu, there is no layman who is both able and eligible to do the work, even if any were willing, because all are disqualified by the church's marriage law.

It is the plight of such parishes that the church as a whole most seriously seems to disregard. Attitudes of despair or of moral indignation are fundamentally irresponsible; yet, outside the revival movement, it is not often that the councils of the church are heard deliberately planning to send the best available men to the least responsive spheres of work. Only a renewed sense of mission and of charity can break through the vicious circle in which these 'depressed' areas of the church are caught. The catechist is not receiving his full salary, so he cultivates cotton and grows half-hearted in his work. The people react to the failure of the catechist by staying away from church and giving even less than before. If the catechist is keen and intelligent enough to be worth a higher certificate, he is taken away from the village which most needs those gifts and posted to one which can pay for a higher-grade man. The people clamour for a better-qualified catechist or for an ordained pastor; but if he is sent to them they fail to raise his salary and he is soon taken away. In the face of this dilemma several of the most thoughtful of the African clergy and leading laymen are questioning the established principle that every church must at least raise the salary of its own minister; the depressed areas of the church in Buganda, they say, are mission fields, and the best available men should be sent there and, for a time, supported by the diocese as a whole. To abandon the principle of local self-support might start a most serious landslide; but to refuse to take that risk may be spiritual suicide.

NOTES

1. The Bataka movement, already mentioned on p. 119, broke out into rioting and attacks upon progressive chiefs in the spring of 1949.

2. The Rt. Rev. Stephen Neill, *Survey of the Training of the Ministry in Africa*, Part I (I.M.C. 1950), pp. 10-11, 21-2, 38-9.

7

The Children of the Church

I N about half the homes visited in Makindu *muluka* there were young children. Some of them were the actual children, or grand-children, of the head of the household; at least as many were the children of brothers or other relatives; and a considerable number were not related at all but lived in the home as domestic helpers and in order to attend the local schools. The same was found to be true in all other parishes that were studied.

During the course of the study 177 boys in five different 'Junior Secondary' schools, or an equivalent standard, in Buganda and Busoga were questioned personally about a variety of subjects. Very careful preparation was made to enlist the most frank co-operation of these boys and to assure them of their complete anonymity. There are sound reasons for accepting the information they provided as reliable. The girls in three schools were also consulted about a different set of topics. Finally the main findings were checked in discussion with several groups of teachers in order that any obvious misinformation and anomalies might be corrected. The tables drawn up as a result of these studies are to be found on page 278-81.

Some of the north-eastern tribes of the Uganda Protectorate impose a severe discipline on the very young children but relax it as the child grows older and more independent. In Kiganda society the reverse is the norm. The infant spends much of its time on a pile of cloths beside its mother's bed; later it is carried everywhere tied on the mother's back or straddled across her hip. Toddlers are allowed almost complete freedom; fathers and other adults dote on them and they are often spoiled. Weaning may not take place until the child is two years old or more, but when it does happen it is often a most traumatic experience, being the sharp severance of a deep physical bond. It is generally true that the mother's link with her child is personal and affective whereas the father's is authoritarian and institutional, as embodying the interests of the clan.

As would be expected, though more girls than boys seem to have felt tension and antipathy in their relations to their mothers, yet the majority of all the children had easy, happy relationships with them. A great many of the boys spoke with deep feeling of their mothers and the debt they owe them; the most shameful insults that can be used in Buganda are all some form of outrageous abuse of this relationship. But from the very beginning the child is made aware that it is not to his mother that he belongs but to his father and his father's family. Once the child is weaned, there is no absolute permanence or stability in the relationship to the mother. An important factor in the experience of young children is the frequency of divorce, desertion or polygamy in the homes. Out of all the boys in the Junior Secondary standards in the five different institutions, 49 per cent. had seen their fathers take new wives, and 24 per cent. no longer had their own mothers living at home. Since that sample included the two leading boarding schools, with a greater proportion of modern and 'enlightened' homes, the average for the whole child population would certainly be a good deal higher.

Security, however, and a sense of belonging come from the father's clan. This is first ratified in the child's clan name. There are today just over thirty identifiable clans among the Baganda proper, and some of the immigrants from neighbouring tribes are similarly organized. Every clan has from half a dozen to twenty names for its own boys and a similar number for girls; in addition, there are a considerable number of names derived from the old hero gods or from proverbial sayings.

In the old days children were formally named at a special ceremony called *Okwalula abaana*, literally, 'the hatching of the children'. It was the special duty of the paternal grandmother, standing by the child, to recite the names of the ancestors of the family, beginning with the dead who were nearest to her son, and going back until the baby laughed. This was taken as a sign that it was the ancestor just named whose spirit would be the child's guardian and whose name was said to be revived or restored in this way. It is very difficult to decide whether or not the Baganda have in the past entertained a belief in the re-incarnation of ancestors in their descendants. Almost all educated Baganda deny ever having heard of it, and it would be too facile to read into the customs of Baganda in the villages a significance drawn from other Bantu societies where such beliefs were explicit. When a baby strongly resembles its grandfather it is commonly said, *yabbukiramu jjajjawe*, 'He has restored in him his grandfather'. The verb *-bbuka* means 'to be restored', referring to some unspecified spiritual entity. So when a person sneezes, someone may immediately call to him, 'Bbuka!' The author has listened to village people arguing whether the spirit of the grandfather can actually be restored by re-incarnation in the newborn child; some said that this was so, but the majority denied, saying that a *muzimu*, or spirit of the dead, has gone for ever from this life, and that only the likeness or character of the grandfather is reproduced in such a child. The idea of re-incarnation is quite a different thing from the belief, which the majority of village people share, that a child or adult may become possessed by the *muzimu* of a dead grandfather. Such possession is always a temporary or spasmodic occurrence.

The synod of the Native Anglican Church forbade the *Okwalula* custom in 1913 in the following minute:

> that the ceremony of giving a Tribal name accompanied by heathen rites be forbidden, but that the Tribal name be given in baptism as a second Christian name and thus prevent the invocation of an ancestor to name the child in a heathen ceremony.

In a church in which the majority of children are for one reason or another denied baptism as infants, this regulation is somewhat un-imaginative. Nevertheless, most Christians today seem no longer to associate the giving of the name with the actual spirit of the ancestor. Many parents, particularly the better educated, choose both clan and Christian names with no other ceremony apart from baptism. But others still use the old customs in varying degrees. The following describes what is fairly common in Busiro and Kyagwe counties.

A child is usually given a name by its parents or grandparents on the day of its birth, for people believe that an unnamed child is sickly and cries a great deal. They will run through the names available for the father's family until the infant stops crying and so indicates that the right name has been chosen. If at a later time the child becomes poorly, a different name may be tried.

One catechist described how his baby daughter had made no attempt to walk long after the usual time. Then one night his aunt dreamed about the child, but in the dream it had a different name. When they heard this the parents re-named the child, saying, 'You are Nalubega'; and from that day the child began to learn to walk

The *Okwalula* ceremony follows after a considerable interval. As this is only done when there are several children of the family group requir-ing it, and these must always include infants of both sexes, it is nowadays usually delayed until some other clan function, such as a funeral wake, has given occasion for a big family gathering. Children participating in

11. Interior of a village church built and furnished by a local carpenter. A farmer takes the services

12. Village church built and furnished by a local carpenter (on the right)

13. Small village school, unaided by grants, run by a local church

14. Full primary school at a pastorate centre

the ceremony, therefore, may be three years old or more, yet their hair may never be cut until this has been done. So shock-headed babies are a common sight in the villages.

The first part of the ritual is a test of the true paternity of the child. For this purpose the umbilical cord of the baby is kept from the day of its birth, wrapped in a piece of bark-cloth. In these days a great many babies are born in maternity centres and there is always the danger of a European delivering the child and throwing the cord away. But most African midwives and doctors ask the mother if she wants it kept. When the test begins, the mothers of the children sit cross-legged on a bark-cloth. They are then asked to produce the cords; if they do so they are congratulated and may be given two shillings as a reward; if one has lost it, she may be beaten. The paternal grandmother now receives the cord and it is smeared with butter or beef fat and dropped into a large waterproof basket-bowl in which is a mixture of beer, milk and water. If the cord floats, the child is legitimate and there is great acclamation. If the cord sinks, it is a sign that the child does not belong to the clan. 'It is not our blood.' The mother is charged to say who is the father of her child. If she names him, the baby will be sent to him eventually; if she denies the illegitimacy, the child may be left in her care or sent to other members of her clan, but it will not be accepted by the father's clan nor named by them. There are very few people in the villages who do not believe in the efficacy of this test.

The second part of the ritual is the actual naming of the children. They are seated on a bark-cloth in the porch of the house. The parents then indicate what names they have chosen, and each child is solemnly named by its paternal grandmother. The children now have their first hair-cut, and there is beer-drinking and feasting, in which the little lake sprats are an invariable feature of the menu. The umbilical cords, after the testing, are usually taken into the garden and pushed away into an incision in the pithy stem of a banana plant. This seems to be a relic of what was, in the old days, a second method of testing legitimacy. Some families simply throw away the cords, but many of the details differ according to the custom of the clan.

African Moslems observe the *Okwalula abaana*, but they drink tea or unfermented banana juice instead of beer, burn an incense stick, and read from their books. Some Christians now doubt whether such a test can be trusted, or, even if it can, whether it is right for them to make use of it; so an increasing number are ceasing to practise it. On the other hand, all the catechists in one pastorate of Busiro, which has a

K

predominantly Baganda population, asserted that it was still widely used and all agreed that it was a valuable means of strengthening clan solidarity and giving the young child a sense of incorporation and security.

From now on the young child, whether boy or girl, is rooted inextricably in the father's family. Not only his father, but all his father's brothers and brothers-in-law are called 'father', and the father's eldest sister, the *ssenga*, is a person of special importance in the family circle. If the father should die, the child has an inalienable right to adoption into some part of the father's family; there are no orphans in Ganda society, except when a father refuses to admit his illegitimate child and the mother dies without indicating who he is. The acknowledged father of an illegitimate child can claim the child and take it away from the mother, even though she may have slaved for years to support it and send it to a good school. This seems unnaturally hard, and indeed the Buganda Government has legislated that this claim cannot be enforced until the child is seven years old if a boy, or eighteen years if a girl; and yet the majority of mothers give their support to the system because they know that this is their child's guarantee of security and of a place in society. Quite often, even when the genitor himself abandons her, his relatives do in fact give help to the mother towards the education of the child.

Against this background it is not difficult to see the possibility of Christian baptism taking the place of the old naming ceremony, and it was clearly the intention of an earlier generation of missionaries and African church-leaders that it should do so. It is attractive to talk about this kind of transfer; but in practice it is not as simple as it may seem. The difficulty arises not from the relics of animism, nor from the test of legitimacy, for these are elements that might perhaps be cut away. The real difficulty consists in the fact that the Church's use of baptism is in one way too widely embracing, and in another way too narrow, to become a substitute for *Okwalula abaana*. On the one hand baptism is initiation into something whose dimensions are far broader than those of a clan. It is true that the idea of the church being the great tribe of Christ is a favourite conceit of many missionaries. A small number of Africans in Uganda, mainly those in the Revival, have borrowed it and are asserting that Christians ought to repudiate all allegiance to the old clans. These Christians set aside the clan names in favour of newfangled ones derived from the language of the Bible such as 'He has overcome', 'His grace', and so on. But this attitude is generally unpopular. In any case baptism cannot pretend to meet the particular sociological needs which *Okwalula* satisfies. On the other hand, whereas every child is eligible for initiation into some clan or another, baptism is conditional. If it were ever to take the place of *Okwalula abaana* it would have to be made available for all, or nearly all, whose parents desire it. The Roman Catholic Church does in fact make an almost open offer, but in the Anglican Church, in spite of widespread anxiety to obtain it, baptism of infants is refused in a very large number of cases. This is a question we shall have to consider in another chapter.

In almost all Ganda homes in the villages the father has his own bedroom to himself, unlike many of the northern and eastern tribes where a man shares a bedroom with his wife. The Ganda wife also has her own room, from which her husband calls her if he needs her company; she may have the younger children with her. The other children sleep as a rule in the dining-room at the back of the house. In the homes of the more educated there are children's bedrooms; village people with ambition also copy this new custom and many are proudly building houses that are honeycombs of tiny mud and wattle rooms. In the same way, even uneducated peasant parents buy wooden beds for their children in place of the pile of bark-cloth which was all a child could expect in the old days. It is still rare, however, to find a child who has a mattress or sheets until he goes away to school, though most adults now use them. The possession of several mattresses is a point of pride for many men, and it is not unusual to find some selfish fathers with three on their own bed, while wife and children have none! This, and much else that follows, is not the case in educated families, where home life in all essentials is modelled on Western patterns.

In the old days the father always sat alone, or with his male guests, for meals. Later he and they were the only ones to be promoted to sit up at a table; wives and children continued to sit on a mat on the floor, either in the same room or at the back of the house, and to eat from a common basket-bowl. Nowadays some men like to have their wives, and even the children, sitting with them; but the natural conservatism of the women tends to resist this change; and when there are more than a few children it is in any case impossible for them to sit around an ordinary table. Attention to children's table manners has always been regarded as very important, though the details which are emphasized in these days are different from past manners. In the old days lunch was a fairly light meal served as soon as the women, who returned from cultivation at about ten o'clock, were able to prepare it. The more substantial evening meal was eaten at about six in the evening. Today lunch tends to be later, and in some homes, larger; tea and coffee drinking provides refreshment between meals; and supper may be any time between nine and midnight. Children who have fallen asleep may be woken up for this late supper. This development is peculiar to Buganda. Tribes in the Eastern Province still eat at about six or seven, though it is thought to be civilized to copy the late meal of the Baganda. Only the very educated homes give the children an early supper, and put them to bed before the adults' meal-time.

In the early morning men, women and children all go into the banana plantation or cotton plot to cultivate. After some time the children are sent back to the house to wash their hands and legs, to eat some of the cold left-overs of the previous supper, and perhaps to brew some tea, before putting on their better clothes and going to school. Sometimes parents may join them at this breakfast, but often the adults do not leave work until later. Many children in the villages are given nothing to eat before they start for school.

The answers of the schoolboys revealed how little most children expect of their fathers. Only 18 per cent. of these boys recorded the fact that their fathers had attempted to give them any sort of instruction. This might refer to their earliest reading lessons, but sometimes it meant no more than information about their clan, or what one boy called 'lectures about character'. Another 14 per cent. remembered, as the most valuable thing their fathers had done for them, the training in good behaviour, including the punishment which they had received. This was particularly emphasized by Basoga boys. The most commonly recorded benefit was the provision of clothes, for this can by no means be taken for granted in peasant homes. Another 12·5 per cent. remembered with gratitude the purchase of some provisions over and above the ordinary staple foods—bread, milk, meat, etc., and a very few mentioned little gifts of sweets or money. Most pathetic were the 10 per cent. almost entirely from the north-eastern tribes, who had never forgotten some special demonstration of affection: 'When I went to meet him on his return from a journey he picked me up.' 'He sometimes made me sit at his feet while he ate his food.'

In many peasant homes the man treats his children, especially his daughters, with a mixture of careless neglect and absolute authority. There are fathers who refuse to pay school fees and have never bought their daughters either clothes or blanket. A girl may be allowed to use a plot in the family garden for her own purposes and from the age of ten she will grow and market her own cotton in order to clothe herself. Her aunt, who is often her champion in such cases, may help her with occasional gifts. Yet, when the child returns from school at midday, she is expected to report immediately to do some household task, and often she is so occupied in fetching water or running errands that she has no time to eat lunch before the afternoon school. The recent introduction of compulsory school lunches in Buganda has been designed to meet this sort of neglect, and though it has met widespread opposition it has certainly resulted in more adults becoming aware of the children's need.

The authoritarian father is the counterpart, within the home, of the absolute power of the Kabaka in traditional Kiganda society. There is a sense in which the first derives from the second. During the two years of the Kabaka's exile Christian leaders were complaining that the very stability of home-life was undermined, since the source of all authority had been removed. The father of the household is still a figure to inspire fear. This is less marked than it was once; many educated parents are seeking to establish a different relationship with their children, and in the country districts it is a major source of concern to the adults that fathers no longer seem able to inspire their school-going offspring with the old awe. Yet of the boys that were questioned, 40 per cent. said that they were definitely afraid of their fathers during early childhood. This figure is to some extent misleading, for there is a big difference between the 67 per cent. boys from the north-eastern tribes who had this fear, and the 24 per cent. only of Baganda; this disparity may be due less to tribal than to educational differences.

Over against the authoritarianism of the father must be set an entirely contrary element in the relationship. As so often appears in African social institutions, a stability is achieved by the counterpoise of opposite emotions. A daughter, or even a son, writing to the father, may address him as *mwana wange*—'my child'. This happens particularly when the child has been sent away, according to traditional custom, to live with the paternal grandfather. Frequently the child and the grandparents develop an extraordinary accord. They are regarded, in some contexts, as belonging to the same generation, and can speak of one another as 'brother' or 'sister'. So the child adopts towards its own father the attitudes and relationship of the grandparents. The influence of this ambiguity of relationship upon Ganda society is very profound. Towards all authority there is a 'looking down on' as well as a 'looking up to'. Girls very early begin to extend towards men in general the attitude they have towards the father, which is both submissive and maternal. Those two words describe also the emotion which great numbers of Baganda, both men and women, seem to feel towards the Kabaka.

It may have been partly because of the tensions of this ambiguous relationship between children and father that in the old tradition it was thought necessary to send a child away, as soon as it was weaned, the sons going to a paternal uncle, and daughters to an older married brother. The custom of sending children away at weaning is fairly common in Bantu society, but the right of certain older kinsmen to ask for a child is peculiar to Ganda society.

Today there is a definite decline of this practice among the better educated and professional families, but it still remains very common. Its purpose, and therefore its pattern, is beginning to change, more noticeably in Buganda than elsewhere. Whereas it used to be mainly a means of maintaining the solidarity and interdependence of the large family-group, today it is sometimes regarded more as a way of getting children to a better school than is available in the neighbourhood of the parents' home. However, this is certainly not yet the major considera-tion, for if it were, one would find that the choice of relatives to whom children are sent would be determined mainly by the locality of the schools, whereas in fact it still is dominated by the old sense of family propriety. I found that of the boys who had been sent away from home 25 per cent. went to live with a paternal uncle. As far as the Baganda and Basoga were concerned, the same percentage also went to the paternal grandfather. (Members of the north-eastern tribes, being for the most part immigrants, had naturally not had grandparents easily available.) The *ssenga* or father's sister was also fairly frequently mentioned by Baganda boys, and even more commonly by the girls, often with a good deal of fear or resentment. These are the relationships that a sense of family obligation would indicate; all others were repre-sented by far smaller numbers. There is little doubt, then, that parents still send children away primarily for the sake of old solidarities and to resolve the tensions of the authoritarian home. The boys themselves seem to think of it in those terms. Of those who had been sent away from home, only a small minority regarded it as a bad thing; the rest approved of it for such reasons as: 'If I had stayed at home I would have grown up impudent and disobedient'—'I knew that it pleased them to have me living with them'—'I learned a lot which I could not have learned at home.'

Of the boys who were interrogated, just over half had been sent away from home at some time before their twelfth birthday. Certain differences are apparent as between tribes; and even more as between those whose background is a professional, educated home and those who come from mainly peasant parents.

	Percentage sent away before 12th birthday	Average years of age when sent	Average duration of absence from home
Baganda boys . .	53·6	7½	3 years 2 months
Basoga boys . .	66	6½	2 years 3 months
Boys from N.E. tribes (mostly of immigrant parents) . .	38·7	9	2 years 6 months
Boys of professional homes . . .	46	7½	3 years 3 months
Boys of peasant homes	59·6	7¼	2 years 9 months

From about the fifth year the Muganda child finds indulgence is replaced by severity whether it is in its own home or elsewhere. Punishment may be spasmodic, but is usually harsh. Far the most common form of punishment is *beating*. Next to this in frequency is the *refusal of food*, in a few instances for as long as three days. It is significant that this form of punishment is twice as common in Busoga, where famine is an ever-present threat, as in Buganda. On the other hand, the Baganda boys reported more often than the others some form of *binding or locking up*; many of them have been locked in the dark of a small storeroom for a whole day, and occasionally one may come across quite a young child with a wrist roped to an ankle. Similar to this, but less physically asserted, are the various forms of *detention*—boys are forbidden to leave the home compound, or to go to school, or visit their friends. It is remarkable that the north-eastern tribes appear to know almost nothing of punishment either by binding or detention. In addition to these four most common methods, a number of boys mention enforced digging or some other task—collecting sand or building materials, removing a termite hill and so on. There are also, as might be expected, in any community, occasional acts of calculated cruelty and terror; children are sometimes locked outside the house at night and told that the *Musezi*, the dreaded Night-wizard, is coming to eat them.

The offences for which children are punished fall into four categories, which we may call Laziness, Nonconformity, Nuisance and Improbity. There are some significant differences in the degree of importance attached to these four types of offence in the various tribes; and also as between the behaviour of homes in which the father has a professional or salaried job and those of village cultivators and craftsmen.

Laziness includes failure to carry out the ordinary household chores and unreadiness to go to school. It is far more frequently punished in the north-eastern tribes than among the Baganda. Fathers in the professions very rarely punish their children for not working in the home or garden.

The second category of Nonconformity includes the child's unwillingness to wash itself, or to remove jiggers from the feet, bad behaviour at meal-times, refusal to run errands, and the whole range of impudent or disobedient behaviour. Under the same head we must mention truancy, and staying a long time away from home. All these offences are punished far more frequently in Busoga than in Buganda, which suggests that the modern Baganda are beginning to value qualities of independence, while elsewhere parents still put a premium on conformity. Wandering from home, however, seems to be the particular *bête noire* of the professionals and is a mark of a growing class-consciousness; a modern chief, for example, may punish his son for playing too much with the village children.

Nuisance includes damage to property, fighting, playfulness and tricks, especially in front of guests, crying and bed-wetting. The Baganda react more strongly to offences of this kind than do the parents in other tribes.

The fourth category can be described as Improbity. This term covers lying; slander, especially of one's own parents; bullying younger children; unchastity; stealing.

It would be a false impression to imagine that the life of the boy or girl in Buganda is entirely made up of lessons at school and severe treatment at home. There is a leisureliness to the day's timetable and plenty of games to play. The group of girls who go together to the stream for water, the goat-boys who meet on the hilltop, will get as much fun out of their occupation as children anywhere else. At certain times of the year the edible ants are ready to fly from their earth burrows; then the village boys build clay tubes leading from the escape holes into pot-traps, and drum on the hard earth to make the ants rise as if the rain had come. At other times they hunt wild birds with traps or throwing-sticks. There is football for the boys on the field by the school, or wrestling at the homestead. There are dances at which the older children can join in and the youngsters take an occasional turn at the drums. There are traditional stories at nightfall, with their appropriate songs. Yet it remains generally true that parents are not much interested in the play of any except the smallest children. Fathers look on their offspring as undeveloped adults and expect them to make themselves useful as early as possible in the daily tasks of grown people; this is particularly the case with their daughters. It is, after all, a comparatively recent idea in the West also, that childhood has its own peculiar needs and patterns of development.

It is, therefore, not surprising that the church in Buganda has so far paid very little attention to the special spiritual needs of children. They are expected to pick up what they can from the patterns of behaviour and the moral judgments of their elders. Whether there is deliberate religious training in the home or not depends on the reality of the parents' faith. In almost all homes there is grace before meals. There may be family prayers in the morning or evening; of the schoolboys who were questioned, 60 per cent. reported fairly regular prayers in their homes, but in Makindu and Kabubiro villages less than 10 per cent. of the householders claimed to do so. In some families there are spasmodic attempts to train children in personal religion. The schoolboys reported that 71 per cent. had been taught how to pray by their parents, but, again, in the village a far smaller number were being helped in this way. It is impossible to assess exactly what is being conveyed in this home teaching.

No doubt in the homes of many catechists, clergy and strongly Christian lay people there is a very fine example given of regular family devotion, and care is taken to teach and discipline the children. But in many of the rural homes Christians seem to fail more than Moslems, or followers of the old ways, in the training of their children. A Christian man who is a polygamist or who is occasionally drunk does not normally labour under a sense of guilt because he lives by the casual standard of the community; but if he sets himself up in the home as a teacher of the Christian faith or ethic, he inevitably introduces a new standard by which he is judged. This often emerges in the quarrels of husbands and wives, in which they openly condemn one another by the standard of Christian teachings. The children are present; and the parent who is so accused feels that he or she has lost face. In the traditional home, on the other hand, children are taught that whatever the father does they are never even to think that he is wrong, and certainly must never say a disparaging word about him to others. So the authority of the pagan father remains intact until his child goes to school, whereas, unless he is a very good Christian, that of the church-member is somewhat discredited. It is, therefore, easier for him to remain silent than to attempt any religious training. The responsibility for that is left to the school and the church.

Young children, once they begin to attend school, are usually made to attend church on Sunday mornings, and in many places they form, compulsorily, the bulk of the congregation. But almost no concession is made to them in the conduct of the service. Even children of under five are expected to sit or kneel through long, incomprehensible services. They learn, in the lower classes of the primary school, to sing by heart some of the most popular hymns, and to chant without comprehension the morning canticles. They repeat the Lord's prayer and, in time, the General Confession. But there their participation in the worship usually ends. A few of the catechists and clergy are shining exceptions, and their preaching reaches out deliberately to the younger members of their flock; but the majority confine their teaching of the young to the special baptism and confirmation classes, of which mention will be made in the next chapter.

Sunday Schools at present have hardly begun to be taken seriously. In the statistical returns for 1950, Anglican Sunday Schools in Nigeria registered 118,000 pupils and in Kenya 36,000, that is in both cases, nearly half the number of pupils in the church schools. The diocese of Uganda showed only 106. The spiritual needs of a whole generation are a very grave challenge to this church which can only be met by lay action. If the laity—which must include more than the hard-pressed school-teachers—rise up quickly to take responsibility for the life of their church, and are allowed to take it, the situation may be redeemed. Already there is evidence of a stirring of the conscience of the church in this direction and in 1957 it was decided to appoint at least two African clergy as diocesan Youth Organizers. It remains to be seen how far the church as a whole will appreciate and support their efforts.

8

Youth and the Schools

GANDA society has never found a wholly satisfactory answer to the problematic relationship between adolescent children and their parents. The tensions between younger children and their fathers were resolved by sending them away to relatives, as we have seen. But in later childhood there was a slow build-up of conflict between the authoritarianism of the parent or guardian and the *mputtu*, or obstinate rebellion of the child. A new relationship was called for, but had not yet come into being. This awkward, half-and-half state was recognized in the custom whereby the older children might not sleep under the same roof as their parents. A small sleeping-hut was built for the boys; and the girls, if they were not living with an older married brother, might sleep in the kitchen-house. These rules are still in operation in the village, though the more educated families prefer, if possible, to build larger houses with separate rooms of the older children.

The advent of school education has greatly increased the problem of this relationship by prolonging the awkward pre-adult period and by liberating the children from the older disciplines. Girls who in the past would have been married off before they could cause trouble and anxiety to their parents are found today in the upper standard of the Primary Schools and may have another three years of school life ahead of them. Boys who would have been apprenticed in the household of a chief, or at the palace itself, where they would have been given enough responsibility, tempered with discipline, to satisfy their needs, are still dependent on their parents or guardians, while defying old authorities and taboos.

It is partly for this reason that not every father is clamouring for the education of his children, as is sometimes suggested. There is a certain amount of disillusionment abroad in the villages. 'Why should he go to school? I never learned to read, but I'm rich enough in these days,' is a fairly common rejoinder. Others say flatly they have better things to spend their money on than in laying up trouble for themselves. If the parents are indifferent, the children sometimes lose interest in their education after a year or two. This happens particularly with the advent of adolescence. Then they say 'We have grown up', and they envy the members of their age-group who are free. None the less, the general picture is still of a pressing demand for more schools, and, since the principle of 'the higher the fewer' operates in the educational system as elsewhere, there is a frustrating bottleneck at every transition from one standard in the system to the next.

The material evidence of the church's existence which is most commonly seen is the wooden sign-board at the side of the road, or at the junction of two paths through the elephant grass, which reads, 'N.A.C.—(or R.C.M.)—Primary School', followed by the name of a village. If one follows the direction indicated by the board one comes, sooner or later, to an open space of short grass, along the sides of which stand one, or maybe two, long, low buildings, which are classroom blocks, another of almost the same shape, which is the parish church, and the houses of a catechist and a school-teacher. All are of mud-and-wattle walls, sometimes sand-plastered and whitewashed, often roofed with corrugated iron. On closer inspection the open field is seen to contain goal-posts for football.

This is the visible sign of the union of the church and the educational system; it is a monument to a remarkable Christian achievement and to the devoted service of great numbers of missionaries, government servants and African teachers. But the unchanging symbol may be misleading when great changes are in fact taking place. A more observant scrutiny of some of these church-and-school compounds may reveal new classroom blocks of brick and aluminium, a new school kitchen in the background, and a brick house for the headmaster. The catechist's house and the church remains unchanged, or a little more dilapidated than before. These things are a symbol of something else—of the £4,000,000 estimated cost of a five-year plan for primary education proposed by the commission of 1952.

No longer are the young school-teachers trained at Mukono, side by side with the senior catechists and ordinands. The only teacher-training that remains there is a small establishment for giving teachers an additional qualification as handcraft and woodwork instructors. This is the only training centre for primary teachers which is still inter-tribal; all general training is now done in regional colleges, affiliated to the church, and staffed by Africans, missionaries and other Europeans.

No longer are the school-teachers the junior colleagues of the local pastor or catechist in the work of the church. Their time is fully occupied with the demands of their own profession, which those of them who are good Christians regard as a vocation. Some of them may be willing to give a hand with Sunday services and preaching, if invited to do so, but the pastor and catechist must not take this for granted, and it is very much resented if they do so.

No longer are the affairs of the classroom, or the private lives of the teachers, the proper concern of the pastor or catechist. There are local education authorities and a diocesan inspectorate, through both of which the church can exercise a considerable degree of control; and for serious misdemeanours a teacher can be suspended or a pupil dismissed. But the local pastor or catechist has no right of immediate access or interference. The schools are ruled more by directives from the Ministry of Education in Buganda than by the councils of the church.

These changes are entirely proper and necessary; but they require a very profound adjustment in the thinking of both the laity and the ministers of the church. Unfortunately they have been brought about mainly through the negotiations of the officers of the government Department of Education with a few specialist officials of the church and mission. This may have been unavoidable in the circumstances, but it means that the church as a whole has scarcely begun to realize or to face responsibly the changed relationship with the schools.

Not only is the church as a whole living in a fool's paradise in this respect, but the mission has signally failed to bring home honestly to the clergy and other leaders the true state of affairs. So far from helping them to understand that the modern classroom has an entirely different aim and function from the old school-church unit, and encouraging them to make a re-appraisal of the place of the present schools in relation to the church's task, the mission seems, generally speaking, to have acquiesced in the unthinking desire to control and possess the educational system. The unreality of the church's apparent control has been concealed in the past by the liaison between the Department of Education of the Protectorate Government and the churches' boards of education. But the recent creation in Buganda of an African Ministry of Education, with its policy of developing more and more schools, and even training colleges, which are independent of the voluntary agencies, must at last compel the church to face up to its responsibility towards the young generation without relying upon a relationship with the schools which no longer exists.

For it cannot be too strongly asserted that what started to happen in the late 1920s was not an improvement of the old schools but the introduction of a fundamentally different thing. The old school-church unit was engaged in a single task, which could never properly be the concern of any government, namely, the creation and upbuilding of a local Christian community within the structure of African society. Partnership with government in the educational field could only come about by separating one aspect of this task from the totality, thereby bringing about a change of function. To turn a catechist into an infinitely better school-teacher can certainly be called improvement, but only by applying a different set of standards. These new standards, and the changed conception of the function of the school which they imply, are those which are common to the Western way of life, which modern Africa is adopting. The schools have become educational centres which initiate the children, not into the local Christian community, but into competitive, bourgeois Western society. Of course, a good educational system, like a good department of community development, and a good medical service, is of benefit to the members of the church. It is also most desirable that there should be good Christians engaged in all these departments of modern society, and the church must embrace and support them all. But as long as a large part of the church has not yet understood and accepted the changed function of the schools, it will not begin to provide any other means of doing those things which the old school-church unit was achieving. This more than anything else accounts for the failure of the Uganda Church to tackle seriously the need for Sunday schools and recreational clubs for its youth.

In the *miruka* parishes themselves everything depends now on the personalities of the pastor, or catechist, and the headmaster. In one village, for example, it was common knowledge that the headmaster of the primary school had a second wife by African marriage, living twenty-five miles away, whom he visited regularly, every week-end. By the rules of the church he should have been suspended, but no one was anxious for that to happen where teachers are so scarce. The pastor, who visited the parish to preach on Good Friday, spent the twenty minutes after the service, before he had to go elsewhere, in browbeating the head-master's wife, trying in vain to persuade her to give evidence against her husband. Rather naturally, in that parish the older children in the school do not feel that the link with the church has much significance.

In another parish, on the other hand, which is also a pastorate centre, there exist the happiest relations between the church and the school. Every morning before dawn the pastor, the headmaster and the catechist meet in the church and, kneeling at the Communion rails, sing a hymn together and pray for the school and pastorate. The pastor has absolute confidence in the school staff and never attempts to interfere, nor to impose on them for help in his work. The school has a strong *esprit de corps*; boys and girls wear an attractive and unusual uniform designed by the headmaster. The staff, instead of being scattered around the village, as is so often the case, live in a single row of small houses, each in a flower garden, and meet together once a week for a talk on some aspect of teaching method. The school plays an active part in the Sunday services, for which it provides an enthusiastic choir. All this is the more impressive in that the pastorate lies well away from any main road from the capital, and is not often visited by inspectors and supervisors. The same pastorate, as might be expected, is one in which many of the village churches are in the charge of laymen. Yet the whole of this achievement might easily fall to the ground with the appointment of a new headmaster who had no religious convictions and no desire to co-operate with the pastor.

It is partly the insecurity resulting from the realization that the destiny of the school is out of their control which leads so many Christians in the villages to complain that 'the mission has given away our schools to the government'. It is not only moral considerations which lead to these misgivings. As was pointed out in Chapter 4, there has taken place a loss of that integration between school and community which the old, low-grade village schools preserved. It is this which makes the 'Day Schools'—unaided and unqualified—so popular. They are to be found in many parishes, close to the church, usually in a ramshackle thatched building. The 'teacher' is often a girl who has recently left the 4th or 5th class of the Primary School, though, on account of low wages, most parents object to their children doing such work. The fees are very small, and many parents still like their children, before going on to the Primary School, to start off in such a class, learning their letters and syllables, singing, reciting a few prayers, counting and weaving grass mats. But their popularity springs from the sense of local proprietorship which these pathetic little schools keep alive.

The same is true, also, of many of the private schools. The majority of these, it is true, are run primarily as a business venture by men who, for lack of qualifications or previous dismissal, are unable to do a job in the official church schools. But such headmasters, unless they rely mainly on immigrant children, must depend in much greater measure than the grant-aided schools on the co-operation and goodwill of the local parents; this means that there is often a sense in which their school 'belongs' to the community and satisfies the need for integration more fully than do the schools of the official system. Occasionally, as at Makindu, a private school may be started specifically as a tribal venture to provide for the children of a large immigrant minority, and in such cases the parents' meeting is virtually the board of management. A comprehensive report of the private schools and their history would make weird reading; yet a minority of them are achieving a very reputable standard, and they are likely to fulfil an important function in the future. Unfortunately the church tends to turn a disapproving eye, officially at least, upon these schools, since they do not apply such strict disciplinary regulations towards the members of their staffs.

Proprietorship and integration with a community, though of quite a different kind, are also inspired by the big boarding-schools for boys and girls. Started by the missions, and still having a concentration of missionaries and other European Christians on the staff, these schools are now more or less independent foundations, each under its board of governors, on which church and government are represented. Existing, as they have always done, to serve and to create the upper and professional class, they are closely integrated with the *élite* of the country, and 'belong' in a most vivid sense to their old boys and girls. They have had, and still have, a profound influence in moulding into Christian patterns the thought and ideals of the leaders of Uganda. Their mission is the mission of the whole church directed towards a special area of society; but inevitably they tend to work in isolation from the main body of the church, so that neither they, nor the rest of the church, seem able always to recognize their essential unity in a common task. The girls' boarding-schools and training colleges appear to maintain, rather better than those of the boys, some sense of responsibility towards the church as such. As one Muganda in high office expressed it: 'At Budo boys are inspired to seek the good of their country rather than the good of the church; but in Gayaza the girls are taught to seek the good of the church by seeking the good of their homes.' This contrast is closely linked with the inherent difference between the personal and intimate relationship of staff and pupils in a girls' school, and the more impersonal and extrovert attitudes of a boys' school, which is bound to be reflected in the type of religious training that is given. So the wife of another leading

Muganda said: 'When we were girls at boarding-school we were taught how to pray and how to maintain our spiritual life. But when we are married, if we want to have a Christian home, we find we have to teach these things to our husbands; and that is not easy, though many of them would like to know.'

It is the special pride of the boarding-schools that they enjoy such opportunities for character training. The great majority of schools, however, have, in comparison, almost none; and so the youth of the villages have to rely for their Christian training on the Religious Knowledge periods in the school curriculum, and on the baptism and confirmation classes run by the local catechist.

Compared with the standard that used to be demanded, the latter have fallen to a very low ebb in most places. There are, of course, some fine exceptions. A few catechists have a quite remarkable gift for teaching, but the majority seem to be not merely incompetent but indifferent. Many of them are content to announce in the church that classes will begin on a certain date, and never attempt to follow up the unbaptized children of the parents in their congregation to persuade them to join the classes. This means that very many of the children who could not be baptized as infants because of the condition of their parents' marriage are in fact never baptized at all.

Before the baptism classes begin there is a little ceremony in church, if the catechist remembers it, whereby candidates are admitted to the catechumenate. Boys and girls aged between eight and eleven stand up in the face of the congregation and are solemnly asked whether they are willing to give up their heathen practices such as fornication, drunkenness and witchcraft and to be monogamists all the days of their life.

The children must possess themselves of a Prayer Book and a Bible or New Testament and are then called to attend church daily at a certain hour for instruction. If the catechist is lazy, they may have to spend a great many hours each week waiting outside the church for his arrival. In one parish a small class reported that in five weeks they had been through the service of Morning Prayer, but had not yet begun to read any of the Bible; while in the same period the confirmation class had read through the catechism in the Prayer Book, but so far there had been no explanation of it.

These classes usually last about six months. For the last month the confirmation candidates are supposed to live at the pastorate centre in order to be instructed by the pastor himself. This is sometimes the only valuable teaching they receive, and some of the clergy are scrupulous

L

in making badly prepared candidates wait until a later confirmation. The knowledge that candidates are likely to be questioned by the Bishop before the service has effectually discouraged the earlier practice of making a last-minute round-up of children to swell the numbers.

When children are ready to be baptized they are supposed to visit the pastor to be tested by him. They are expected to pay 50 cents on this occasion, 'for the blessing', and Shs. 4 for the baptism fee.

It is a serious matter if the positive Christian influence of the combination of church and school upon the youth of the community is weak; because, weak or strong, it has to be set in the balance against the negative and disruptive influence of the schools upon traditional disciplines. In their funds of traditional wisdom there is nothing to tell the older people how to deal with youths who have passed what was once considered the proper age for marriage but who are still dependent on their parents' or guardian's home, though quite unprepared to accept their discipline. The freedoms and perplexities of a modern society have toppled the balance of what was, even in the old days, a precariously poised relationship. Adolescence unaccompanied by responsibility is a comparatively new feature in Ganda society, but its delights are such that even the young men and girls of the village who no longer attend school may prefer to prolong their irresponsible independence rather than take up a definite job or found a home.

It is possible to spend a great deal of carefree time strolling from one beer-drink to another. In the old days many of the feasts were held by daylight, but now there is no time limit and they can last through the night. It is commonly said that 'the feasts have been turned into markets'; drink traders arrive and set up their stalls wherever a big feast and dance is being held.

In the old days, again, women and children were expected generally to drink only what the menfolk allowed them, but today things are very different. It is not surprising, then, that many of the youths drift into a series of casual relationships and postpone indefinitely any idea of a serious marriage. One boy of fifteen, who spent his days loafing around the landing-beach and the fish-market, when asked if he did not want to earn some money so as to be able to get married one day, laughed, saying, 'Why should I marry? I can always get a girl for a shilling or two; I prefer to be free.'

It is against this general background of breakdown that the older children in the Primary and Junior Secondary schools have to be understood and helped by their church, in the persons of the clergy, catechists and Christian teachers. It is universally recognized in these days that the sexual indulgence of boys and girls in early puberty is very common. This is not a new thing; at the same time it is not to be supposed that traditional Ganda society was indifferent or light-hearted towards pre-marital intercourse. It would be truer to say that the conventional adult attitude was severe and anxious over the misconduct of the young but somewhat ineffectual at preventing it. It was the unchastity of a daughter rather than of a son which was felt as a disgrace, and preg-nancy therefore was the crime that really mattered. The girl was forced to tell who was the cause of her trouble, and the man was fined first and then, if possible, made to give the marriage-payment and marry the girl. Even if the girl did not agree to a marriage, she had to live with the man's relatives until the child, which was theirs, had been born. After that there was a ceremonial meal to re-establish her relations with her own parents. But, as Roscoe says, 'such an incident did not prevent a girl from marrying, nor would her husband think less of her; but it prevented her from being taken to wife by a chief, or anyone of import-ance; consequently every measure was taken to keep the girls pure until marriage.'[1]

Today all the instability of a society in transition, the blurring of tribal culture-patterns through immigration, the discrediting of parental authority through the education of the children, and the avenues of escape opened up by public transport, have combined to relax even such sanctions as existed in the past, and to induce a confused and amoral state of mind. It is true that many elements in the Christian ethic are very slowly gaining ground, most noticeably in the revival movement and the educated bourgeois class. But while people generally think they know what Christianity says about the obligations of married people, they are less clear about what it has to say concerning the behaviour of adolescents. In former days girls of about twelve were given a very thorough course of sex-training by an older woman; but because the manner of some of the detailed instruction was offensive to the mission-aries, the church frowned on this without providing anything adequate to take its place. Today nothing of that tradition remains except, strangely, the one physical element in the old preparation, whereby many young girls are still taught to produce by manipulation a certain elongation of the genitals. Otherwise one meets today among adol-escents in Buganda the same extraordinary mixture of experimental knowledge and bewildered lack of understanding which is the despair of social workers amongst British and American youth. The main difference is that wise and unshockable social workers are at present almost non-existent in Buganda.

Of the boys in the five schools who discussed this question and gave information,* more than half said that they had had intercourse with girls. Figures based on the whole sample would be misleading because there is great disparity in the average age of boys in this standard in different institutions. But, taking only boys from fourteen to seventeen years old, it appeared that of the Baganda 43 per cent. had had such experience, of the Basoga 56 per cent. and of the north-eastern tribes 77 per cent. (It should be remembered that in this sample all the boys from the north-east were immigrants and this always produces a weakening of normal *mores*.) These differences may be due to educational standard and status in society as well as to tribal characteristics; of the boys of all tribes whose fathers are in a professional or salaried job only 44 per cent. had had experience.

It can safely be said, then, that sexual intercourse is widespread among boys of fourteen years and over; below that age it is much more rarely known. Girls are generally first involved in these liaisons when they are between twelve and fourteen years old, though a considerable number begin their experiences much younger. No figures are available to show what proportion of young girls are involved; probably it is smaller than that of the boys, particularly in the professional class. Nevertheless, judging by conversation with adults and children in several villages, the number is certainly very high. Many of the girls are prompted, at first, by curiosity and the desire to become 'grown-up' like their older friends. In the villages, also, there is the attraction of some small reward; girls of ten and eleven reported having received a shilling or two from a man, a handkerchief or a belt from a boy. These are gifts, but they come to be expected, and constitute a real temptation to a child who receives no clothes from her parents.

It needs to be remembered that these children have grown up in an atmosphere of ethical ambiguity in this matter. It is known that traditional morality and the rules of the church agree in condemning premarital intercourse. To be 'caught in the act' arouses an intense sense of shame. Yet, on the other hand, in the villages, the knowledge that 'everybody does it' is insidious, and quite clearly a great number of boys and girls do not feel that such behaviour is seriously wrong. There are, of course, children whose minds have become unhealthy or shameless, but there are others who in spite of their sexual encounters preserve a

* See Appendix C.

sort of animal innocence which is very difficult to convey to Western minds. In the questionnaire which was submitted to the schoolboys, very many who admitted that they had often had intercourse and that nothing had yet occurred to make them try to avoid it, stated that they intended eventually to marry one wife only 'because I am a Christian and want to keep the law of God'. One boy of fourteen who has already had five different girls said that he wanted to be a bishop when he was grown up!

In regard to this matter the church resembles the traditional society in that there is a very wide gap between the standard that is laid down and the actual expectation of achievement. Such a situation naturally tends to drive the guardians of morality into negative attitudes of anxiety. There is nothing peculiar about the Uganda Church in this respect, for the same is true, in varying degrees, almost everywhere. It is only a small minority of clergy and laymen who point out that to expel one child from a school every few years for being discovered in an offence which it is certain that one boy in every two has committed is unrealistic and calculated to confuse rather than educate the conscience of the rising generation. At present the majority in the church have not progressed beyond the attitudes of the traditional morality, and appear to concentrate on preventing or punishing what they pretend are exceptional lapses from the normal standard. There are, however, a few clergy and some of the African teachers in girls' secondary schools who are beginning to think that the true task of the church is to give loving support and direction to boys and girls who are struggling against the tide to achieve an ideal which is not yet commonly accepted.

This change from the negative to the positive attitude must bring the leaders in the church, first to marvel that so many adolescents are in fact fighting, and succeeding in their fight, for chastity, and next to consider what are the factors which tend to militate for or against them in this struggle. To this end a careful analysis was made of the differences which appeared between the home background of those boys who had resisted successfully this temptation and those who had not. No one factor stands out beyond the others, but cumulatively the evidence is impressive. Without burdening this paragraph with statistical details, the following are the factors which appear to favour a boy's resistance. He is definitely more likely to achieve the Christian ideal in this matter:

if his relations with his father have been based on friendship rather than fear;

if his childhood punishments did not include beating, starving or binding;

if he was taught by his parents to pray privately;

if he remained in his parents' home till his tenth year;

if his parents have been regular churchgoers;

if his parents clearly indicate disapproval of such conduct;

if his mother has not been separated from his father;

if no other wives have been introduced into the home during his childhood;

if there have been regular family prayers at home;

if both parents are of the same religious denomination. (See Appendix C.)

It seems clear, therefore, that the church would be wise to approach this area of its responsibility from two sides; more understanding pastoral guidance of the young (for no manipulation of conditions can eliminate the primary element of individual moral decision), and an overall effort to bring about certain changes of attitude and relationship in the homes of its people.

The majority of the young adolescents in the villages of Buganda have a definite ideal of goodness and of a better pattern of life, though for the most part it is too shallow to become a dynamic compulsion in their lives. They greatly admire kindness, honesty, patience and the courage to stand by one's convictions. Among the youth of the villages there is generally a longing for enough self-mastery to stand clear of the messiness of mutual mistrust, drunkenness and sexual indulgence which they find surrounding them. Almost all put up some sort of struggle against these temptations, but they are afraid of the loneliness which is the price of 'not joining in', and are defeated by a deep-seated moral fatalism.

Now and then an individual makes a pathetic attempt to break away from the downward drag of the environment. Some of them join the baptism classes with this motive, particularly some of the children of nominally Anglican parents who take themselves off to a Roman Catholic station some distance from their home and stay there for the three months of the catechumen classes. The denominational differences mean nothing to them; it is the opportunity to escape temporarily from the home village which attracts them.

It is this element of escape, as well as the desire for education and a salaried job, which underlies the urgent scramble of the boys to get into secondary schools. That opportunity is at present beyond the hopes of most village girls, however. Numbers of them, therefore, adventure into the big towns from exactly the same desire for escape and a better life. For many of these it is a leap from the frying-pan into the fire. The aunts to whom they go for accommodation prove sometimes to be little better than procuresses. Not by any means untypical is the story told by a probation officer in Kampala of a thirteen-year-old girl who came one day to his office in desperation, because she could not stand any longer the life she was living. She had come in from the country a year before, and was staying with an aunt almost in the shadow of the Anglican cathedral. The aunt rented a dormitory to seven men, and the girl was required to sleep there to be used regularly by them all.

Sometimes it is the parents themselves who send even their younger children from the villages into the towns to earn money for them. Recently a young Musamia boy from the eastern province was sent by his mother, when only nine years old, to go forty-five miles away to Jinja to see what he could pick up. The boy got a job as nursemaid to an Indian's children at Shs. 40 a month. After the first month the mother arrived, took Shs. 35, and sent the boy to Kampala to see if he could do better there. Wandering round the streets on his arrival, he saw through an open window some sugar and cigarettes on a table, climbed over the sill to take them, and was caught by the police. Now, fortunately, he is in a remand home.

It would be absurd, of course, to imagine that the large towns are nothing but a moral quagmire. There is probably a greater concentration of devoutly Christian African homes in Kampala than anywhere else in the country. Moreover, the youngsters from the more cultured and sophisticated homes know their way around in a modern environment, and discuss the problems of the Christian boy or girl in very much the same terms as are familiar in the West.

Opinion is very much divided in the church, and in African society, on the question of Western dancing. The majority of the older Christians, and some of the younger, regard it as wholly evil. But for most of the younger generation discussion is concerned only with the questions 'Where?' and 'With whom?'. Some dance halls are regarded, with good reason, as undesirable. But even if a girl limits her dancing to the reputable places and occasions, there still remains the problem of how to conduct the friendships which naturally develop. Society, which is in transition and has not yet made rules of propriety that extend to the new situation, is unkind to a young couple who want to have further opportunities of meeting one another without being committed to a serious relationship. The fear of insinuation and scandal usually drives the friendship under cover, in a series of secret meetings, which the young people, finding themselves individually at a loss with no familiar *mores* to guide them, often cannot handle without emotional and moral calamity.

There are at present very few leaders in the church who have yet realized that if they want to see recreational facilities with a decent reputation provided for the younger generation, then it is the church in its laity which has got to set about providing them. The need for such facilities is most evident, particularly for the hundreds of young clerks and semi-skilled workers who live, perhaps, in a village ten miles out of the town. Having no opportunity for games or other recreation after office hours, and only a village in darkness to look forward to, these young men begin street-corner gossip as soon as they are outside the office, stroll on with friends to an eating-house and then to a bar, and arrive home quarrelsome and out of pocket with no time for a family life. One or two of the voluntary recreational associations for youth have been active in Uganda for some time. The Scout and Guide movement has had considerable success in the schools, and more recently the Y.W.C.A., through the energetic drive of a very few people, has established a number of groups. But neither of these efforts is wholly succeeding in satisfying the more adult needs of African youth. If the barriers of suspicion that have most unfortunately been erected between the clergy and the department of Community Development could be broken down, greater consultation and co-operation between them might lead to something more creative and truly relevant than has yet appeared.

NOTE

1. J. Roscoe, *The Baganda* (1911), p. 79.

9

Men and Women

THE church in Buganda, from its highest officials to the lowliest
baptized member, is anxious and at a loss with regard to the
instability of marriage relations throughout the country. There
is good reason for this concern, as there is in many other parts of the
modern world. To be worried is far better than to be indifferent, but
there are grave dangers in over-anxiety. There is a point of despair
beyond which it is perilous for any society to go, for that way leads to
the ultimate loss of heart, when all standards are cynically abandoned.
Probably the greatest contribution the church can make in this area of
life at the present time is to be completely undismayed, as well as clear-
sighted; pastorally scientific rather than moralistic. The anxiety is
nothing new. It would be possible to quote from the past missionaries
of every decade from 1880 to 1950, words which seem to be a precise
description of the present state of affairs. It is better to remember
Mackay's observation that, 'in nature the greatest things grow slowly,
and we can expect no other mode of operation here'.

The majority of Christians in Buganda are married in accordance
with traditional African custom. Since all the modern variants, including the marriage of Christians in church, are in fact modifications of
this, it is necessary to understand what normally takes place in a
properly observed Ganda customary marriage in the present day.

A good African marriage is never a private arrangement between two
individuals, but a carefully prescribed meeting-point between two clans.
It is undertaken with a deep sense of responsibility toward both the past
and the future generations and therefore its object is primarily to
produce children. But while this is basic, it still leaves room for strong
affection and even romantic love, and very few marriages take place that
are not based on the consent of the two parties.

Occasionally a girl marries against her will because her father or her
aunt threatens her with a curse, and sometimes a boy who lacks initiative
will allow himself, with apparent indifference, to be guided solely by

the advice of an older friend in the choice of his partner. But normally the first step towards a marriage is taken by a boy asking a girl to be his wife.

In the villages the age of marriage for girls appears to be lower than it used to be: between thirteen and fifteen is quite usual, but a few are married at eleven years old. According to the laws of the Buganda African Government, intercourse with a girl under fifteen, with or without her consent, is punishable according to the circumstances, but this is one of many instances where the law, under Western influences, does not accord with common practice and so is rarely enforceable. A man prefers to marry a girl who is a virgin, and in present conditions he believes this is only possible if she is very young. This preference is particularly strengthened by Moslem influence. Early marriage was also more common in some of the neighbouring tribes, and immigration has therefore tended to lower the average age in certain areas. In the towns, however, and among the more educated families everywhere, the age is a good deal higher, especially if the girl has been to school. Boys also marry later than they used to do, partly because a young man need no longer marry in order to win his independence, and partly because he has to work for several years before he can earn the increased marriage payment that is demanded.

If the girl accepts the boy's proposal, she normally tells the news first to her brother, who passes on the information to her parents. The boy then has to write a number of letters, in each of which he must enclose a few shillings, one to the girl herself, one to her paternal aunt, or *ssenga*, one to her brother, and finally one to her father. If all goes well the girl replies, saying, 'Your letters have pleased us.' The boy follows up his advantage with a present of meat, sugar and salt, worth from Shs. 30 to Shs. 50 in all. If the father accepts the salt, this formally signifies his consent for the betrothal to proceed. The next step for the boy is to go with the girl to buy her the clothes she is expected to wear for the formal betrothal. In the old days a new bark-cloth was *de rigueur*, but today she will expect from Shs. 150 to Shs. 300 worth of cotton or silk goods from an Indian store.

For the actual betrothal, or *okwanjula*, the various members of the girl's family who are concerned usually gather, for convenience, at the one household, otherwise a great deal of going to and fro is involved. The suitor approaches the girl's *ssenga* and asks her to speak on his behalf. She then takes him to the girl's brother, and kneeling before him speaks as though she herself were the girl, saying, 'I have grown up and this is the man who wants to marry me.' The brother then demands a gift of beer, or Shs. 30 as a substitute. On receiving this he goes with it to his father, where the discussion over the marriage payment begins. Sometimes the brother goes to and fro between the father and the suitor until agreement has been reached. The formal acceptance of the beer by the father seals the betrothal contract, but he may not touch it until the girl has indicated her willingness. Sometimes, if he has already been informally advised of the amount, the suitor will pay the whole marriage payment immediately; otherwise a day is fixed for the payment, or part payment, and when this has been made over, the father very often will write an official receipt. This is not legally necessary, since the evidence of witnesses is accepted in the African courts in case of a claim, but it is becoming more customary. A feast is held to celebrate the betrothal and acceptance of marriage payment, at which the formal gift of beer is drunk by the witnesses; the suitor himself is present at the feast, but does not eat any of the food.

Much discussion goes on in the villages as to whether modern parents are asking too much marriage payment, or *omutwalo*, compared with earlier days. There has always been considerable difference between the customary amounts demanded in different tribes. The Bavuma are reputed to have asked always a much greater amount than the Baganda, while the Badama regard five cows and five goats as the statutory gift. The influx of such tribes is sometimes blamed for the inflation of marriage payment in Buganda at the present time. In the old days Baganda parents, if they liked their daughter's suitor, would often be content with only a formal gift of beer and salt; but it is generally agreed that the statutory amount at the beginning of this century was a goat, a bark-cloth, five gourds of beer, salt and ten rupees. By today's values that amounts to roughly Shs. 400. (Average prices of a goat Shs. 200, bark-cloth Shs. 35, gourd of beer Shs. 30; a rupee was 1s. 4d.) Moreover, cash in those days could purchase at least twelve times as much produce or livestock as it can today. In actual value, therefore, the old marriage payment was not much less than the usual amount asked today, which ranges between Shs. 300 and Shs. 600, though much lower and much higher sums than this are often quoted.

The modern use of a cash payment in place of other gifts inevitably tends to turn the transaction into a sale, and the girls in the villages quite often use that word in these days, saying, 'My father wishes to sell me.' But it still remains true that the majority do not think of it in these terms. It is primarily a deposit, made as a guarantee both of the good faith of the bridegroom and the good behaviour of the bride. It is also a solemn recognition of the transfer of the services, though not the person, of a girl from one clan to another. It is, however, an interesting peculiarity of Ganda society that marriage payment does not confer on the husband the right to all the children of the wife. It is the *genitor*, not the *pater*, who owns a child, so the child of a casual union can be claimed by its true father's clan.

In the villages the majority of girls seem to approve of the institution of the marriage payment, and if a father waives it, his daughter often feels that he undervalues her, and that her husband does not love her. Many of the educated girls, however, with their new concepts of free individualized personality, object strongly to the marriage payment, saying that it gives the husband proprietary rights over his wife which spoil the idea of partnership in marriage. Moreover, such girls, unlike their sisters in the villages, hope that the economy of their home will be based on the pooled resources of both partners, and therefore do not want to find their husbands burdened with debt at the start of their married life.

After the giving of the marriage payment the boy and girl are not supposed to meet each other until the wedding day. This is still fairly strictly enforced among the Baganda in the villages. Several of the neighbouring tribes, however, regard it as normal for the girl to visit the boy occasionally, and have intercourse with him, before the actual marriage takes place, and the mingling of cultures through immigration naturally produces confused and weakened disciplines in this respect today. In the towns, among educated families, many of the European customs of courtship and engagement are being combined with the traditional African patterns.

Though the contractual element in the marriage has virtually been completed in the betrothal and giving of marriage payment, there remains the wedding ceremony for the actual consummation. For a week before the wedding the girl is kept in seclusion, very often in the inner dining-room of her elder brother's house, and is washed several times a day by her aunt or mother, and rubbed with butter to make her skin supple and glossy. On the last day it was usual for the mother to give her daughter advice concerning the art of marriage, particularly in its physical aspect, but in these days this is sometimes reduced to a few perfunctory words just as the lorry is arriving to take her away.

On the morning of the wedding the bridegroom is supposed to visit once more the home of the bride's mother in order to give her a present to console her and to compensate her for all the care she lavished on her daughter when she was only an infant. This special gift is known as *Kasuze katya?*, or 'What sort of night has the little one had?', in memory of the sleepless nights that the mother once spent watching over a wakeful child. In the old days this gift was always a gourd of beer, because the mother would have consoled herself during long night watches with drinking; in these days the charming custom is maintained by the gift of a tin of paraffin oil to refill the lamp that was so often burning all night when the child was wakeful.

The girl's parents play no part in the wedding itself, though they often give a feast for the relatives of their own generation. The girl is taken to the bridegroom's home by the guardian brother and the aunt, who wears her sash diagonally over one shoulder, and carries a peeling-knife. The bride is usually wearing a white bridal dress, veil and tiara, hired from an Indian trader. Other brothers and sisters, and at least one chosen bridesmaid, accompany them, and the party sets off, often in a hired lorry, with one or two drummers sounding their *omubala*, or clan beat, and singing traditional wedding songs. The bride, however, is supposed to look subdued throughout the proceedings.

Meanwhile a considerable party has gathered at the bridegroom's home, consisting of his relatives—mainly of his own generation—and other friends. There the drums beat the *omubala* of the bridegroom's clan. As the bridal party approaches, a group of the bridegroom's friends rush out to meet them and bar the way. The girl's brother then asks for a gift of money or a chicken in payment for bringing her, and a long time may be spent in haggling over the amount. At last he leads her forward to a mat of woven palm leaves which has been spread in the courtyard before the bridegroom's house. She kneels, and her brother takes her hand and places it in the hand of the bridegroom.

Then follows the wedding tea-party. The bridegroom leads his bride to the 'high table', set under a shelter of poles and thatch in the court-yard. The guests take their places, those of the bride's party on one side and those of the bridegroom's on the other. The bride's brother makes sure that enough chairs have been provided for his party, and if this is not done a serious quarrel may break out between the two sides. Tea and bread are served and a wedding cake is cut by the bride. Speeches are made to the bridegroom, stressing the moral obligations of faithful-ness and kindness to his bride, and hospitality to his relatives. All this may occupy a long time, but when it is over most of the bride's party take their leave and go. Her aunt and the chosen bridesmaid, however, stay behind.

The marriage feast is now prepared. By this time it is already evening and the drinking and dancing are likely to continue throughout the night. While food is being prepared and the drumming is warming up, the bride is taken into her husband's house by his sisters and her aunt, and her wedding clothes are taken off. After some time the husband joins her to consummate the marriage. Before doing so he is expected to give her precise instructions regarding any taboos of his clan or family, and also to lay down quite clearly the pattern of behaviour he wishes her to observe in her household duties. Failure to do this is often quoted as the reason for subsequent misunderstanding and quarrels in a home. If a girl is unfortunate enough to have married a man who is secretly a sorcerer, this is the moment when he will reveal it to her, sometimes by demanding that she perform some ritual act, such as squeezing herself through a long incision in the stem of a banana plant. Even well-educated girls know that this is a calamity that might befall any unwitting bride.

The bride must remain in the house for the rest of the night, but the bridegroom, having changed into his everyday clothes, is expected to join in the drinking, singing and dancing which are going on outside. There is often a good deal of licence and the bridegroom may indulge himself quite promiscuously.

In the early morning the bride's aunt goes inside to examine the bridal sheet or bark-cloth. If the girl was a virgin the aunt takes the sheet to the girl's parents; and the bridegroom goes to their home with a young female goat, which he leaves secretly in their courtyard, and runs off without showing himself. If the girl was not a virgin her husband's relatives cut a hole in the sheet and send it to her parents as a mark of disgrace. These customs are not always observed in these days.

For a week after the wedding the bride is secluded in the house, treated as a guest, and served by her husband's relatives. The end of this 'honeymoon' is marked by a ceremonial visit to her parents, called 'the return of the butter'. After spending a day and a night with them she goes back to her husband accompanied by a procession of her relatives bearing bunches of plantains, button mushrooms and simsim, firewood and a cooking-pot, perhaps a goat or even a cow. In these days the party may hire a lorry if the distance is great. The bride, however, must approach her husband's home in the evening, carrying a chicken in her hands and with one plantain-bunch balanced upright on her head; these must be cooked and eaten entirely that night. The other gifts are cooked, either that evening or the following day, as a congratulatory feast for the husband and his friends. The bride herself takes no part in preparing the food, but thereafter she enters upon her normal duties as a housekeeper.

What has been described is a properly conducted marriage by African custom as it is commonly observed in these days. There are, however, many variants representing a greater or lesser degree of the breakdown of disciplines. The first thing to go is the formal betrothal. The man anticipates the contractual arrangements by persuading the girl to come and sleep with him. After some time, if both still wish it, they may decide to become formally married. The man arranges with her parents the amount of marriage payment that is to be given, and the girl returns to live with them until the whole, or an agreed instalment, has been paid. The marriage ceremonies will then take place in the usual way. The prospective husband, having already abducted the daughter, is in a strong bargaining position, so this method of obtaining a bride is growing more frequent as a reaction to the inflation of marriage payments. It is a short step only to the complete breakdown of the contractual element in marriage. Having persuaded a girl to live with him, the man may refuse to give any marriage payment except the formal beer and salt, and even that may be omitted. This has no legal status, yet it is coming to be regarded by many Baganda as a kind of marriage by mutual consent. Sometimes such unions remain unbroken for life, but there is inevitably a strong tendency for them to dissolve as casually as they were formed. So there is appearing in the villages, as much as in the towns, a completely lax pattern of serial liaisons, described as 'roaming' (*okutambula butambuzi*) on the girls' part, and as 'repetitive marriage' (*okuwasawasa*) on the part of the men.

In the sample of 76 households at Makindu and Kabubiro the types of marriage of the heads of households were divided as follows:

Percentages	Out of 61 1st wives	Out of 36 2nd wives	Out of 19 3rd wives
By African custom . .	51	61	53
By abduction . . .	22	28	32
By Christian rite . . .	22	0	5
By Moslem rite . . .	5	11	10

In a survey of 24 pastorates in Buganda it was found that 25 per cent. of the married Anglicans had had a church marriage. In 8 Ankole pastorates the figure was 42 per cent., reflecting that keener adherence to Christianity which we have already noticed in connexion with church attendance there. In the towns, owing to the greater prevalence of Western social patterns, there is a greater number of church marriages, but it is impossible to generalize. For example, the majority of those who work in the Katwe district of Kampala live a little way outside the town and have a Christian marriage, whereas in Kisenyi and Mulago districts the majority are resident and have only serial liaisons.

It is important to recognize that in the majority of church marriages exactly the same customs are observed, from the betrothal to 'the return of the butter', as take place in a customary union. The only difference is the addition of the church service in place of the handing over of the bride by her brother in the courtyard of the bridegroom's house.[1] Otherwise everything is the same. The bride's parents remain at their home. The two parties arrive by lorry at the church, with drums beating the *emibala* of the two clans, and sometimes bringing their gourds of beer on board with them. The bride's aunt stands as matron of honour, and her brother gives her away, and, after the service, off they go to the bridegroom's house to take up the customary routine at the point when the wedding tea-party begins. There are some Christians who will try to exclude beer-drinking, to play gramophone records instead of the bawdy marriage songs, and to bring the party to a finish before dark. This, however, is almost impossible when the church service, often many miles from the bridegroom's home, rarely finishes before four in the afternoon. The members of the revival movement like to turn the tea-party into an occasion for testimonies and hymn singing, and make a special point of the freedom and evident happiness of the bride. But all such modifications of the traditional pattern depend entirely on the Christian convictions of the individuals taking part. They are not a necessary feature of what is called Christian marriage, which can, and often does, include the whole traditional ceremony, but with the addition of the church service.

The second generation of missionaries, from 1890 onwards, mis-understood and disliked the use of marriage payment. Under their influence the church council passed a resolution, in 1897, in favour of abolishing the custom. A few of the leading Christians did in fact give it up, but otherwise it was maintained. Several Christians tried to explain that the custom did not imply that they were selling their daughters.[2] Among them was Sir Apolo Kagwa, according to Robert Walker's account.

'I remember once Pilkington preaching against this custom; he said it was the same as selling the women. The Katikiro waited on him in the vestry and discussed the matter with him. When Pilkington heard the whole matter he did not think it so objectionable as it at first seemed. The Katikiro pointed out that the girl was not forced to go against her wish, but that she liked to see how much the man cared for her, and also there was a reasonable prospect of her being taken good care of when she had been obtained at some cost to the man. . . . The chiefs are now considering what limit should be put to the amount of presents to be asked for marriage.'[3]

In these days a number of educated Christian parents waive the marriage payment; but generally speaking the custom is still observed by the majority of Christians and often a higher marriage payment is asked for a girl who is to be married in church. Unless a girl is of age the consent of her parents is required before the church will marry her, and this consent is usually tantamount to an acknowledgment that the marriage payment has been paid.

Marriage with the Christian rite is regarded almost everywhere as the ideal. The majority of adolescents say that they hope to have a Christian and monogamous home; the majority of Christian parents would like their children to have a church wedding, though a few say they will not allow them to be 'bound' by the Christian rite. But the basis of this ideal is social rather than religious. People say about Christian marriage such things as, 'So and so has married like an educated person': 'The woman with a ring cannot be played with'. The important feature is the ring itself, and some people buy rings from the Indian stores purely for the prestige they confer. Yet, like the Christian names adopted by pagan parents, these are thought to have no real efficacy unless they are given with the proper ceremony of the church.

It seems strange, therefore, that 75 per cent. of the Anglicans who have been married have not after all had a church wedding. Various reasons may be found for this reluctance.

In the first place there is the additional expense. This may often be quoted merely as an excuse. Nevertheless, it is true that the hire of a lorry for each of the two parties to and from the church is an additional expense which in most cases is quite unavoidable. Not every local church is registered for celebrating marriages, and even when a parish church is so registered (as is the case at Makindu), the ordained minister

M

may be unwilling to go away from his pastorate centre to take the service, especially if there are other weddings on the same day. Hired clothes and photographers are certainly not essential in the view of the church, yet when society insists that certain appurtenances are *de rigueur* it takes a very single-minded Christian to refuse to conform. Then there are the fees demanded by the church. Officially these amount to Shs. 10, but almost always more is required. Since everyone who is closely concerned with the marriage is receiving gifts from the bridegroom, it is not surprising that the hard-pressed clergyman should make the most of this opportunity. He first ensures that the couple have paid all their *buzimbi* dues up to date; until they have the full set of receipts they cannot be married. Then he names certain subscriptions which he reckons should be paid into whatever fund is causing him most concern at the time. One couple from Kabubiro, for example, were required to pay Shs. 15 each for the repair of Ngogwe church; another young man from Makindu had to give five shillings to the fund for sending clergy to England for further training, and one shilling for building the Rural Dean's house. After all this, the couple are handed envelopes in which they are expected to put a free-will offering 'for the chairs'—the statutory fee is called, 'for the table' (on which the registers are signed)— and Shs. 6 is regarded as a suitable amount for each of them to give. If a couple arrives late for the wedding, some of the clergy exact a fine of Shs. 10. There is one further financial consideration. By the marriage laws of the Buganda Government a man married by African custom can legally claim the return of the marriage payment if his wife clearly deserts him without due cause, and such cases are quite often brought in the *Gombolola* courts. But if the man has been married by Christian rite, any such claim is invalid, since marriage payment is not recognized as part of the Christian contract.

A very frequent cause of Christians marrying by African custom only is that the church rite is practically forbidden whenever an Anglican marries a Roman Catholic. The Roman Church, as elsewhere, will only marry such a couple when an undertaking is given that the children shall be brought up in that church. The canons of the Anglican Church in Uganda rule that its members should not marry persons of another confession, *if* such conditions are laid down. Unfortunately the official Luganda version of the canons mistranslates that phrase as '*because* such conditions are laid down', so turning the canon into an absolute prohibition. Whatever the rules, the *de facto* use in all the parishes of Buganda is to disallow all 'mixed' marriages. But, because of the past history of religious affiliations in Uganda, the fact is that in any district a high proportion of the eligible marriage partners will belong to the 'opposite' denomination. Indeed, since a considerable number of one's co-religionists in the locality are members of one's own family or clan, and therefore disqualified as marriage partners by the rules of exogamy, the chances that the person one chooses to marry will be a member of the other denomination are very high. Yet to ask one or other of the partners to change the religious affiliation in which he or she has been brought up is to expect a degree of independence which is rarely found in village society, where marriage is still a contract between two clans. The result is that large numbers of 'mixed' marriages take place, and the partners are given no option but to marry by African custom only.

A third reason for the reluctance to have a church marriage is the fear of the total commitment involved. This does not mean that most young men enter upon their first marriage expecting it to break down or deliberately making allowance for the possibility of other wives at a later date. There are certainly some who do this, but most of them hope to have a monogamous home.

But it needs to be more clearly understood that in the mental attitudes of many African peasants there is no sharp distinction between hope and intention. In Luganda the words 'to promise' mean 'to cause someone to hope'. For the village people every relationship in the world of things as well as in the world of people is personal, and therefore arbitrary. They are more intensely aware of their inter-relatedness with everyone and everything than are Western Europeans, and consequently less conscious of their individual self-determination over against the rest of existence. Their total awareness of the present moment is far more vivid, but this is achieved at the expense of foresight and reflection. Therefore their whole concept of volition and intention is far less positive and unconditional than is normal in Western minds. This can be seen in the matter of personal conversion. Much Western evangelistic preaching emphasizes the individual act of will and decision; but the more typically African attitude was expressed in the words of a Muganda catechist who, describing his own conversion, said: 'I told God that I was ready to be saved, and three days later he did it.' The same difference of outlook is shown by a comparison of the Moravian doctrine of assurance, which has played such a big part in the Wesleyan revival and in Anglican Evangelicalism, with the special emphasis of the Uganda revival movement on being in a condition of salvation at the present moment. This is demonstrated in the preference they have developed for the word *okulokoka* (being in a state of salvation) rather than *obulokozi* (salvation), which focusses attention on a spiritual experience in the past. This insight is clearly indicated by the words of one schoolgirl who wrote: 'Many people in our school were saved and a short time after were no longer saved.'

This obviously opens up some fascinating fields for theological exploration. But for the present purpose it reveals why it goes against the grain to pledge the future. Vows are not unknown, but always involve an invocation of the supernatural, both to aid the fulfilment, and equally to curse the breach, of the promise. For this reason the church was opposed to the custom of the *omukago*, or blood-covenant, because of the curses under which the participants lay themselves by their oath. It can be seen, therefore, that to a man and woman who belong to this background, whatever their hopes may be for their marriage, to vow a lifelong and exclusive fidelity must appear both presumptuous and dangerous.

Diametrically opposed to these attitudes is the position which the Anglican Church has taken up, the basis of which is the axiom that African customary marriage is 'potentially polygamous'. The church did not immediately reach this conclusion. In the early days the practice of the missionaries was ambiguous. For example, in 1883, Nikodemo Sebwato and Yokana Mwira were required only to promise that they had given up all but one wife, before being baptized; whereas, at the end of the same year, Zekaliya Kizito Kisingiri, had not only to do this but also to marry his one wife with Christian rites. According to the Rev. F. Rowling's report to the Conference of Missionaries in 1904, the custom up to that time had been to recognize and register the unions of those married by African custom before their baptism, provided that both parties stated that they had married by their own free will and promised to adhere to it always. At the Conference, however, Bishop Tucker successfully introduced a motion that 'when baptism completes the conditions necessary for the solemnization of matrimony in church the parties be required to come and be married in church according to the rites of the Church of England as soon as possible'. The Bishop seems to have been very largely responsible too, for the terms of the original marriage ordinance of the Protectorate Government, gazetted 15 November 1902, which, as George Wilson, H.M. Deputy Commissioner at Entebbe, wisely pointed out, seriously questioned the validity of native marriages and 'would retard that work (of the Missions) in promoting morality, by discouraging marriage among the masses of the population'. Wilson, after drawing attention to the many difficulties that the ordinance would place in the way of ordinary peasants who wished to legalize their marriage, remarked that, though perhaps the baptized Anglicans 'might be compliant under Tucker's influence', the 250,000 unbaptized adherents would not agree to the delay and travel.[4]

As Wilson had foreseen, the implications of the Marriage Ordinance, and of the attitude of the Anglican mission which lay behind it, had a disastrous effect on the already weak stability of the family throughout Buganda by debasing the currency of African customary unions. It is now widely believed, even by educated Baganda, that African customary marriage is not recognized even by Buganda Government law, though this is not in fact true. In the Protectorate law provision is made for converting a 'native marriage' into a 'legally binding marriage', but the former has no legal status, and all those whose marriage is of that kind are officially described on governmental forms as *abawulu* (literally 'bachelors'), a word which in these days indicates any irregular union. But it is in the official view of the church that African customary marriage—the marriages, that is to say, of four-fifths of the population —are most completely discredited. All who are married in that way, including the 75 per cent. of married Anglicans, are regarded as living in sin, whether they are monogamous or not, and are automatically excommunicated. Among the brethren of the revival such marriage is commonly called 'pagan', and a wife married in that way is referred to as *malaya*, the word for prostitute. So far is this sort of marriage discredited that men or women who have lived for years in an African customary union may eventually dissolve it and afterwards marry someone else by Christian rite on the grounds that the first was no marriage. Such cases feature quite often in the conversion stories of the revival movement.

It was this anomaly, appearing soon after the decisions of 1904, which so offended Bishop Willis that early in his episcopate he tried to reinstate to some extent the validity of African customary marriage. To him belongs the credit for seeing that, while African marriage is potentially polygamous, it can equally be described as potentially monogamous, and it is more positively Christian to do so. At his request the Government appointed a special commission to enquire into the question of native marriages in their bearing on Christian baptism, and in 1914 a new marriage ordinance provided some of the necessary remedies. By the same token Bishop Willis introduced in 1917 the following two canons, which are still the law of the church:

'1. A native customary union between non-Christians, although potentially polygamous, or potentially dissoluble, is to be regarded as a good marriage, capable of becoming exclusive and lifelong, in virtue of the baptism of both parties to it, and *ipso facto* becoming so if the baptism takes place. Parties to such a marriage are not to be re-married after baptism, but the fact of marriage, its lifelong nature, and its indissolubility, shall be publicly acknowledged, and the appropriate certificate issued, and the parties to it shall receive the church's marriage blessing before being admitted to Holy Communion. . . .

'2. A marriage potentially polygamous or potentially dissoluble is not raised to the level of Christian marriage by the baptism of *one* party. If after such baptism the Christian partner be deserted by the non-Christian, the Bishop shall determine whether the Christian partner is free under the *privilegium Paulinum* (I Cor. vii. 12-15) to regard the existing marriage as dissolved and to marry again with Christian rites. This privilege applies only when a Christian partner has been deserted by the non-Christian; if the Christian drive away the non-Christian, the privilege cannot be claimed.'

Unfortunately here is an example of the ineffectiveness of centralized legislation to change the thinking on the circumference of the church. In spite of the clear intention of these canons, the general attitude of the church towards African customary unions has remained unchanged. The version which is repeated in the villages is that 'Willis tried to persuade the church to recognize marriage by African custom, but the old clergy refused what he wished to do and defeated him.' The canons in any case do not envisage the marriage of baptized Christians without the rites of the church, which is the central problem today.

A church in which the majority of adult members are permanently excommunicated is a monstrosity which demands the most serious re-appraisal of basic assumptions. Whether it is right to exclude such Christians from Holy Communion is a question that must be faced in a later chapter. At this point the weakness which most clearly emerges is the lack of discrimination in the wholesale branding of all who are married only by African custom. In the Makindu parish, for example, there is the case of the old catechist, mentioned in Chapter 6, who was in charge of a village church for twenty years, but who, a few years after the death of his first wife, married again a woman who is a Roman Catholic and was at once disqualified from officiating as a catechist because the marriage was by African custom. In the same parish are two sisters who were both communicant members of the Anglican Church. Each married a man who was also a communicant. They would have liked church weddings, but the girls' father objected to this, and without his consent the clergyman could not have taken the marriage. They were, therefore, married by African custom. Though for ten years the two couples have remained monogamous, they have been condemned as 'living in sin', and their children, as 'children of fornication', have been refused infant baptism. The recitation of more cases would become tedious, but enough has been said to suggest the state of moral confusion which the present practice of the church has created.

Everywhere in the Buganda Church this topic causes acute anxiety and dissatisfaction. To look back into the past and see how the negative policy of the church and missions has been largely responsible for wrecking the disciplines of Kiganda marriage does not provide any answer to the problems of the present. Unfortunately all discussion of practical remedies is crippled by the fear of lowering standards, and since the policies of the church are naturally determined by those who have had a church marriage, there is not much sympathy with the point of view of those who have not. In 1957 an important step was taken towards the alleviation of this anomaly when the Anglican Church declared that an African customary union between previously baptized persons is to be regarded as a valid marriage (though not as a Christian marriage),[5] provided that the two parties promise solemnly that it will be a lifelong union and monogamous. Only a simple declaration, either in a civil registry office or in church before the pastor, is required, and must be registered in any suitable book. They are then re-admitted to Holy Communion, if already confirmed, and their children are accepted for baptism. In some districts outside Buganda there has been a big response to this new opportunity, but in Buganda only a few couples have so far taken advantage of it. It must be remembered that when Bishop Willis introduced the canons of 1917 they were rendered ineffective on this issue by the resistance and disregard of the older clergy. The *de facto* position is now so rigidly established in the pastorates and parishes that it will not be altered by a merely *de jure* change. Nothing can redeem the situation short of a determination to go out 'into the highways and hedges to compel them to come in'.

By attaching so much importance to its marriage service the church gives the impression that the ring is indeed a guarantee of monogamy. The facts do not support that view. In twenty-four pastorates in Buganda, only half the marriages that have been celebrated in church are still monogamous (52 per cent. in the parish congregations and 48 per cent. in the village congregations). Once again there is a marked contrast with Ankole, where 81 per cent. of all church marriages are still monogamous. In Makindu parish, out of thirty-three church marriages, fourteen are monogamous at the present time (42 per cent.), but on closer examination it was found that of these fourteen, four have taken second wives by African marriages but have subsequently sent them away, and two had had previous African marriages which were dissolved before the church wedding. There is no evidence to show whether the same might be found true of the monogamous households in other parts of the country or not.

Polygamy is definitely on the decline, though the causes for this are mainly non-religious. Though only fourteen monogamous homes in Makindu parish had had a church wedding, there were thirty-eight monogamous homes which had been married by African custom, a majority of whom are generally reputed to have remained strictly monagamous throughout their married lives.

Kiganda tradition asserts that the early kings of the present dynasty were monogamists. It was the period of imperial expansion which produced the royal harem. Though, on account of war casualties, women generally outnumbered men in the population, most of the surplus must have been taken up by the Kabaka and chiefs. The early missionaries give contradictory reports as to the prevalence of polygamy among the peasants in their day, but the chiefs certainly had large numbers of women.

But, in the early days of the church, many of them enthusiastically gave up all but one of their wives in order to be baptized. This was a real sacrifice for the man, and certainly made things difficult for the wife who remained to manage the home alone. African clan society absorbed without difficulty or disgrace the wives who were discarded, so that their hardship was much less than has often been supposed. Missionaries of a later generation tried to rule that a polygamist, when discarding his wives, should always retain the first, but the synod refused this on the grounds that by African custom all were equally his wives and he should, therefore, choose freely which one he would keep. But the first enthusiasm began to pass, and many of the chiefs, particularly when they found they were no longer trusted with much responsibility in the church, began to have second thoughts. In south Kyagwe, according to one old chief who is still active, 'Yonasani Kaidzi was the millet that fermented the beer. He had kept only one wife and he persuaded them all to do the same. But when he went they found that their nature had never really accepted the new way.' For the chiefs, certainly, there were real difficulties. Most of them had several private estates in addition to their *ex officio* holding, and the usual way was to have a wife in charge of each food-garden. The transfer to the use of men stewards was costly, and many were unwilling to undertake it. The lapse of the chiefs led naturally to a general relaxation.

In spite of this, polygamy steadily grew less. The changed economics of the country have reduced its advantages and the population trend is in favour of monogamy. In 1911 the number of married African women in Buganda exceeded the number of married African men by 15 per cent., in 1931 by 10 per cent., and in 1948 by only 2·6 per cent. Throughout Buganda, however critical men may be of the church's regulations in many respects, practically no one suggests that the Christian ban on polygamy should be relaxed. Today the problem from the point of view of the Christian Church is not polygamy but a succession of marriage partners, one by one. The real battle is not between one established pattern of marital relationship and another, but between stability and social disintegration.

There are five main factors which are making it difficult for men and women to achieve a successful monogamous marriage in these days.

First is the economic factor. We have already seen, in the case of both catechists and chiefs, that the easiest way to maintain several estates or plots of land is to have a wife in charge at each place. It is general knowledge that this is being done even by a few of the most respected leaders in church and state. Slowly, however, the pressures of economics are changing, and so also is the popular idea of the economic function of women. A man still has to provide his wife with her *kadde*, or digging-frock, and if the marriage is dissolved she is expected to leave it with him though the rest of her clothes are her own property. Nevertheless, the attitudes expressed in this custom are disappearing. Most Christians when facing the decision whether they should take a second wife or not, though they know the church's regulations, do not think of it primarily as something that is intrinsically wrong, but consider the question in terms of the feelings of the first wife—shall they or shall they not do something which will injure or anger her? Economic advantage is balanced against a new valuation of their relationship with each other.

Second, and of far greater importance today, is the problem of sterility. The incidence of this among the Baganda is notoriously high, as has been remarked from Lugard's time to the present day. It has usually been attributed to venereal disease—and this certainly accounts for most cases; but recent research has suggested that dietary deficiency may be a secondary cause. A childless woman, just as much as her husband, after four or five years of marriage, is most severely tempted to try again with another partner, and public opinion will not disapprove if she does so.

Among the more educated Christians it is suggested that many marriages break down from failure to achieve sexual satisfaction. Opinion is divided, some saying that there is not much deep incompatibility, but that men who form a habit of greedy promiscuity in their youth cannot learn to be content with one woman in marriage. There is, nevertheless, some reason for taking this factor seriously. The widespread demand for books giving sexual information cannot be entirely pornographic, and the failure to provide anything in place of the detailed instruction given to adolescents in the old days has been a serious omission. It has for a long time been a rule of the church that clergy shall interview and instruct every couple before celebrating their marriage, and the theological college at Mukono has tried to equip ordinands for this part of their ministry. But, even if full confidence could be placed in their ability to do this, the clergy have a most inadequate opportunity of giving this information since they rarely know that a marriage is contemplated until the couple come to put up the banns three weeks before the service. The problem, in fact, is precisely the same as in the parishes of the older churches.

The fourth reason for marriage breakdown is the failure to adjust to the social change which has laid upon both men and women an unwonted burden of individual liberty. In the past a woman was wholly dependent either on her husband or on her father (or brother). If she ran away from the former, she had nowhere to go but to the latter, who, since he would have to make good the marriage payment if she deserted, took pains to effect a reconciliation and persuade his daughter to go back to her husband. But in these days public transport and relaxed social conventions have opened many doors of escape to the disgruntled wife. At the same time a few years in a primary school, instead of working in her parents' home, have prepared many a girl to expect more of her married life than was her mother's lot. Most men, on the other hand, have not in the least adjusted themselves to the changed relationship of give and take. Knowing only the old pattern of mastery, they have little skill in winning and holding the affection and respect of their wives. Both men and women alike are too readily suspicious and lack the reserves of patience and forgiveness which a relationship of mutually free partners demands. Few have yet learned how to quarrel and achieve reconciliation; and when the dispute reaches a serious deadlock the church courts are found to be so dilatory that very few Christians bring their cases to them. They therefore take the easy way out. Not many men take the initiative in divorcing their wives except for unfaithfulness; it is simpler for them to bring another woman into the household. On the other hand *okunoba*, or desertion, by the wife is very common, and the most acute problem is presented to the church by the great number of young husbands who, usually through their own foolishness, find themselves left to choose between a life of involuntary celibacy or excommunication.

The last, and most thorny, factor threatening the stability of marriages in these days is the lack of commitment of husband and wife to each other. It is at this point that the great strength of the revival movement lies, with its insistence on spiritual partnership. Among educated Christians in Kampala the weekly discussion-group which meets at Namirembe fulfils an invaluable function because husbands and wives, having started to discuss a topic there, continue to share in free discussion afterwards in their homes. Generally speaking, however, even in the marriages of educated Christians, men and women are still groping towards a new relationship which is strange to them. The church as a whole is turning its attention more and more to this aspect of the problem, and one gets the impression that a widespread spiritual wrestling is taking place. Sometimes, in the villages, people give expression to their sense that they are confronted by a choice between two types of relationship. One man in Makindu parish said, 'To love is one road, and to rule is another. But the way of love fails. If I used force with my wife, she would understand it and respect me: because I have tried the way of love she despises me.'

Again, many others fasten upon the question of inheritance as symptomatic of the problem. As one catechist said, 'In the church you say you give all to your wife but in fact you do not. It would be good if all who marry in church first signed a contract or a will.' This referred to the fact, often discussed in this context, that a wife does not automatically inherit from her husband. By Ganda law his property belongs to his clan, as hers belongs to her clan. If, however, either makes a will settling the whole or part of the inheritance on the other, this over-rides the claims of the husband's or the wife's clan. This is not very often done; the husband's clan, however, in the absence of a will, may settle an amount on his widow if they think it good to do so. Some years ago the then Katikkiro proposed to the synod that it should legislate that all church marriages should automatically establish the wife as her husband's heir, but the motion was rejected on the grounds that it was totally unacceptable to the majority of people at the present time, and would only result in still further disparaging the Christian marriage rite.

Some of the intelligentsia in the church are seeing still wider implications in the same problem, and assert that the clan system must go completely before the new concept of partnership in marriage can make headway. They point out that at present both husband and wife are far more committed each to his or her clan, than they are to one another. When any Muganda wife says, *Ewaffe*—'our home'—she is invariably referring to her parents. The marriage is no stronger than a precarious contact between two clans which, lacking the older sanctions and solidarities, very easily springs apart. Therefore, they say, it is necessary to break completely what is left of the system in order that men and women may make a more real commitment to one another in marriage. Such arguments may be partly prompted by the natural impatience of the young, well-to-do married couples with the unreasonable demands which their relatives make upon them. They are arguments also which shock the ears of modern missionaries, who are aware of the dangers in such cavalier dismissal of old social structure. Yet these are questions to which the church, not the missionaries, must give the answer.

That the church is alive to the demands of this problem there can be no doubt. In recent years the diocesan marriage-guidance committee has shown a greater sensitiveness to the pastoral needs of those who have failed. The Mothers' Union is a very well-established organization, with branches in hundreds of parishes. Though at first sight it appears, in the villages, to provide nothing but a dull repetition of unimaginative meetings for pathetic little groups of women, these gatherings are in fact the one spiritual consolation which great numbers of Christian wives have to rely on. Fighting to maintain the Christian standard in difficult homes, and fiercely tempted to avenge themselves on unfaithful husbands, they gladly walk five miles or more in order to sit for a couple of hours with a few others engaged in the same struggle, because they know that it steadies them enough to endure for another week. It is widely felt, however, that the Mothers' Union can only partly alleviate the difficulties because it caters for the women only. In several districts the church has spontaneously introduced the keeping of St Peter's Day for services and conferences for the married couples in the pastorate.

Out of this movement there are also growing up, in several places, monthly meetings for married people.

The problem, however, is far too massive for such piecemeal remedies to solve alone. The recovery of a whole society in dissolution is a task that calls for supernatural faith and wisdom; but these have to show themselves in strong nerves and common sense. At present the church in Buganda shows rather more anxiety than apathy towards the problem. In many Christians the anxiety verges on despair; in a smaller number it is turned to a profound wrestling with the question. But both these reactions spring from a conscience that is alive. Therein lies the hope that this church, in spite of every cause for dismay, will make its creative response to the challenge and the call of God.

NOTES

1. The Roman Church treats the betrothal ceremony seriously and has a rule that a priest or his representative must always have been present at it if there is to be a church wedding.

2. R. H. Leakey, Letter to Stock, 21 Oct. 1897, in C.M.S. archives.

3. Archdeacon R. H. Walker, Letter in *C.M.I.* 1900, p. 341.

4. George Wilson, Letter, 6 Jan. 1903, in Government archives, Entebbe.

5. This distinction is surely theologically unjustifiable in the case of those who make the required declaration in church. It is certainly a reversal of the intention of the canons of 1917.

10

The Traditional World-View: I

DURING the time of the Kabaka's deportation, 1953-1955, the leaders of the church were greatly exercised about the resurgence of paganism throughout the country. The number of those attending church dropped alarmingly in some areas and the word was going round that the Europeans' religion was only used to soften up the African people but had no integrity in it. Groups of diviners, especially around the capital, were announcing that the powers of their fetishes and of the old hero gods would restore the Kabaka; along the lake shore, in Buddu county, prayers were offered to Mukasa, the god of the lake and chief divinity in ancient Buganda; and a prophet appeared who claimed to be possessed by the spirit of the hero Kibuka, who had died fighting for a Kabaka against his enemies and had become the national god of war. When the Kabaka returned, large numbers of diviners stood in the crowd that awaited him at the airport, and, on his triumphal tours through the counties of his kingdom, he was in many places greeted by mediums shaking the divination rattle and showing their fetishes.

Yet, in spite of appearances, it is very doubtful whether this could rightly be called a resurgence. There was a small section of one of the political parties which attempted to create a 'back to paganism' platform, but without much success. The drift away from church was not in fact as wholesale as was sometimes made out. The truth is that these phenomena had never been absent from the life of Buganda, but that, in the heat of emotion and under the weakened authority of the African administration, they came out more boldly in the open.

Constantly, throughout the history of the Anglican mission, reports show that aspects of the old cult were still alive. Every now and then a shrine was discovered and destroyed; or an individual came and burnt his fetishes or charms. During the early years of this century Islam, though it appeared to be a spent force as a rival faith, was instrumental in reviving the traffic in charms and fetishes. In the first year of his episcopate Bishop Willis instigated a commission of enquiry into the life of the church as a result of which the synod of 1913 passed a long list of regulations designed to put an end to practices associated with the old beliefs, and more than eighty houses of Christians were burned down around Kampala as reprisals against people who had given information to the commission.

Legally there is a uniform law of witchcraft covering the whole Protectorate of Uganda, though the different African administrations have interpreted it differently in their application. The Witchcraft Ordinance of 1912 says that 'whosoever holds himself out as a witch-doctor or witchfinder or pretends to exercise or use any kind of super-natural power, witchcraft, sorcery or enchantment', and anyone who imputes witchcraft to another 'otherwise than by laying information before a court', is liable to punishment. In Buganda and Bunyoro this has been interpreted as a total ban on all traditional supernatural activity, with the result that divination has been carried on in an atmosphere of secrecy, but in Busoga the law has been applied only against sorcery and the imputation of sorcery, while spirit-mediums have been allowed to operate quite openly, since their activities are not witchcraft in the meaning of the ordinance. From time to time cases are brought in the *gombolola* courts in Buganda and men are im-prisoned for the use of witchcraft and their instruments are burned, but charges are difficult to substantiate and people are usually afraid to give evidence.

Neither the law of church nor state, however, nor even the zealous burning of magical objects, is a real answer to this problem. For all that is contained in the vague word 'magic', however ugly or exotic its manifestations may appear to be, is primarily a way of looking at the world. It has its own logic and its own rationale. To one who lives within that traditional world-view there is nothing occult or demonic in the cult. Everything that is done has its reasonable place in the process of coming to terms with, and living within, that kind of world which it is believed to be. It is only after the advent of Christianity, and especially the conception of dualism which it implies, only after the undifferentiated unity of existence has been broken, that magic takes on, as it did in Europe, the fascination of darkness.

Even that does not mean that the church is now justified either in laughing the traditional world-view out of court or in merely waging against it a battle to the death. Something of both those things may have to be done. But the primary need in this confrontation is to understand and (dare one say it?) to sympathize. There are three reasons for this.

First, the church, instead of hitting out blindly, should be able to see where its own understanding of truth must conflict with this other world-view, and why it has to differ. Secondly the church can only help people pastorally by standing where they stand and taking as seriously as they do the things which trouble them. Thirdly, even when the practice of the old ways comes to an end, the world-view which lies behind them remains. Certain elements in it may approximate more closely to Biblical insights than does the European world-view. In any case it is into this world-view that Christ comes when the African peasant receives him, and out of that world-view, transformed by Christ, the theology of the African Church must be born.

TABOOS

In a world in which the relation of cause to effect is never understood merely as mechanistic continuity, but always presented in terms of the arbitrary personal will inherent in all aspects of existence, it is enough to know that certain actions bring an automatic retribution without having to understand why or how this happens. There are still a number of *mizizo*, or prescribed acts, that are commonly observed, mainly concerned with food. Women and girls avoid eating eggs, chickens or mutton since it is thought that to do so may result in sterility. During pregnancy other foods are prohibited as endangering the life of the child. Certain contacts between relatives-in-law, the *bako*, may produce death by palsy. One member of the congregation at Makindu believed that he was being attacked in this way because he had taken up residence in a house in which his brothers' children had previously lived with their wives. To the same category belong the taboos concerning the totems of the various clans, which members may on no account eat. The synod of 1913, which received the report of the commission that Bishop Willis had set up to enquire into the moral and spiritual condition of the church, and passed a number of regulations dealing with the observance of pagan practices by Christians, tried to legislate about the clan taboos. It recorded its conviction that to eat the totem is harmless, but went on to say that 'inasmuch as the totem preserves the integrity of the tribe (*sic*), it should be preserved in such ways as giving tribal names, and using the totem on notepaper headings and signet rings or as an emblem on the walls of houses'. In these days the observance of taboos in the villages is certainly not as universal as it was, but the change is due to new ways of looking at the world rather than to an extensive use of notepaper or signet rings!

OMENS AND MARVELS

Modern Western, or Westernized, man, having surrendered to the scientific specialist the duty of giving the explanation for so many phenomena, is prepared to take a great deal for granted. Assuming a mechanistic causation in every event, he can afford to let a multitude of incidents pass as accidental without any sense of insecurity or wonder. Not so the African peasant. For him any occurrence may be significant for his personal well-being, and therefore needs to be explained. There is no such thing as accident. It has been said that the African conception of the universe is just as rational as the European, but while the European idea of causation deals with the question 'how?' the African idea of causation deals with the question 'why?' At Makindu, for example, two men set off to travel twenty-five miles by bicycle. One of them almost had an accident through a broken brake-cable. When that had been mended they went on, but half an hour later the same thing happened to the other's bicycle. Whereupon they gave up their journey since it was clearly unpropitious to travel that day. Individuals have their own code of omens: some will turn back if the first person they meet on a journey is a woman, others if it is a man. Any marvel or monstrosity calls for comment. The birth of a child which has already cut its teeth calls for a propitiatory feast and beer drink, as something potentially threatening. The birth of twins also is regarded with a mixture of joyous pride and fear, and is celebrated with complicated rituals that have been fully described by others.[1] At Buikwe a three-legged goat was displayed in the market. The owner was turning it to good account as a fair-ground attraction, but he had first consulted the spirit-medium to learn what it portended and what he must do to avert the danger. Another expression of this attitude to events is the sacrifice that is frequently offered when a man builds himself a new house, especially if it is of brick or has an iron roof. The question, 'to whom is it offered?' cannot be satisfactorily answered, except by saying it is to that element of personal being inherent in all existence.

CHARMS AND MEDICINES

In almost every market there are the sellers of charms with their wares spread out on a mat. Some of these we should call medicinal, others magical, but the distinction implied by the two words is meaningless in the African context. There are long porcupine-quills, sections of which, sliced off and placed on the person or in the house, are a pro-

N

tection against smallpox. Large disk-like seeds placed on the bellies of children take away stomach-ache. A chip of resinous gum flaked into a cup of tea is a cure for hernia, and the small scales of the *lugave*, or scaly ant-eater, can be administered in the same way to help women to bear children. There is a large fibrous root sold as a cure for malaria, and small stringy roots as an aphrodisiac. The trailing tail-feathers of the Whydah finch are a charm to help a man to gather in wealth, as the bird collects twigs for its nest. Small hedgehog quills are sold to plant in the soil at seed time to make the crops grow. More definitely magical are the *nsiriba*, little packets of some concoction, or wooden charms, sewn up in cloth. These are attached to a person's clothes as a protection against ill-fortune.

In the fish market at Golomolo the regular salesman of such 'medicines' is a baptized member of the Anglican Church who knows his Bible quite well and attends church sometimes. His work is purely a financial concern. Yet he does recognize some kind of conflict between his business and his Christianity, for when a clergyman visited the market and some bystanders called out asking this man if he had anything that would bring the pastor luck, he replied, 'He believes in God: these are the things of Caesar.'

That charms of various kinds are widely used by Christians was shown during the diocesan mission in 1957 when converts who had been church members all their lives brought their charms and fetishes and burned them publicly. Egg-shells are fastened under the eaves of a hut to make the hens more productive, or little bundles of groundnuts to make that crop grow. A particular species of wild bird may be suspended there to bring good luck, which usually means one of three things— wealth, children and the love of women. Another type of small bird is a protective charm; hung up by its neck it will render an enemy harmless without killing him, but, suspended by its leg, it will bring about his death.

On one occasion a man passed through Makindu village full of jubilation over the capture of a thief. He had placed a protective 'medicine' beneath the threshold of his hut before going on a fishing expedition. Now word had reached him that a thief had broken into the house and taken a goat and other property; but as he was going out with them the medicine had worked and his foot had become fixed on the doorstep so that he was unable to move. He had already been there for two days and the owner was on his way to beat him and extort a confession before releasing him. A previous headmaster of the Anglican primary school at

Makindu had similarly thrown a protection around his house—the word used, *okusibaga*, means to immunise—which was reputed to make it impossible for anyone to steal his chickens.

SORCERERS AND DOCTORS

A certain number of charms are generally known and, like patent medicines, can be procured without consulting a doctor. But, for those who can afford it, more reliable results can be obtained through a professional expert. These are of two kinds. The *mulogo*, or sorcerer, deals mainly in destructive medicines or poisons; the *muganga* is a doctor who deals mainly in antidotes and protection against spells. There is also the *musawo*, who is generally a herbalist, and occasionally also a bone-setter, and whose concern is the healing of bodies. But in these days no clear distinction can be drawn between these three, nor between them and the diviner, whom we shall consider later. Most practitioners are prepared to turn their hand to anything that is required.

Protective medicines work by injuring a man's enemies. It is a short step to change a defensive weapon into one of aggression, and the *mulogo* deals particularly in murder and mischief, either for a client or on his own account. The most common method is to plant some malignant 'medicine' secretly in the house or garden of the victim, and to ensure that he learns, in some indirect way, that he is being bewitched. Often the psychological attack is sufficient. But the *mulogo* is also a poisoner, and is able, if necessary, to support his magical assault by physical means. Two members of Makindu congregation paid £30 to a *mulogo* for poison intended for another member, but were foiled through the intervention of the *mulogo*'s wife and, later, reconciled to their intended victim. People, however, prefer to avoid this method if possible for, as one who had tried it pointed out, poison can often be traced to the poisoner, but 'medicine' is safer to use because it is supernatural. 'Medicines' include such things as a snakes' head, a cow's horn, a toad, a tuft of human hair, or even a pen or a pair of spectacles. Hardly anyone in the villages wholly disbelieves in the efficacy of these things. When a woman died in Makindu parish the leader of the Mothers' Union passed on the information that 'they bewitched her with eggs', which had been planted in her garden on the previous day.

In cases of misfortune it is of the first importance to discover the physical instruments of bewitchment, if possible, and get rid of them, and also to learn who is responsible in order to take counter-measures.

This obviously presents opportunities for fraud, and it is widely recognized that a professional racket is carried on. In Makindu parish, for example, lived two Moslems who made a speciality of this. An old Christian woman who had contracted leprosy became very scared of her condition. These two approached her and, after asking a rigmarole of questions, assured her that someone must have used witchcraft in order to kill her. They easily persuaded her to consult a friend of theirs who had a number of fetishes. He first demanded a fee of Shs. 60, a black goat and a white hen. They then went into a seance and it was revealed that a quantity of 'medicine' had been planted in her garden and would cause her death in three days if it was not removed. They next offered to come as soon as it was propitious to hunt for the bewitchment, but they waited for two days and called her to a second seance before doing so. In the meantime they had gone by night and buried a goat's head, an egg and a snail-shell beneath her threshold. When eventually they arrived for the search, arrayed in ceremonial charms and wreathed in the vines of the magical *bbombo* creeper, they searched at great length all over the house and garden. Suddenly, as they crossed the threshold of her door, their leader collapsed and seemed to be dying, and was only revived when some antidote had been blown into his mouth. Whereupon they all refused to continue the search until the old woman, in a panic, gave her remaining goats to enable the fetish to increase its protective power over them. Then with an iron spike they probed the ground until the hidden 'medicine' was discovered, carried away into the bush, and rendered harmless.

The actual power of the 'medicines' seems to reside not in themselves as physical objects, but in what might almost be called an attached spirit. The objects themselves are sometimes called *byookoola*; but the meaning of this word can be better understood from the belief that a man may sometimes have the misfortune to marry a girl who has a *kyookoola*. He may not know this, but if he should drive her away the *kyookoola* is left to haunt him, crying and wailing in the house. It is not her soul, or *muzimu*, which is left, for without that she would soon die. It is something of herself which has yet an independent entity. Sometimes the man tries to procure 'medicine' to exorcise the spook, but more often he goes after the girl and pays her to recall it so that it will not trouble him any more. It is a *kyookoola* which resides in the 'medicines'. This concept of an *anima*, inherent in an object, yet having an entity of its own, is important to grasp, since it throws light on what follows.

FETISHES

The word for a fetish in Luganda means, simply, a horn, because most of them consist of the horn of a cow or buffalo, a horn-shaped gourd, or clay cylinder, into which has been packed a concoction of magical substances mixed with clay. Through the ritual application of the blood of sacrifices this becomes the habitation of a 'familiar', which is personal but in no way human. Some fetishes elaborately decorated with beads, are many generations old, and, in earlier days, the most powerful of them were the royal fetishes. These had the same power to possess people as had the spirits of the dead kings, and it may still be said of a case of possession, *Aliko Lukenge*—'Lukenge (one of the royal fetishes) is upon him.' They were housed in the palace enclosure and the Kabaka had to inspect and commune with them at every new moon. Many of the most famous fetishes were destroyed in the early days of Christianity. Others were placed in the Uganda Museum, which is commonly known as 'the House of the Fetishes', and is certainly regarded by some of its visitors as a repository provided by the British Government for these still powerful objects.

As an agency of witchcraft a fetish may be concealed in the house of the victim in the same way as the 'medicines', or hung in the owner's home as a protective charm. More often the fetish, as a physical object, remains in the possession of the practitioner and only the familiar is 'sent forth on an errand' (*okusindiikiriza*) to do the mischief. Usually the practitioner is quite specific, and dispatches the fetish to burn down a house, or to cause death by drowning, or by lorry. In these days many believe that there is a greater efficacy in fetishes obtained from neighbouring tribes—Busoga, Kigezi, Congo—possibly because the Witchcraft Ordinance has been applied less drastically there than in Buganda. One well-authenticated incident in 1956 was that of a Muganda girl who was taken to hospital with what appeared to be a partial stoppage of blood to the brain. She was discharged uncured, and a *muganga* was called in. When he had administered medicine and repeated a spell, she started speaking rapidly in Luciga, a language of which she had no knowledge. The *muganga* then diagnosed that the girl's sister had procured a Muciga sorcerer to send a fetish to attack her. Antidotes were applied and the girl recovered.

One of the landowners at Makindu was involved in a dispute with a family of Basoga who claimed that they were being defrauded of a part of his property which his father had given to them. Having lost their case before the *muluka* chief, instead of taking it to the *gombolola* chief they retired to Busoga, saying only, 'You will see what we shall do.' Some months later the man's sister, who lived in a house by herself, was woken in the middle of the night by deep voices which seemed to be speaking in the rafters of her house, saying 'We have come to take away your brother's spirit.' The next morning she ran to tell her brother, who then began to fall into a decline. He consulted an Indian doctor in Kampala, but without much faith. He rapidly lost weight and exhibited the symptoms of severe shock. He was a member of the local congregation and welcomed the prayers of the catechist on his behalf, but was convinced that his only hope of recovery lay in procuring the help of a more powerful fetish in order to recover his spirit which had gone from him. The suggestion that such a belief could not be reconciled with Christian prayer he regarded as quite unreasonable, retorting, 'If a sick man is taken to the European doctors can you not at the same time pray God to heal him?' He proceeded to pay £90 to a local sorcerer for the help of his fetishes, but to no avail. He then entered the Government hospital in Kampala but continued to grow worse. Finally he capitulated to the Basoga, giving them not only the twenty acres they had originally claimed, but twelve head of cattle, many goats and chickens, a house with a corrugated-iron roof, and all the furniture in it. He thereupon made a quick recovery. In this and many similar cases the resort to fetishes may be regarded as an extra-judicial means of redress through trial by psychological ordeal.

Fetishes may also be consulted for oracles. Two or three practitioners work in partnership for these seances, which always take place indoors at night, and often a curtain of bark-cloth separates them from the enquirers. Beer is drunk freely and the company sings the songs that are associated with witchcraft, while the *nsaasi*, or gourd rattle, maintains an insistent rhythm. Under cover of darkness the practitioners fit together several lengths of hollow castor-oil stems, with a calabash trumpet on the end, and speak through this in a growl or a high-pitched squeak so that the voice sounds from the rafters. At the same time a smouldering twist of bark-cloth, fastened, together with little rattles, to the end of a reed, is made to dance and chatter above the heads of the on-lookers to represent the familiar itself who is speaking to them. Window-shutters fly open and are slammed shut again, small objects may be flung across the room, and an atmosphere of terror and excitement is engendered in which people believe they can hear their own disembodied spirits speaking with the familiar and begging for its help.

It seems to be universally acknowledged that the fetish séances are full of fraud, and yet everyone seems to know of cases in which accurate information was unaccountably produced by the familiar, and so credulity is kept alive.

NIGHT PROWLERS

One other type of sorcerer is known in Buganda—the dreaded *musezi* or night prowler. He fulfils no professional function but is the typical anti-social 'witch' whose malevolence is directed quite indiscriminately against anyone who may cross his path. He is associated particularly with leopards; sometimes he is said to ride on a leopard, sometimes he transforms himself into one. No doubt the sound of a real leopard outside a man's hut at night is often interpreted as being a *musezi*; on his part the *musezi* himself imitates the beast, prowling through the gardens wearing only dry banana leaves and uttering the hoarse snarls of a leopard. It is generally believed that the *musezi* is a cannibal and eats the flesh of his victims, though no informant could actually confirm this except by hearsay. He is credited with supernatural powers which are thought to emanate from a *kitambo*, or familiar spirit, which takes possession of him, so that he is not humanly responsible for his behaviour and may even be unaware by day of what he does at night. There are other kinds of possession by *bitambo* which seem to flourish particularly in Buddu county.

ANIMAL CHILDREN AND ANIMISM

Reference has already been made to fears concerning unnatural births, or even twins, but there is an unlimited range of weird beliefs and old wives' tales circulating continually with regard to supernatural generation. It is widely believed that a human child may be born with an animal twin. Sometimes this disappears immediately after its birth, vanishing like a ghost, but often it remains materially present. Then a little shrine, like a miniature hut, is built for it in the garden, it is placed inside, and the mother tends and feeds it. After about a week it disappears into the forest and they say, 'he has gone to collect firewood'. If the creature dies at the house, its spirit is likely to return to possess some member of the family and speak through him. Things that are most commonly born in this way are leopards, pythons, lions, frogs, rats, rivers or lakes. People say that it is the frogs and rats which most frequently die in infancy, which may point to premature fœtus as a possible explanation of the grounds for these beliefs. If the creature, for example a leopard, returns and kills some of the family's goats, they will not attempt to kill it. Several catechists, when asked to express an opinion on these things, agreed that they happened less frequently now than in the old days, but were quite dogmatic that it is not simply a legend.

There may be an association between these ideas and the belief that all the creatures mentioned, with the exception of the frogs and rats, are often regarded as supernatural beings. A python is believed to be an incarnation of the *lubaale* Magobwe, and people finding one coiled in some spot in the bush leave small offerings of eggs or coffee berries. They do not kill a python unless it is taking their goats; then they may excuse themselves, saying *ngusse lwa bubi*—'I have killed it for wrong doing'. A story was circulating at Makindu about a school-teacher, one of the Christians of the revival, who had killed a python that lived in a rock off the road from Bwoya to Ngogwe. Within two months three of his children had died.

It may seem strange that rivers and lakes are included with animals among the creatures that may be born of woman. It is very typical that no distinction is made between what Westerners would call animate and inanimate beings. Several rivers are reputed to have originated in a human birth. At the source of the Sezibwa, close to the place where the teacher killed the python, is a conical rock from the base of which the spring emerges. The story is told of a girl who had been deserted by her lover, and in her pregnancy was travelling towards Ziba, when she stopped to rest in a shade of a tree. But, as she slept, the sun moved on and shone full on her, so that in her exhaustion she gave birth to nothing but water, the twin rivers of Sezibwa and Mubeya. A priest still lives near by to accept the offerings that are brought there. The *lubaale* of the place is particularly powerful to help women in childbirth. Women are known to go straight from the Anglican maternity centre at Ngogwe to pay their vows at the source of the Sezibwa. A little later they will be saying in church, in the service of the Churching of Women, 'I will pay my vows in the presence of all His people.' Both acts express an equal thankfulness, and if one challenged them they would probably reply, 'God created all things.'

There are many other natural features, besides rivers, which are believed to have their *genius*, or indwelling *lubaale*. In many places the huge, glacier-borne, granite boulders are regarded with awe. The pastorate church of Kasawo was built in the midst of a tumble of rocks, once regarded as the dwelling-place of the goddess of hunger, Nagawonyi, to whom people brought offerings of plantains, beer and goats when they needed rain. Recently the headmaster of the primary school was asked by a young couple, who had obviously had some education, where 'the throne of the hill' was, because they were childless. When he understood what they wanted he told them that God is not to be found in created things like rocks, and recounted his own experience of salvation. But later he saw they had found the ancient place of offerings and had left some cents there.

At Girimbo on the shore of the lake in the Makindu parish are a series of caves cut in two tiers into the face of an overhanging cliff, crowned with a patch of virgin forest from which a curtain of trailing vines hangs over the mouths of the caves. This mysterious place is the shrine of the *lubaale* Kokola. The lower caves are filled with the property of Bavuma fishermen—bicycles, nets, paddles, tins containing cash—left there, maybe for six months or more, unguarded save by Kokola himself. There is no thief, however irreligious, who will dare to steal things that have been left in the keeping of the *lubaale*, for those who have attempted it have always been struck dead. A mile away lives the owner of the estate, who is also the priest of Kokola and will become possessed by the *lubaale* to give oracles, for those who pay his fee. He bewails the neglect of the shrine, remembering the days when each cave was cleanly carpeted with fresh-cut grass, whereas now they are covered with at least a foot of dusty bat-dung.

These *balubaale* of rocks and rivers, waterfalls and great trees may have been the earliest of the 'gods' of the Baganda before the advent of the dynastic *balubaale*, whom we shall consider in the next chapter. With them should perhaps be grouped the great gods of natural forces —Gulu, the sky god who had neither priest nor temple until recent times, Kitaka, god of the earth and underworld, Walumbe, god of death, Musoke the rainbow, and Kiwanuka the lightning. Many of these animistic *balubaale* were associated only with particular clans on whose estates the rock, tree, waterfall, or whatever was their dwelling-place, was found. The *bataka* or heads of such clans were, and are sometimes still regarded as, the priests of their particular *lubaale*. This applied later to many of the 'dynastic' *balubaale* also.

So far the charms and fetishes, and the *balubaale* of natural pheno-mena, which we have noted have all been supernatural powers of a non-human nature—though, in saying that, it must be remembered that the distinction is far less significant to an African peasant than it appears to a European. We must turn now to what are the dominant elements in the traditional Kiganda world-view, all of which are linked with the belief in the *mizimu*, or spirits of the dead.

NOTE

1. See J. Roscoe, *The Baganda* (1911), pp. 65 ff.; Lucy P. Mair, *An African People in the Twentieth Century* (1934), pp. 43-53.

The Traditional World-View: II

THE words which have been used since Mackay's day to translate the Christian concept of soul and spirit originally bore a purely metaphysical sense (*omwoyo*=spiritual character; *obulamu*=life), or a purely physical meaning (*emmeeme*=sternal cartilage, *omutima*= heart; both, *per ext.*=seat of the emotions). By Christian usage they have become stereotypes, and this now conceals the fact that the traditional Kiganda conception of man saw him, rather as the ancient Hebrews did, as an essentially this-worldly creature, consisting of a material body in which was a semi-material *muzimu*. The *muzimu* had no very important function as long as life remained in the body, though as we have seen in the case of the bewitched landowner, if the *muzimu* was removed the body would pine away and die. Some villagers living in more remote parts are still terrified of cameras, believing that they are a means of capturing a man's *muzimu*. The Kiganda ideas of the manner of existence after death are also somewhat similar to those of the Hebrews. In a physical sense the *mizimu* are small (tiny houses can suffice for them), cold (the funeral wrappings are sometimes considered as a protection), and weak, needing a physical agent through whom to do their will. But considered as active, psychic entities they are immensely powerful. In the old days it was thought that the *muzimu* of a dead peasant was of no account, but today, since there is less distinction between the chiefs and the commoners, the *muzimu* of any person has to be treated with respect.

FUNERALS

In any country where men believe that the well-being or contentment of the spirit of a dead person is partially dependent upon the proper observance of funerary rites, death and burial will always be attended by a multitude of customs, the significance of which may not be generally understood though no one dare omit them. The arrival of the Christian gospel soon challenges the most obviously meaningful customs, such as offerings to the dead and the building of a little house for the spirit. Some of these were expressly forbidden by the synod of 1913. But a great number of customs, none of which, considered separately, has an obviously pagan connotation, have remained. A keen minority in the church, including the brethren of the revival, make a particular point of turning the funerals for which they are responsible into an occasion of positive witness to the Christian belief about death. Others, including most of the clergy, adopt a somewhat negative attitude of disapproval towards any funerary customs other than strict obedience to the Book of Common Prayer. To the majority of ordinary Christians who have not grasped the fact that Christianity is not simply an alternative ritual, Christian burial by itself seems a bare and inadequate ceremony. They tend therefore to regard it as an addition to the usual customs, in the same way as they do the Christian marriage service. The same, of course, is true of a great many funerals in Europe and America.

In Buganda the dead are usually buried in the banana plantation behind the home, or in the clan lands in some other place. (Very occasionally a clergyman, or some Christian leader of long standing, will be buried near the pastorate church.) Immediately after death the widow and the brothers or sisters of the deceased wash the body with the juicy, inner pith of banana stems (*binyiinyinsi*), wrap it in small bark-cloths, leaving the face uncovered, and lay it on a bed, usually in the front room of the house. The family, and friends in the neighbourhood, begin at once to gather together at the house for the prolonged 'wake', known as 'Keeping Death', which may last for several months. During this period the widow and the daughters neither wash nor cut their hair and nails; at night they must sleep on the ground and all sexual relations are forbidden. The sons also leave their hair uncut. The widow and daughters, and some of the brothers and sisters, may spend the whole period of the wake at the home of the deceased. Shelters are erected in the courtyard and in the banana plantation, and there they sit and chat by day, and at night they sleep on the dry banana leaves wrapped in their blankets. Other friends and relatives come for a few days only, some arriving in the evening and returning at sunrise to their work, for the essential thing is to spend the night there. Everyone who comes is expected to bring beer, or a gift of money, and to contribute food to the general supply. Girls who live in the neighbourhood spend their days there to cook for the assembly. Every night a lot of beer is drunk, but there is no singing. There are spasmodic outbreaks of wailing, especially by the women, who gather around the body in the house. Much of this wailing is purely formal, though it rises now and then to a climax of sharp, ejaculatory cries as they call on the name of the departed. Those who feel most deeply are generally quieter, though by not expressing grief aloud one risks the displeasure of the *muzimu*. If the deceased has had twins, even if they have died, a small drum is beaten whenever the wailing breaks out, and this is called 'the voice of the twins'. The other sons and daughters in that case wear a wreath of *bbombo* creeper round their hips, as in the celebration for twins. During the short period between death and burial no one in the neighbourhood will do any cultivation. Most of the neighbours, even those who are not keeping the wake, will pay a visit of commiseration, saying, *Musibye mutyano mu naku? Ee, olumbe, kyekitalo!*—'How are you in your grief? Ah, Death, it is a wonder!' Then a small gift of money is made to the eldest son, who acts as treasurer.

On the morning of the burial a large crowd gathers and the pastor and catechist arrives with their robes. The body is wrapped in a bark-cloth and, as the wailing rises to a crescendo, the close relatives take their leave of it. Then the face is covered and the body is carried, feet first, from the house into the courtyard, because, it is said, the will resides in the head, but this walk is not taken with the man's volition; it is a vain journey. Then the corpse is expertly wrapped in bark-cloths and whole bales of white calico. Since the number of cloths used is regarded as an indication of respect, very great quantities may be used. At the funeral of one of the landowners at Makindu in 1956 the grave-clothes consisted of 43 bark-cloth sheets, 6 cotton sheets and 108 yards of calico, and the winding lasted for one hour. The clergy then lead the procession to the grave, singing a hymn. During the burial service wailing sometimes continues in the background and rises to a climax when the body is lowered, with twisted strips of bark-cloth, into the grave. Several of the men climb down after it to ensure that it rests according to the traditions of the clan. In some clans, for example, a man is laid on his right side and a woman on her left. In a few places Christians follow the Moslem custom of cutting out a vault at one side of the main pit, placing the body there and boarding it up so that the loose soil shall not fall upon it. As soon as the body is in place, the pastor finishes the service and then hymns are sung while the grave is being filled in. This may take some time, but as soon as it is completed several banana stems are chopped down—beer bananas for the men and ordinary plantains for the women—and everyone present washes hands and feet with a handful of the watery pith.

The company then returns to the courtyard, where the eldest sur-
viving brother reads aloud the accounts of the funeral gifts and the
amount of cash left by the deceased. After this the main crowd begins
to disperse. Those who are keeping the wake gather at some distance
from the grave for beer drinking.

Every Christian adherent is very anxious to have Christian burial, and
great distress is caused whenever this is refused, as happens in cases
when the baptism certificate of the deceased cannot be produced, or
when he has lapsed from church attendance for several years, or,
occasionally, because he has failed to pay his *buzimbi*. The reasons
given for desiring Christian burial are very vague; usually it is simply
'because I am a Christian', but sometimes people say, 'in order that I
may be at peace' or 'so that I shall rise again'.

A bizarre dispute was raging, in Kyagwe county only, during 1955
and 1956, as to whether the body should be carried to the grave for
Christian burial head first or feet first. It had arisen from an occasion
when a local leader of the 'Bataka' movement had been buried near
Ngogwe, and the mourners had insisted, in place of the hymns, on
shouting in chorus a nationalist slogan of that time, and had wanted to
carry the body to the grave feet first because it was the traditional
custom. The pastor hotly resisted both proposals and continued thereafter to demand very pointedly, at every funeral that he took, that the
body must be carried head first. People, who until that time had given
so little thought to the subject that their accounts of past customs are
completely contradictory, were roused to passionate loyalty either on
behalf of Christian standards or of nationalist sentiments. The dispute
has since spread to other counties, and the senior clergy have ruled that
Christians must take a confessional stand and accept only the head-first
position at Christian funerals.

After the funeral the wake continues at the house, though mourners
no longer keep up their concerted wailing, until the rite known as
Okwabya Olumbe, or the dismantling of Death. If it has not already
been done, the heap of earth on the grave is now beaten flat and a pile
of stones is raised over it. But the central function of this rite is the
installation of the heir, and there is a form of prayer authorized by the
Anglican Church which many clergy use in order to bring this important ceremony under Christian auspices. The installation ceremony
is traditionally followed by a beer drink and the singing of songs
associated with death and the spirits of the dead. The *okwabya* is the
most important occasion for the gathering of a family, and owing to the

development of transport greater numbers come together in these days than in the past. It is often convenient to hold a children's naming ceremony at the same time.

THE SPIRITS OF THE DEAD

The majority of Christians in the villages are caught in an ambivalent attitude regarding the spirits of the dead. They accept the Christian teaching about life after death, which on the Anglican side is necessarily somewhat vague, but they also take into account the, to them, incontrovertible evidence that the *mizimu* are real and active in ordinary life. The official teaching in the churches and schools tends to deny, or at least ignore, the objective existence of such beings on the grounds of a superficial 'scientific' outlook; but in the Bible, on the other hand, Christians find them taken quite seriously. The witch of Endor is often quoted, and throughout the Gospels the word *mizimu* has been used as the translation for *daimonia*. In an attempt to eliminate the associations of the word *muzimu* the synod of 1913 ordered that *daimoni* should be substituted, and this is done by all readers in church, though no change has been made in print; but since the new word conveys almost nothing it has not much power to change existing concepts. Many Christians now say that the *mizimu* are probably not the souls of dead persons, and the name Satan in its plural form is used to define them. But the majority prefer to keep an open mind.

It is widely believed that for some time after the burial the *muzimu* of the dead person remains in the vicinity of the grave. Noon rather than midnight is regarded as the witching hour when the spirits are most likely to approach. The sudden gust of wind in the midday stillness that rattles the banana leaves and lifts spirals of dust to dance on the paths is said to be a *muzimu* moving through the garden, and children run back to their huts in fear. Sometimes after a funeral the heir will consult a spirit medium to find out how best to please the *muzimu* of the dead. Then he may be given precise instructions as to how he should build a miniature hut or shrine in the garden as a dwelling-place for 'the old ones', and little offerings of coffee berries or beer, and occasionally a chicken, are placed there.

Many stories are told of haunting by the *mizimu*. Daudi Waiswa, the Christian leader at Nkompe who is mentioned in Chapter 6, had solemnly laid down, before his death, that none of his property was to be taken by any but his own children. For eighteen months after he died his house stood uninhabited. Then a brother took the corrugated iron from the roof and sold it to another man. Shortly after it had been fixed in this man's house he began to hear a chattering sound and a knocking on the roof night after night. Finally, on a still night, the iron sheets were suddenly ripped off the house and fell into the garden. The man returned the iron to Daudi's children, who replaced it on their father's house. But, in the meantime, the brother who had sold it had died. For some years after this Daudi's widow lived alone, but eventually she took another man, and within three weeks she was dead. Everyone in Makindu parish knew this story and all attested its truth.

SPIRIT POSSESSION

The most usual way in which the *mizimu* are thought to manifest their power is by possessing a living person. Possession may be of three kinds. There is that which is regarded as a malevolent attack from which the victim can only be saved by the use of supernatural means of exorcism. There is possession by the *muzimu* of a dead king which is regarded as a call to the individual to dedicate himself or herself to lifelong service at the royal shrine. And there is supernatural possession of a medium for purposes of divination.

There are not many adult Christians in the villages of Buganda who have not at some time met the phenomenon of possession. The most common forms of involuntary seizure are said to be of wives by deceased husbands, or children by grandparents or aunts. It is said that a *muzimu* cannot possess anyone with whom it has no personal acquaintance, but the victim may not know whose spirit has possessed him and will need to consult a diviner to find that out. Women appear to be more liable than men to possession of all kinds, and almost always some acute psychological tension or frustration is a precondition of the involuntary attacks. Epileptic fits, known as *nsimbu*, are recognized as a disease the incidence of which is due to the action of the *muzimu*. Sometimes the possession of the victim produces violence; she rushes from her hut frothing at the lips, tears off her clothes and runs through the banana plantation on all fours. The attack is generally healed by giving the victim medicine to drink, though often it is necessary for the *muzimu* to speak through the victim and make known its grievance before it will depart. It is not only the uneducated who are subject to these attacks. In 1955 a young girl pupil at a mission boarding-school, who had very unhappy relations with her parents, was seized by what the Government hospital diagnosed as acute hysteria. For three weeks she was speechless and stared fixedly before her, and, according to several African members of the staff, occasionally spoke in a voice other than her own. The hospital specialist declared that her condition was curable but that it would take a very long time. Her father, however, instead of leaving her at the hospital, took her home, asserting quite positively that 'the sickness is from her aunt'. Two weeks later he returned her to the school, where she has continued under observation with no signs of a recurrence.

THE SPIRITS OF DEAD KINGS

The most deeply impressive relics of the old cult in Buganda today are the *masiro*, or royal tombs, from which the county of Busiro derives its name. On many of the hills can be seen a great conical thatched hut, built in the old style with richly plaited reed-work, within which the lower jawbone of one of the dead kings or princes, as they are often called, is preserved, together with his spears, drums and other insignia. The interior of the great house is dim, lit only by the daylight that streams through the low porchway. From the blackened coils of reed-work at the apex of the roof a curtain of dull crimson and blue hangs thirty feet high, and at its foot stands a fence of polished spears. Near by are the ancient royal drums, and other insignia hang from the tall poles which are wrapped in bark-cloth. The floor is carpeted thickly with new-cut grass. It is a presence chamber, and beyond the curtain lies the decorated jaw bone of one of the dead kings. The rest of the body was usually buried in some other place; but Mutesa I, under the influence of Islamic teaching, disinterred the bodies of several of his ancestors and had them buried where their jawbones were preserved. Beyond the line of spears stands a low box-frame, draped in patterned cloth, within which the gourds of beer are 'set before the king' whenever one of the special feasts is celebrated there.

Living in the enclosure around each royal shrine is the entourage of wives and household staff which has been maintained ever since the death of that king, which, in some cases, took place at least four hundred years ago. At some of the less important shrines there may be only one 'prince' and one 'princess' left in charge, but at others a great company are to be found; when one dies, his or her clan has to send a successor to fill the place. They live there in celibacy, cultivating the plantations that surround the shrine, brewing beer for the feasts and repairing the structure. Every night, at the larger establishments, three women and two men sleep as guardians in the shrine itself.

On special nights connected with the king's history a feast is held inside the shrine, when great numbers of the 'princes' and 'princesses' assemble for drinking and dancing to the royal drums. Then many of them may be possessed by the *muzimu* of the dead king. There is one person, however, at every shrine who is the officially recognized medium through whom the king makes known his will. He is called the *mukongozi*, which is the title of the bearer on whose shoulders the Kabaka, during his lifetime, is carried on ceremonial occasions. When being possessed (*okusamira*), he falls into a trance and speaks in a strange voice that is said to resemble that of the dead king; the similarity is also manifest in certain mannerisms and facial expressions. These likenesses are taken as signs of the genuineness of the oracle. So Mutesa I, in speaking of his own death and burial, is reputed to have said:

> 'Whenever there shall be a man who presumes to say "I am possessed by Kabaka Mutesa", you shall give him this book of the Koran which I read; if he always reads it then it is I, for I am a literate man. I do not wish to be spoken for by deceivers. But when you see that he has not read it, then he is lying.'[1]

George Pilkington added that some time after Mutesa's death a medium was proved false in this way and soundly beaten for his pains.[2]

The divination of the mediums at the royal tombs is carried on for the benefit of the reigning Kabaka. The present Kabaka often receives such messages from the various *masiro*. Sometimes they are weird and apparently illogical, but usually they contain straightforward and somewhat obvious advice. Other mediums besides the official *bakongozi* bring their messages to the Kabaka. He is not, however, thought to be dependent upon oracles or omens inasmuch as he himself belongs to the same order of beings as those from whom the messages are supposed to emanate. In the old days, however, the Kabakas frequently followed the advice of their ancestors regarding the appointment or dismissal of chiefs. Speke was informed that if Mutesa ever dreamed that his father was directing him to kill someone as being dangerous to his person the order was religiously kept,[3] and Ashe noticed that whenever a man was promoted to a chieftainship he offered his thanks not only before the Kabaka, the Queen Mother and the Royal Sister, but also at the tomb of the late Kabaka.[4]

Sometimes a person, generally a woman, who lives many miles from the *masiro* may suddenly be possessed by the *muzimu* of a dead king and called to devote herself to his service. In a psychotic state she wanders across country until she reaches the shrine of the king who has possessed

her. There she is questioned by the members of the entourage, who ask
her to tell them the precise relationship in which each of them stands,
and the tasks they have to perform. If she cannot answer as one who is
familiar with the establishment, she is sent away as a mad woman; if,
in spite of having had no previous contact with them, she answers as
if she knew all about them, she is accepted as another woman whom the
dead king has desired to have. This happened, for example, a few years
ago, in the pastorate of Masulita. A married woman, a communicant
member of the Anglican Church, who was childless, was suddenly
seized by the *muzimu* of the prince Luyidde, son of Kabaka Mulondo,
whose shrine stands on a hill not far from her village. From her body,
which was stiff and numb, two voices spoke, one repeating, 'I am
Luyidde', and her own saying, 'I am a Christian: I cannot go.' For days
the psychosis continued, no one seemed able to help her, and eventually
her brothers and her husband, also a communicant, agreed that nothing
could save her but to let her go. She is living now at the shrine on the
hill, separated from her husband because she belongs to Luyidde. Once
in a while she is possessed (*okusamira*) and speaks with his voice, but
otherwise she is quite normal, regularly attends church, and is still a
communicant. This story, and indeed the widespread occurrence of
possession in all its forms, suggests that there is a very serious need for
the church to reconsider its pastoral responsibilities. The development
of some properly safeguarded ministry of exorcism may be the right
approach. Such a proposal might be resisted by the *évolués* in the church
who have grown up to deny any objective reality in such phenomena.
This question has far-reaching implications that require thorough
theological examination.

DYNASTIC BALUBAALE

It is probably impossible to define in any terms satisfactory to
Western logic the distinction between the dead kings of the present
line and the *balubaale* or hero gods. Quite apart from the question of the
supposed nature of the living Kabaka, which can probably best be
described as 'prospectively supernatural', it might almost be said that
the *mizimu* of the Baganda kings are in process of evolution towards
the status of the *balubaale*. That they have not quite reached the same
status is evident in several ways. The *masiro* are rarely referred to as
biggwa, or temples[5] (though both resemble the palace of a king), nor
are they looked after by *bakabona*, or priests, as were the shrines of the
balubaale; and the royal *mizimu* are not usually called *balubaale*. Never-

theless, the same word, *mmandwa*, is used of the medium both of a dead king and a *lubaale*; and many of the diviners in the villages say that the *lubaale* who possesses them is one of the royal dynasty. One woman medium at Makindu, for example, explained that her *balubaale* are Prince Kaliro and the two kings, Juko and Kyabagu. She also declared that 'all the greatest *balubaale* are princes' (i.e. royalty). Very often it is said of one who is possessed, *aliko mulangira*—'a prince is upon him', which is synonymous with *aliko lubaale*. So also, when there is an outbreak of plague or measles in a village, people may say, *omulangira atukyalidde*, 'a prince has visited us'.

The reason for this is not merely that the dead royalty of the present dynasty are regarded in the same way as the *balubaale*, but, conversely, that the great *balubaale* of the traditional religion are in fact the *mizimu* of an older dynasty of human rulers. Exactly who they were is a fascinating problem of history which awaits a satisfactory solution. Some would identify them with the Bachwesi, who were the equivalent of the *balubaale* in the old culture of Bunyoro-Kitara, and who were certainly an ancient line of kings. In legend they are associated particularly with the Sese Islands in Lake Victoria, but whether they represent an earlier branch of the Hamitic dynasty that has ruled for so long in the interlacustrine kingdoms, which was driven out when Kimera founded the present line of kings, it is impossible to say.

This island dynasty appears to have sprung from a warrior called Bukulu, who, according to one tradition, came into the country with Kintu, the semi-mythical ancestor of the kings of Buganda. The descendants of Bukulu are set out opposite, with the names of those who became *balubaale* written in italics.

At a later period both *Serwanga* and *Kyobe* came to be thought of as separate individuals, both *balubaale*, the former worshipped as a python god on the lake shore in Buddu, and the second as the god of woodcutters.

Mukasa is also said to have married *Naku*, who was the wife of Kabaka Kayemba, and whose deformed child, *Kawumpuli*, became the *lubaale* of plague. This sort of correlation between the two dynasties is tantalizing and confusing, for one can never be certain, in the stories of the contacts of the Baganda kings with this Sese Island dynasty, whether they were dealing with the original human king, or with the priest or medium who acted on behalf of him as a *lubaale*. However this may be, it does not alter the truth of Sir Apolo Kagwa's statement that 'we understand clearly that every single *lubaale* was a human being.'[6]

Bukulu

Wanga		*Musisi*
Was called to help Kabaka Juko at the eclipse of the sun 1680.		Was stricken with palsy, so is regarded as the god of earthquakes.

Nambubi = Wanema = *Nagaddya*		*Wamala*
Also called Mairwa; settled on Bukasa Island.	Became the goddess of the marriage of women.	Quarrelled with his brother and came to Singo county where Lake Wamala lies.

Serwanga, called Mukasa = *Nalwanga*	*Kyobe called Kibuka*
One tradition says he was a companion to Lukedi the Conqueror of Bunyoro. Became the greatest *lubaale*, the god of the lake. Always spoke of the Kabaka as his son-in-law.	Sent by Mukasa to help Kabaka Nakibinge against Bunyoro. Flew into the clouds, hence called Kibuka, but was shot down and fell into a tree at Mbale Mpigi, where he died. Became the *lubaale* of war and storm.

Nende	Kirabira	*Mirimu*
Brought to Kyagwe county after Kibuka's death. Became the god who defends the eastern frontier of Buganda as Kibuka defends the west.		Became a *lubaale* whose shrine was at Ndeje.

Many incidents in modern times confirm this conclusion. Ashe was informed that both the *balubaale,* Kibuka and Budo, were human mummies, though in Roscoe's time the shrine of Kibuka contained only the umbilical cord and other human organs.[7] In 1903 the shrine of a *lubaale* called Kihringa was discovered hidden in the bush near Ndeje. Inside the temple was found the mummy of a man with two spears and a wand decorated with beads and shells. Samwili Mukasa Naganafa, the Kangawo, burned the place down to the consternation of his father who feared the vengeace of the *lubaale*.[8]

It becomes clear, then, that the ancient 'gods' of the Baganda are the spirits of dead kings, and their relationship to men is the same in essence as that of all *mizimu*. They reveal their displeasure through mediums or by direct possession; they can be propitiated with offerings and by promises. But they have never been worshipped in any full sense of the word. There have been practically no occasions for large congregational ceremonial or public celebration in connection with the cult, for religion has been a matter of 'occasional offices', individuals or families turning to the supernatural at each point of need. In one sense it would be true to say that in this traditional world-view all living men and spirits of the dead, natural objects and supernatural beings, were so closely inter-related in a single, this-worldly plane of existence that there was no place for a transcendent God. It may be that the *lubaale* Katonda, the Creator, to whom no offerings were made and who spoke through no medium, represented a dim conception of the otherness of the Source of all being, though it is impossible, without further evidence, to be certain whether any idea of absolute godhead existed before the coming of Islam. But, if it did, it lay completely outside the realm of effective experience which was contained in the perfect unity of the here and now. The Swahili word *eddini*, religion, which includes Christianity and Islam, speaks of that new way which stands over against the traditional world-view, and the difference focuses upon the concept of a transcendent God.

But that concept cleaves the perfect unity of existence with the vast gulf between God and not-God. And the Incarnation has been presented only as an isolated crossing-over rather than the closing of the gulf. God, therefore, remains so far beyond as to induce despair, and men try to close again the circle of the unity of life by ignoring what lies beyond the gulf. This attitude is epitomized in the report once made by the old retired clergyman in Makindu parish when, early in this century, he had been on a preaching mission to the people of Bugala Island. These are some of the things that were said to him: 'My fire is my God, for it cooks the food I eat.' 'Perhaps your father and mother may arise from the dead; mine will not, woe is me.' 'Our God is our food and our pipes, nothing else.' A blind man said, 'The reason why I refuse to believe in God is because he has blinded my eyes.' A woman said, 'the reason I don't love God is because he slew my five children.' And another man retorted, 'I know God, he made all things, but I don't want to worship him, you can teach the children.'[9]

So, as long as God seems to lie mainly outside the circle of the here and now, there will be a place for those contacts with the supernatural which have an immediate relevance. The ancient shrines, with their sacred objects and bevies of priests and mediums, have gone; the large-scale sacrifices are no longer offered and a great deal of the terror has passed from the land. But the *balubaale* remain, reduced in stature yet still alive and real in the experience of many people because, through the seances of the mediums, they fulfil certain functions and appeal to certain desires which the Christian Church does not at present seem to be satisfying, as it once did, *in the terms in which the people themselves feel their need.*

THE DIVINERS

Divination (*okulagula*) is the means *par excellence* through which the old ways continue to operate. There are various methods of obtaining the oracle: small squares of leather, seeds, or bones may be thrown; a fetish may be consulted; or the diviner may merely give a pronounce-men on the basis of a thorough questioning. But by far the most common means, which some would say is invariably included, is spirit-possession. The diviner or *mulaguzi* induces a trance, most often through prolonged shaking of a gourd rattle, so that the *lubaale* or *muzimu* who is his familiar may possess him and speak through him.

In earlier days distinctions were perhaps made between the various agents of the supernatural. There was a difference between the *musawo* or herbalist and the *mulogo* or sorcerer, between a *mmandwa*, or medium of a *lubaale* or *mulangira*, and a diviner working for consultants. But in these days the general practitioner has replaced the specialist, and the same man will be diviner, sorcerer, doctor and fetish-owner according to demand. Because women seem to be more prone to possession than men there are more female than male *balaguzi*. Most diviners build a shrine-house behind their own home in which to conduct their seances, though some use the main room of their houses. Usually an entrance fee is demanded, and further payments are expected if the consultation leads to success. Private consultations are most common, but the better known *balaguzi* have so many applicants that twenty enquirers may be present at one seance. Numbers of the *balaguzi* are members of the church. One man who practises near Jinja, and fills his shrine daily with enquirers, turns everyone out of his consulting-room at midday on Saturday, saying, 'Now I must get my clothes ready to go to church tomorrow'.

At the beginning of a seance the diviner puts on the magical necklace of cowrie shells, wild-banana seeds and wooden charms, and perhaps also a beaded head-dress. The persistent sibilation of the rattle, and the monotonous, rapid singing of the songs that welcome the *lubaale*, have a most hypnotic effect, after which the startling, jerky utterances of the various voices that speak through the tranced medium, often in a foreign dialect, are undeniably impressive. Weird injunctions and fantastic acts create a world with a dream-like logic of its own.

It is no new thing for the Baganda to recognize that fraud plays a large part in these seances. One of their proverbs says, *Ekkubo lya mulimba likala manju*—'The path of the deceiver is trodden hard at the back of the house', and there are several others like it, referring to the trickery of the *mulaguzi* and the sense of shame which makes enquirers hide the fact that they are visiting him. At the same time no one is ever going to understand this phenomenon who has not reached a condition at least of scientific agnosticism and an open mind towards it. Some of the *balaguzi*, at least, are more than mere quacks; they are the equivalent of the 'wise woman' of the European village of the past. Watching and listening, they know the secrets of every home and so their diagnosis is often uncannily apt. It seems possible, also, that when the trance is upon them the thing that speaks is their unconscious awareness of the mind of the community, instinctively recognizing the guilty member of society or the points of social maladjustment in an individual, and expressing these insights in the symbols of dream and fantasy. However that may be, the advice of the *mulaguzi* is everywhere attended by enough success, or coincidence, to convince almost everyone that 'there is something in it'. When there has been a death there is a deep-felt need to know the cause, for it is generally thought that no one dies except through the will of someone else, living or dead. So also sickness and misfortune have their causes which only divination can discover. Above all sterility, more than anything else, brings Christians to the *mulaguzi*. As one woman at Makindu exclaimed, 'Of course there is divination: if there were not, would you ever have been born?'

Large numbers of Christians try to keep away from divination, but there are not so many who have never at any time made use of it. The old clergyman in Makindu parish is much admired for his steady resistance to the pressure of his friends, who, seeing that he suffers from the trembling of old age, urge him to seek the advice of the *mulaguzi* in order to escape from the *lubaale* Musisi, the earthquake god, who has evidently seized him. He replies, 'Then I must die, for I shall certainly not begin to go to the deceiver after all these years.' But not all are like him. One pastor who used to work in south Kyagwe never rode a bicycle because a diviner had told him that, if he did, he would be killed (a not improbable augury for the roads of Buganda). A catechist who had been in charge of Makindu church had consulted a *mulaguzi* about his impotence and been cured. Nor is it only the uneducated or rural population to whom divination appeals. The *balaguzi* are very popular in the towns and some attract a large Indian clientele besides their regular African patients. From time to time one or other of the young Christian professional men at the capital receives a letter or a word of advice suggesting that, if he wants promotion or greater success in his business, a particular diviner will be able to help him. One or two African commercial companies employ a *mulaguzi* as well as an auditor. Although Christians try to conceal their consultations, the village community almost always knows, and is tolerant in its judgment. If gossip reports that some well-known Christian leader has been to a diviner people may express surprise, but will add the proverb, *Omanyi ki ebigneda ekiro nga Kangawo yetika?*, which might be rendered, 'Who knows what goes on at night? Even the proud Kangawo carries a load once in a while.'

NOTES

1. Sir Apolo Kagwa, *Mpisa za Baganda*, p. 17.
2. C. F. Harford-Battersby, *Pilkington of Uganda*, p. 220.
3. J. H. Speke, *The Discovery of the Source of the Nile*, p. 463.
4. R. P. Ashe, *Two Kings of Uganda*, p. 109.
5. The accounts of the early missionaries are misleading. Ashe, for instance, says that the repository of the royal jawbone was a sacred temple, but he is confusing the word *kiggya* (tomb) with *kiggwa* (temple)— *Chronicles of Uganda* (1894), p. 67 *note*. This confusion may also underlie Mackay's entry in his journal for 17 May 1885: 'The Katikiro sent for me one day to see him. He was building a shrine to the memory of Mtesa. He called it a *temple*, Mtesa's ghost being the god, where he could sit and reflect when in low spirits.' *C.M.I.* 1885, p. 725. All the same, the impression that the missionaries give is almost right; the dead Kabaka just falls short of being a *lubaale*.
6. Sir Apolo Kagwa, op. cit., pp. 216, 229.
7. R. P. Ashe, *Chronicles*, pp. 96-7. Probably the mummy of Kibuka was intact until the Moslem uprising of 1893 (*Uganda Journal*, vol. 21 (1957), p. 119), though Apolo Kagwa suspected that the clan heads of an earlier generation had substituted a carcase of dried meat for the mummy (*Mpisa za Baganda*, p. 222).
8. *C.M.I.* 1904, p. 601.
9. Sir Albert Cook, *Uganda Memories*, p. 186.

12

The Congregation

H AVING seen a few of the factors which make up the total
encompassment of Christians, particularly in the villages, the
time has come to look again at the church in the parish, not now
as an organization but rather as a congregation and a community within
the community. As in every other part of the world, the church becomes
visible mainly in its Sunday worship—whether that should be so or not
is another question—so we shall first look briefly at the worship of the
Anglican Church in Buganda, remembering as we do so the background
of life and thought against which it is set.

THE CONGREGATION AT WORSHIP

Regular public worship, as we have seen, did not exist in the old religion
of Buganda. It was the Arabs at the palace of Suna and Mutesa I who
first introduced it, translating their Arabic prayers, and readings from
the Koran, into Swahili which a growing number at the court were
learning to understand. It was they, undoubtedly, who set the pattern
of worship by recitation, which Christian liturgical prayer and Bible
reading, conducted first by Dallington Muftaa and later by Swahili-
speaking missionaries, must have seemed so closely to resemble. This
conception of worship persisted. In 1897, for example, Baskerville
visited Makindu for a Sunday service at which, he says, 'a man of mine
who was a Mohammedan but who is now one of our teachers, read the
prayers at a great pace and in a shrill voice, only stopping for breath;
he has evidently not got out of his old Mohammedan chantings of the
Koran.'[1] This tendency to assume that the Islamic manner of conduct-
ing public worship was also the model for Christians must have been
strengthened by the surprising fact that for the first fifteen years of the
Christian mission all teaching was carried on in Swahili, and at worship
the Swahili Bible was used, being translated into Luganda by the reader.[2]
    It is significant also that, apart from small reading-sheets, the first
Luganda book which the church possessed was an abridged version of the

Book of Common Prayer. This was produced shortly after the first out-break of persecution under Mwanga. Commenting on it, Mackay wrote:

'Doubtless you will say, why have we not put a Gospel into print? I certainly thought that by this time we should have done so, but we feared expulsion any day, and after due deliberation we decided to print the prayers, etc. first. The Gospels will now be better done.'[3]

That book was first printed by Mackay in 1885. Two years later it was published in England by the S.P.C.K. with fresh additions. In 1894 Ernest Millar wrote that it was the favourite book among the Baganda. Being in large type, it was the first to be taken up after the reading-sheets, and small boys were often to be seen spelling their way through the marriage service![4] In 1893 Pilkington revised and completed the whole Prayer Book and this, the first officially authorized version, was published in 1897.[5]

The recitation of Morning and Evening Prayer on Sundays has therefore been the mainstay of the devotional life of the local congrega-tions in Buganda for seventy years. This has certainly meant that, even when the catechist gave an impoverished and distorted version of the Faith, the essential outline has been preserved for all the people. It has to be admitted, nevertheless, that very often the recitation is done without a great deal of comprehension. The hortatory sentences with which the service begins (universally known as the *Omuntu omubi*, 'the wicked man', because of the first words), are often read in greater numbers than was ever intended, seven or eight of them being a not unusual ration in some churches. The psalms frequently prove too much for the literacy of the catechist, but are nevertheless recited in full. But perhaps the greatest weakness is the complete lack of all those acces-sories to Prayer Book worship which have come to be taken for granted in other parts of the Anglican Communion. The parish churches in Buganda know of no other lectionary than that provided in the Calendar of 1662, and no additional prayers beyond what are in the Prayer Book. There are, it is true, several excellent small books of occasional prayers in Luganda, but these are rarely found in the parish, or village, churches. It has probably never even occurred to most village Christians that their Sunday worship might be relevant to the concerns of their daily lives.

The supreme asset of these liturgical offices in the village churches lies in the regular reading from the Bible. Many Christians try to read their own Bibles at home. But, lacking any sort of guidance, they tend to start at the beginning and read straight on, with the result that many of them get bogged down in the book of Leviticus. Frequently they exclaim: 'The Bible is an ocean', a proverbial reference to its ambiguity, for the ocean drowns those who fish and those who do not. They feel defeated by it, and Anglicans sometimes express envy of the Roman Catholics because, although they only have the *Evanjiri*, or Gospel, to read, yet they are given more help in understanding it. It is therefore of priceless value that the Sunday services include a systematic reading of Bible passages of some length. It is all the more to be regretted, therefore, that whenever there is more than one minister taking part in a service, the reading of the lessons is always relegated to the most junior official. One of the most far-reaching, yet simple reforms that could be introduced by the Uganda diocese would be to make the reading of the lessons the central and most venerated element in these services. But, in order to do that effectively, a new lectionary, designed primarily for Sunday mornings only, would have to become obligatory, accompanied, if possible, by short explanatory notes to be read before each lesson.

The second element in the worship of the congregation which has had as deep an effect on the growth of the church as its liturgical prayer is the singing of hymns and canticles. The hymns, like the prayers, of the first converts were in the Swahili translations made by Bishop Steere of the U.M.C.A. From his pen had come the version of that hymn which became the theme-song of the Christian household-clusters and which may have been sung by the boy martyrs on their way to be burned. But in the year of their martyrdom the first hymns in Luganda were printed by Mackay. He wrote in May 1885: 'We have tried our hands at Ruganda hymns. This has proved no easy matter. I enclose a few, which we now use in church and at daily prayers. We are slowly increasing the collection.'[6]

In 1892, at Bishop Tucker's request, the S.P.C.K. published an edition of these hymns. But in the meantime George Pilkington had made his first free translations of nine English hymns. All of them, very slightly revised, are still in regular use.[7] They were printed at Nassa, at the south of the lake, and in October 1891 Pilkington wrote: '. . . after a hasty meal, I sing with all the boys who care to come (teaching the adults to sing I have given up as hopeless, so have the French priests); I am teaching them hymns I have written.'[8]

In 1896 the C.M.S. published an edition of seventy-two of Pilkington's hymns, which formed the nucleus of the greatly enlarged collections which followed in 1907, 1911 and 1928. The difficulty which he experienced in teaching his boys to sing them continued to confront the missionaries for a long time. They were not always aware of the source of their problem, which was simply the fact that their pupils' ears were attuned to the African scale of five equal intervals and could not easily adjust themselves to the European diatonic scales. Cyril Gordon, while he was stationed on Bugala Island in 1900, had taught the children to sing hymns which he set to traditional canoe songs and drum beats.[9] Undoubtedly this would have been the more creative way had it been accepted by the rest of the church and mission, but it appears to have remained an isolated experiment. The other missionaries committed their pupils wholeheartedly to mid-Victorian hymn tunes. At first they tried teaching them by constant repetition, reinforced when possible by a harmonium. The first of these instruments to reach Ngogwe arrived there on the heels of Miss Pilgrim and Miss Bird early in 1897, and singing classes were started on three days a week. About that time Miss Chadwick introduced the Tonic Sol-fa method so that her pupils at Namirembe might begin to read music for themselves, and this was adopted later in Mr Hattersley's normal school. It was not, however, until 1928 that a Sol-fa edition of a Luganda hymn book was published. This was the work of the Rev. J. M. Duncan, to whom the church in Uganda owes an immense debt. As organist of Namirembe cathedral, serving in an honorary capacity, from 1928 to 1936, Duncan not only lifted the Luganda hymn-book on to a higher musical level, but he created an entirely new standard of worship at the cathedral which has gradually influenced the whole diocese.

Duncan accepted the tradition of European music in the Uganda and set himself to raise it to a worthy standard. It was Dr K. P. Wachsmann who first seriously reopened the question of indigenous musical expression in the life of the church, and initiated an annual schools music festival in which African and European music, secular as well as sacred, were treated with an equal seriousness. The grounds and the objective of his experiment were spiritual.

'The Church in Uganda was unfortunate in that its tradition could not draw new life from its own soil, but had to turn to Europe for its inspiration. When this became difficult, Africans committed to European expression found that their roots could not support them because indigenous music in the meantime had been put outside the pale. Thus the position can be viewed from two angles—first, European forms of worship kept the African dependent on music from abroad, and secondly, the exclusive use of Anglican music in worship appeared to stigmatize African music as something unsuitable and undesirable for Christians.'[10]

The dogged perseverance of missionaries and African school-teachers has planted the diatonic scale firmly in the Ganda consciousness, and the hymns, albeit with certain indigenous subtleties, are sung not only in church but at family prayers, and by individuals at their daily work. The Church Canticles, however, have proved a greater stumbling-block. The Rev. F. Rowling first printed the canticles pointed for singing to Anglican chants in 1897, and a short time afterwards we find Baskerville struggling with them at Ngogwe.

> 'It is hard work. You cannot talk of notes but "voices", and then the accentuated syllables are "the syllables on which you stand for a little while". They are printed in italics, and you speak of them as "those letters which are falling over". However, after an hour this afternoon we got about three people to understand, and I hope they will be able to explain to others. We had another hour practising the *Te Deum* today, with not much perceptible result.'[11]

To the inherent difficulties of Anglican chanting, which defeat so many choirs in Britain, is added in Uganda the overwhelming complication that Luganda is a semi-tonal language. The fitting of prose words to an Anglican chant is bound to destroy both the rhythms and the intonation of normal speech with the result that the meaning is effectively concealed. A few trained African musicians have been tackling the problem in recent years and one may hope that eventually a solution will be discovered and adopted by the church as a whole. In the meantime the passive acceptance by the congregation of an exercise that is so devoid of intelligence only serves to deepen the impression that worship is the ritual recitation of a form of words that does not necessarily have to be meaningful.

The third element in Sunday worship, after Prayer Book recitation and singing, is the sermon. The standard of preaching varies enormously from one man to another. There is fairly widespread agreement that there are fewer good preachers than there once were, and the most common criticism of present-day preaching is that it is too denunciatory. From examination of observers' reports on a large number of sermons, it clearly appears that at the present time many preachers are negative and on the defensive. The note of 'these evil days' is constantly being struck, and there are a great many references to 'silencing the enemy', and the National Congress is often specifically mentioned. In two places thoughtful Christians, speaking of the grumbling tone in the preaching of these days, quote the proverb: *Bya kuno tasenguka: agoba abajja*—'He who is always complaining about "the state of things here" doesn't clear out, yet he drives away others from coming.' The note of recall is often sounded; perhaps the most popular text is, 'O foolish Galatians, who hath bewitched you?' Another that is often used is 'How hardly shall they that have riches enter the Kingdom of God', and there are many references to Lot's wife, Judas and Demas. A comment that is sometimes made by older Christians is that 'in the old days they told us what God had done for us, but today they only tell us to repent'. The preachers who are members of the revival fellowship are as varied in quality as the others, but they have usually a clearer grasp of how to use Biblical texts appropriately, which they owe to their fellowship meetings. One interesting feature of their preaching is the tendency to reiterate a set theme. Some years ago the metaphor of the pit was likely to occur in three out of five sermons preached by *Balokole*; in 1955-6 the recurrent theme was 'Christ our Hope'.

It is, however, impossible for a European to generalize or judge aright in the matter of preaching. Only one thing can be emphatically asserted—and as a past theological tutor in Uganda the author does so as one who discovers his mistakes too late—namely, that the true standards by which African preaching is to be judged are not those of a European. For there *are* good preachers, though they may not be so many as they once were. Their education is of only secondary importance, though obviously the man with more extensive knowledge, especially of the Bible, is better equipped. When a man is good at preaching, simple villagers and the most highly educated are in complete agreement in calling him good. The ones of whom they approve, and whom they will sometimes go out of their way to hear, include second-letter catechists as well as one member of the cathedral staff. It is certain that these 'good' preachers prepare themselves carefully, but their preparation does not consist in the things that a European preacher must do. A great deal of their skill lies in the idiomatic use of good Luganda, colourful, proverbial, full of piquant analogies, and often symbolical and allusive. It is totally impossible for any European to teach this indigenous art; and the unremitting effort that has sometimes been put into the task of training clergy to preach short, three-point sermons may, in fact, have done more harm than good.

THE CONGREGATION IN THE COMMUNITY

At a meeting called by the *mutongole* of Kigaya in the parish of Makindu the subject of the weakness of the Anglican Church and the need for catechists was being discussed, when one man who was present—he was a little drunk at the time—addressed the company fervently, saying, 'What we Christians need is a society of our own. There is a society (*kibina*) of the Congress, a society of the Farmers, a society of the Club (welfare). In these days without a society nothing goes forward. Why do we Christians not have one?'

His remarks met with admiring assent. It was a good idea and there was a long discussion, though eventually nothing was done. But it never occurred to anyone there that the church, or the local congregation, was *ipso facto* such a society as they were looking for.

In that parish there were only two widely separated members of the revival fellowship. But in other parishes where they are strong they clearly constitute a visible Christian community within the community. As has already been said, their social pattern resembles the household-clusters of the first generation of the church, gathered on the estate of a landowner, who is one of the 'brethren', or living as near neighbours to a Christian trader or school-teacher. Their rallying point is the fellowship meeting, usually held at some time on Sunday, and on one other evening of the week. After an initial singing of the *Tukutendereza* chorus (see Chapter 4, page 101) and an opening prayer, the meeting begins with mutual 'walking in the light', as individuals share with the meeting the failures and recoveries they have experienced since the last meeting. When this basis of 'openness' has been established, one of the natural leaders turns to a passage of the Bible, which is read aloud by various members, taking a few verses each. The leader then expounds the passage; but in fact this exposition usually concentrates on one verse and quickly turns to an account of some personal experience of his own. Then others follow, usually picking on the same verse, but sometimes referring to another verse in the passage that has been read, or in some other part of the Bible. The basis of every contribution is a testimony of thankfulness for some aspect of the truth of that verse which has been revealed in the speaker's own experience. The result, very often, is a thorough and revealing 'digestion' of the one verse, but not much understanding of the passage as a whole, or in context. Whenever a contribution stimulates the sense of thanksgiving, there is a burst of singing, always of the *Tukutendereza* chorus. The meeting then turns to extempore prayer, concentrated usually on the theme that has emerged from the Bible study. After this a little while may be spent in exchange of news received by letters from other groups elsewhere, or the discussion of plans for larger joint meetings or conventions that may be in the offing, and sometimes in further confession, if some individual's conscience has been convicted during the meeting. There is a final round of singing during which members may sometimes greet one another with the African embrace before separating and going their ways.

The quality of the revival community can best be conveyed by relating the stories of three people, who live within a quarter of a mile of one another in one village, told as they recounted them.

The first was a middle-aged woman whose grandfather had been a chief. Though her mother was a good Christian, she 'played with sin', and became a 'prostitute' for four years (this refers to her marriage by African custom). She left her husband and became a cook at a mission station, where she met her present husband. They were married in church, and she tried to be a good woman. Eleven years later, when in hospital, she heard the preaching of a missionary who 'showed her hell'. Though she knew that her first sin was forgiven at her church wedding, she was now convicted of having consulted a *mulaguzi* about her sterility, and above all, of anger. She saw that she was 'in the pit'. When the woman in the next bed died in childbirth, she was filled with guilt but heard the voice of God saying, 'No more "medicines" to cause conception'. In that way she was saved. Later on her husband was saved, but afterwards went back and has often been unfaithful. But she has overcome the temptation to leave him. She has been threatened by attacks from *mizimu*, but has been given 'rest' concerning this. Jesus has saved her from the sorrow of sterility because 'she received Jesus as her child'.

The second was a younger woman. In her youth she loved God much and yet went to the diviners and owners of fetishes and was married by African custom only. She was saved after hearing a leading Christian preach at Namirembe, but 'Jesus came to me without the help of any man'. The verse which helped her was, 'Lay not up for yourselves treasures upon earth'. She then understood that Europeans had not got the true religion, which was simply 'being saved'. After her conversion people accused her before the *gombolola* court, but she won her case. Her husband noticed a difference in her, and she tried to win him, but he died, and then 'she had no debt'. She now lives, as a widow, at the homestead of a Christian man who is no relative of hers, except in the 'brotherhood' of the revival.

The third was a Munyaruanda labourer who had lived in a labour camp with a casual woman and had been a heavy drinker. He was saved by the text, 'Come unto me all that are weary'. He at once sent away his

P

mistress, gave up his beer, and came to Kampala, where he met the man on whose estate he is now living. This shows that 'Jesus makes people meet each other'. His wife is a Musoga, trained as a nurse. While she was working at a dispensary a man offered her Shs. 1,000 and a house on the Entebbe road if she would be his mistress. While she was considering the offer she heard 'mission' preaching and was saved. Both are amazed that Jesus should so overcome racial pride that a Musoga girl should marry a Munyaruanda.

It can be seen that the revival presents a clear-cut gospel and an immensely strong fellowship. Indeed, it offers a security, and a sense of belonging, greater than any other in Ganda society at the present time. For this reason a considerable number of people attach themselves to the fellowship, repeating the spiritual jargon with partial sincerity, only to find after a short time that they cannot keep it up. This accretion of hangers-on has led some of those who are not in the movement to accuse the 'brethren' of hypocrisy.

Remembering the quality of the life of the church in general, it is easy to sympathize with the point of view of the 'brethren' themselves that only in them is the true congregation of Christians to be found. Here is the *kibina* or society—they do in fact use that word to describe themselves—which is the living Christian community. The whole Gospel is related to their fellowship: repentance means, virtually, to confess sins; 'brokenness', as the pre-requisite of a state of grace, means not only surrender towards God, but, as a corollary, compliance to the group; and any salvation is suspect which does not involve wholehearted membership in the revival.

Occasionally a party of the 'brethren' visits one of the weekly markets to preach. The hubbub of the milling crowd compels them to shout, as each in turn enumerates the sins from which he has been saved, and the sins in which his hearers are still perishing. There is no congruence in this preaching, no *approchement*. Indeed, any attempt to woo their hearers is so completely lacking that they seem either to be deliberately emphasizing the gulf of separation which only the miracle of grace can enable the convert to leap, or to be preaching in order to satisfy their own inner necessity to get rid of their indebtedness.

But the great gulf fixed between the gathered community of the revival and the undifferentiated mass of the church is not the only spiritual frontier, nor is that miraculous leap the only decision by which the church grows up into Christ. Even in the parishes, such as Makindu, where there are few, if any, of the 'brethren', the Christian community within the community does exist, though it is extremely hard to discover.

One reason for this disconcerting lack of distinctiveness in the Christian congregation is that it is deeply confused. A lot of the Christians who attend church, and a considerable number of those who don't, are reading the Bible by themselves, and finding it baffling. The older generation grasped a few simple fundamentals and had a lifetime in which to think about them and put them into practice. But the present-day Christians have a confused smattering of many kinds of knowledge, and, as some of them say, it is easier to read the vernacular press or turn on the radio than to study the Bible. If there were catechists and teachers to help them in their fumbling attempts to understand the faith, they might know more certainly what they stood for. Moreover, many of them feel themselves to be under judgment, not of their own conscience, but through the legislation of the church. That, and the effect of the revival preaching, makes many uncertain whether they are still in the church or not, and so they are inhibited from making any stand.

But they are certain of one thing—that they believe in God. What is often lost sight of by missionaries, and by all the more spiritually and intellectually advanced Christians, is the enormous significance of this faith in God. It has to be seen against the background of the old world-view, in which the whole of existence was 'consubstantial', with no fundamental differentiation drawn between inanimate, human and super-nature. To say, 'I believe in One God' is suddenly to see a gulf appearing between the here and now, and the beyond; further, it is to see the known network of inter-relation, which consitututes my life, terrifyingly related in some way to him who is independent of those relationships.

For some half-sensed implications of this faith are so deeply disturbing that they fall back into the self-contained circle of the old world-view. Those who maintain faith in this God who is the point of reference beyond the circle are thereby set over against all others. In this there is no difference between Christians and Moslems. They have religion—*eddini*—and, as is often repeated, 'all religion is one'. The adherents of the old cult, on the other hand, are always called 'those who have not religion'.

In Makindu parish a group of the stronger and more thoughtful Christians were asked what they believe God is like, and they gave these answers, slowly, and in this order. 'He is different.' 'He never changes.'

'He is patient.' Then followed quickly, 'He is Eternal—Wise—the Lover of all creation.' Several repeated, 'He does not get angry.' The earliest convert in the parish, a slave who had been redeemed and attached to Baskerville's household, said, 'He answers prayer and likes to hear prayer.' When the same question was asked in other pastorates, almost the same answers were given.

The belief in the patience of the Christian God has relaxed many ancient fears but without substituting a strong sense of the claims of God's righteousness. Though the whole natural universe is felt to be a realm of diverse personal wills, the Biblical concept of the will of God, as something to be obeyed or disobeyed, is not given primary emphasis. The Luganda language itself cannot easily indicate a distinction between the will and the love of God. Moreover, if God's will implies choice and preference, then it follows that God cannot will everything equally, and a dualism is introduced into the fabric of existence which is only accepted with profound reluctance. There is a theoretical belief in heaven and hell, but the fears of the village people are more for this world than the next. Even habitual drunkards say, 'Jesus has made us free: we have nothing to fear.'

Nevertheless, though the question, 'How can I please God?', is not often asked, there are considerable numbers who have a real love for God. This is the most common phrase by which 'good' members of the Christian community are pointed out—'He loves God greatly.' It may sometimes be admitted of the same person that he gets drunk now and again, or consults the diviners, and he probably has not got a Christian marriage. Yet it is asserted unshakeably: 'He loves God greatly', and the words evidently have a real meaning, for they are only used of certain people. When pressed to explain further, informants have added —'He enjoys the Bible'—'He prays every day'—'He loves to talk about God in his conversation.' In a community which is quick to detect hypocrisy it would not be possible to maintain such a reputation on false pretences.

Village people do not find it easy to talk about their prayers. But without doubt the experiences of some of them in private prayer have a deep mysticism. 'I have seen once in church a great shining road in front of me leading to God.' 'Once or twice, in my prayers, everything in front of me has become shining and I knew I was talking with God.' One very simple man told of a vision of God which filled him with an unbearable longing, but his account was quite incoherent, except for the statement, 'I spent all the night in the bush and didn't want to go home.' Others have a more plodding experience. One man said prosaic-ally: 'From 1934 to 1937 I felt very clearly in my prayers that I had a friendship with God. But now for a long time I have not felt that God is there: I pray in the dark.'

The answers to questions about Christ were almost always quotations from a catechism. Nevertheless, most Christians have a truer grasp of the personality of the historic Jesus than might be supposed. They think mainly of his divinity and his miracles; but they also have a surprisingly clear picture of his humility, compassion, forgiveness and suffering for others. Yet few of them admire these qualities in one another. In general there is a feeling that Jesus, like the Bible, is ambiguous. 'He is an ocean!' 'He is too much for us.' 'The thoughts of Jesus are difficult'. The average Christian knows about the Cross, and the salvation of his soul, almost to the point of glibness. But the whole of the theological content of the faith seems to him too remote from his daily life, which is scarcely surprising, considering the fewness and incompetence of his teachers. If his wife bears no children; if he is about to build a new brick house on the foundations of which it is usual to kill a sacrifice; if his son is insolent in the home; if he is in debt and the tax-collector is his enemy; at such times what has Christianity to say? Repentance, salvation, the blood of Jesus, the Holy Spirit—he can remember all the words, but they do not seem to mean very much. That is when the spirit-medium, and the powers he represents, seem much more down to earth and concerned with him *as a man* than the Christian God. In quite a number of cases the catechist appears to think so too.

But the factor which, more than any other, makes it hard for the Christian congregation to have a visible entity of its own, apart from Sunday worship, is that solid resistance to all differentiation which, as has already been said, is so deeply rooted in this society. Although it is impossible to define anything that is so inarticulate, it might almost be called a type of monism. It is the old belief—or rather it is an awareness, for there is little that is cerebral about it—that there is an essential unity in all created things. The most commonly quoted phrase in village discussions on almost any topic is the sentence with which the first catechism of the Anglican Church in Uganda begins—'God created all things'. It is a blessed phrase, by which, while still maintaining *eddini* and believing in the one God who is beyond, man can almost restore the broken circle of the unity of all existence. Everything in the circle is undifferentiated; everything is included in the vivid realization of the present moment; and God is the Creator of the whole. The phrase is applied to the *balubaale* and to the *mizimu* which may possess the living. It is applied to differences of custom between Moslems and Christians, and to the tensions between Africans and Europeans. It is said of the mysterious haunted caves of Kokola, and of the power of a drum over a human dancer. This is not to be understood as an article of faith but as a way of looking at things which sees no rigid distinction between subject and object, a way of feeling about people which can best be expressed in the word, 'I in them and they in me.'

The hard shell of individuality begins to grow in the schools, and is found almost complete among the fully Westernized. It is, in some ways, easier for Christians to make an individual stand in the towns than in the country, where the pressures of the collective are so much stronger. Yet even the most *évolués* feel that they differ from Europeans above all in this respect, that their sense of belonging to, and being involved in, the whole is so much stronger. The attitude which is most intensely disliked is called *okusosola*, which means to make distinctions or sort people into groups. Not only is it resented, but it is felt to be positively a sin.

Among Christians, as much as anyone, the idea of goodness is primarily social. When it was said that some villager is 'good', further enquiry always produced the same general pattern of values. A good villager is trustful and trustworthy, kindly and frank, merciful and helpful. These values are focussed in the elusive Luganda phrase *obuntu bulamu*, which means, literally, a living humanity or manhood, but which includes the whole range of social virtues from good manners to altruism. But *okusosola*, or discrimination, and *okwepanka* or self-flattery, setting oneself up, are an offence against *obuntu bulamu*.

The ideal of the good Christian is one who has these social virtues but is also a lover of God. Of course, the concept of goodness has itself been altered in many respects by the leaven of Christianity in society during seventy years. The older generation remembers a time when it was no disgrace whatever for a man to beat his wife; now, though he may still do so, there is some shame attached to it. It is contrary to the pattern of goodness. In any community the broadening of social conscience is always a slow process, and the new Christian ideal can only be built upon the existing foundation. In the ideal of *obuntu bulamu* there were certain recognized 'works of mercy'. For example, anyone who heard the *nduulu* or alarm-call was expected to run to answer it, whoever was in trouble. For women to lift one another's water-pots on to, or off, their heads was an act of courtesy. These, and all acts of neighbourliness, were stressed by the Christians as being also typically Christian acts. To them were added new values. We have already noted, for example, how early in the story of this church the grace of humble work in menial tasks, even by the aristocratic, was regarded as a demand of Christ. Today this local, small-scale, social conscience is just beginning to awaken to wider implications, but it is a slow process. There are many grave social ills that cry aloud for a prophetic voice to be raised by the church. There are a small number of bad slums growing up within the area in which the public health ordinance could be applied; the prisons of the African administration, and the treatment of offenders, fall far below the standards of normal humanity and decency; yet these needs do not, as yet, appear to have stirred the conscience of many Christians in Buganda. The educated women seem to be somewhat more sensitive and courageous than the men in respect of such things, and they have shown already a reforming zeal concerning the very crude methods that have hitherto been adopted in dealing with the problem of prostitution in Mengo African township. The greatest hindrance to the development of such social action comes from the exclusive concentration of all African leaders upon the simple issues of self-government, and the fear that any efforts to bring about purely social reform may be misconstrued as political disloyalty. This confronts the Christian educated layman with a difficult choice.

Yet although their deep sense of solidarity and lack of individuation causes the majority of Baganda Christians to think it wrong to separate themselves and stand apart from their community, or to adopt any attitude of spiritual or moral superiority, nevertheless, on closer acquaintance the disconcerting homogeneity of the mass of Christian adherents reveals, below the surface, many lines of demarcation, many points of personal and communal decision, at which some, choosing painfully to obey the voice of God, stand apart from the rest, and, in that stand, find fellowship with other confessors. The occasions of these moral and spiritual battles are innumerable. In the previous six chapters of this book some of them have been indicated. In the parent-child relationships, and in the temptations of adolescents; in the choice between drunkenness and loneliness; in the decisions about betrothal and the type of marriage, and in the struggle for stability in the midst of much marital breakdown; in the encounter with the old world-view and the needs which magic appears to meet; in the challenge of political tension, when the choice often seems to lie between irresponsible pietism or a total surrender to the slogans and emotions of propaganda;

in all these and a hundred other 'valleys of decision', men are confronting the demand inherent in the Gospel and the frontiers are being drawn.

If that be true, if these are indeed the growing points at which the church in Buganda is moving towards maturity; then it must follow that the theological concept of the 'gathered community', or of the 'confessing church', is not to be looked for only in the spiritual *élite*, who are conscious of where they stand and what they are doing, but in all the imperceptible choices by which men are detached from their older loyalties and habits, and in all the unseen resolutions which are being made continually within the totality of the church. The real 'responsibility' of the church consists in this multitude of tiny responses to the Spirit of God working invisibly within the fabric of the divine society.

In a strange way the majority of thinking Christians in Buganda today are aware that this is so. A surprisingly large number of the educated younger generation, when asked to describe the finest Christian they have known, speak of some quite obscure villager, as often as not outside the revival fellowship, who is nevertheless living out, in the terms of his normal African environment, the fulness of Christ. He was brought to that degree of discipleship, not usually by one miraculous leap, but by a long series of hard decisions, won out of conflict. The impulse which brought him out of the sphere of apathy and set his foot upon the first step of the long process might have arisen from an endless variety of causes. One chief suddenly found himself politically suspect and was ostracized by his friends: in his loneliness he turned to the local pastor. Another man was involved in a drunken quarrel in which he thought he had killed his neighbour: in an access of fear he started coming to church.

If this is true, then the processes of spiritual growth that are of most account in these days are, after all, precisely the same as those which we have seen were operative during the first fourteen years of this church's life—congruence, detachment and demand, culminating periodically in some crisis which *God* precipitates. This means that the primary need of the present day is the recovery of congruence, and a new spirit of *approchement* in the official counsels of the church, towards the great body of the discredited and partly un-churched Christians.

The church in the Uganda diocese is confronted with a choice. Either, accepting its own second-rate totality in the forgiveness of God, it must lovingly adapt itself to the spiritual stature of its people, as the prophet Elisha cramped himself over the body of the Shunamite's son, in the faith that, concealed by that close embrace, the inner processes of growth will work again. Or it can decide that the time has come for the condition of crisis, when church and society have sprung apart, to be permanently sustained, and for the gap between them to be kept open and visible in order that the church in Uganda may be a 'gathered' community, standing apart from society with standards uncompromised, demanding that men should leap the gulf by the miraculous power of Christ. The history, and the present condition of the Buganda Church, seem to suggest that the former way is the right one to follow. It is fundamentally a theological decision. It is also an act of faith.

NOTES

1. G. K. Baskerville, Journal, 25 May 1897, from MS. copy in the possession of the Bishop of Uganda.
2. E. Millar, *Uganda Notes*, Jan. 1913, p. 20.
3. A. M. Mackay, Journal in *C.M.I.* 1885, p. 726.
4. E. Millar, letter in *C.M.I.* 1894, p. 452.
5. Pilkington's revision, published in 1897, is virtually the Prayer Book in use at the present time, apart from a few additions incorporated from the 'deposited' book of 1928. The most interesting of the alterations made to Pilkington's version are in the Prayer of Consecration in the service of Holy Communion. The S.P.C.K. had made Pilkington substitute the Swahili word *omugati* (bread) in place of the only possible Luganda word, *emmere* (food), which is used in the 'Bread of Life' passages in St John. Events have proved the wisdom of this change, since bread is in common use throughout Buganda today. Pilkington also gave the S.P.C.K. committee an assurance that the Luganda word *omwenge* was a correct translation of 'wine'. In this he was right, for all the early missionaries had spoken of the local *omwenge* as 'banana wine', and Bishop Tucker had authorized its use at the Holy Communion rather than spend the funds of the church on importing European wine. But later versions substituted the latinism, *envinyo*, used by the Roman Catholics, since there is no grape-wine produced in Buganda. Similarly Pilkington used *ndeku* (gourd cup) and *ng'unda* (long-necked gourd vessel), which were both in common use, but these words have since been replaced by the foreign words, *kikompe* (cup) and *mudumu* (jug), for the communion cup and chalice. Other changes are not easy to understand, and, on the whole, Pilkington's Luganda was the better. He reaches his highest pitch of perfection in the Collects.
6. A. M. Mackay, Journal in *C.M.I.* 1885, p. 726. One of Mackay's hymns, *Mumikono gya ISA*, seemingly based on 'Safe in the arms of Jesus', is printed at *C.M.I.* 1884, p. 760.
7. Pilkington's first nine translations were of the following hymns—the figures indicate their numbers in the present Luganda hymn-book: 'Art thou weary?' (204); 'There is a fountain' (228); 'There is life for a look' (227); 'Onward, Christian soldiers' (152); 'Look, ye saints' (30); 'I heard the voice of Jesus' (216); 'Grace, 'tis a charming sound' (215); 'I lay my sins on Jesus'

(128); 'Just as I am' (218). With these Pilkington also wrote a tenth hymn in Luganda based on the Bible story of Moses and the rock of Kadesh (52). Ten more were printed the following year.

8. C. F. Harford-Battersby, *Pilkington of Uganda*, pp. 151-2.

9. Sir Albert Cook, *Uganda Memories*, p. 186.

10. Dr K. P. Wachsmann, Article in the *Uganda Church Review*, No. 73, 1946.

11. G. K. Baskerville's journal, *C.M.I.* 1897, p. 838.

III

THE FUTURE

'It is somewhat the fashion just at present to take a despondent view of things, and to think that because new temptations are crowding in upon the people, that therefore of necessity there must follow spiritual degradation and decadence, if not actual ruin. I cannot and do not take this view. To do so would be to limit the power and to doubt the love of God the Holy Ghost.' Bishop Alfred R. Tucker, *Eighteen Years in Uganda and East Africa*, vol. ii, p. 120.

13

Pastoral Questions:
Word, Sacraments and Ministry

I F this survey has revealed one thing more than any other it is the vitality which lies within the body of the church in Buganda. It is a body which is fighting for its life against diseases which could be fatal, but the hidden forces of health are wonderfully at work in the conscience, and in the daily decisions and struggles of a great number of Christians. Those forces need to be supported and called out into a conscious and co-ordinated will to live. Faith in the Holy Spirit, and a sober appraisal of what is actually taking place in the life of the church, lead one to expect to see its inner vitality and responsiveness moving the whole church towards a fundamental reorientation of its concern and realignment of its strategy.

Such realignment must consist of a planned and persevering reversal of the tendencies which make for disengagement in the life of the church and enervate the forces of vitality and growth. This means that the principle of tutelage and bureaucratic supervision will give place to more local responsibility and freedom of action. It is bound to mean, also, that more and more laymen participate in the leadership of the church as well as in local pastoral ministrations, not as official representatives of 'the laity', but because they have, in fact, the *charismata* which the church needs. The innate vitality of the church is already expressing itself in this direction.

Realignment will also mean decentralization. Because the pattern of the church has for so long been a pyramid, it may take some time to screw up enough courage to look upon the *muluka* parish as the real unit out of which the structure is built, and to grant to the pastorates such a measure of autonomy that they will largely stand or fall by the decisions which they make. No part of the church can, of course, be self-contained, but the inter-relationship between the several parts and the whole should consist primarily of prayer and assistance rather than of control. The living link between the pastorate and the diocese must be found in the spiritual reality that 'whether one member suffer, all the members suffer with it'. This demands that if the church in a particular pastorate is weak or defeated, the concern of the rest of the diocese should be expressed by coming to the rescue with financial support or the supply of men, and the organization of the church must be such as to make this mutual responsibility possible. As the church is Anglican, this caring of the whole for each of the parts is symbolized in the bishop, and a great step of decentralization was taken when the synod of 1956 subdivided the diocese of Uganda into four suffragan areas, which may eventually become separate dioceses, so making possible a more intimate relationship between the bishops and the pastorates under their charge.

At first sight the pastorates in Buganda may seem to be unqualified to bear a greater burden of autonomy and freedom of decision than they have at present. But in fact there are very few pastorates which do not contain among the senior catechists and educated men in secular professions, and in the rank and file of ordinary Christians, enough men and women of wisdom, fervour and simple goodness to rise to this responsibility if only they are sought out and entrusted with it. But such a burden will certainly prove too heavy unless they are able to draw upon the resources of the Word and the sacraments. Without these, all 'response' within the church will be merely a reaction to stimuli and not a real responding to the living God.

In its Bible the Luganda-speaking church has an inestimable treasure. Unlike many translations, the Luganda version was written on the basis of long experiment. Mackay's caution was well rewarded. O'Flaherty had been pressing forward with his own one-man translation of the Gospels, but, because Africans had not shared sufficiently in the work, Mackay and Ashe rejected it as premature. In 1886, however, Mackay printed the first thirteen chapters of St Matthew, and completed that Gospel early in 1887 with the help of Henry Duta and Andereya Kaddu. Soon after this Ashe translated St John's Gospel,[1] and Mackay was working on a revision of this up to the time of his death. The revision was completed in 1891 by Cyril Gordon, Henry Duta and Sembera Mackay, who also were the translators of St Mark and St Luke. Ashe was responsible for most of Genesis, Walker for the Acts and Crabtree for the Minor Prophets. Besides the Africans already mentioned, Mika Sematimba and Nuwa Kikwabanga gave expert assistance in translation from the Swahili. But the presiding genius of the Luganda Bible was

George Pilkington, who revised all previous work and completed the whole Bible before the end of 1896.

After their return to the country the Roman Catholic Fathers were not far behind in producing their translation of the Gospels. Matthew and St Mark appeared in 1894, St Luke and St John two years later. They were published in France and seem to have been more exclusively the work of one or two missionary scholars, so that Africans were less responsibly involved in the making of them than was the case with the Anglicans. It was this long preparatory period of experiment, prior to Pilkington's arrival in the work, which gave to the Anglican Church their unique grounding in the Scriptures. Pilkington frequently referred to this.

'There were none of the ordinary difficulties of searching for words to translate the important terms and phrases of the Gospel; these were not only at hand, but so far stereotyped by extensive use that any radical changes, had I wished to make them, could hardly have been justifiable. This fact made the work possible, and it also makes me hope that the translation (thanks not to me but to my predecessors and to the Waganda themselves), is a better one than a first translation into a new language generally can be; it has been really beaten out during many years by the best brains among the Waganda themselves, with the help of Mackay, Ashe, Gordon, Walker and the others who have been here.'[2]

The result of this was not only a version of the Bible which revision committees have twice reported to be almost beyond criticism, but a church which had been built up on a foundation of concentrated Bible study. This accounts for the extraordinary grasp of the Christian faith which those first Baganda Anglicans clearly enjoyed, on the basis of which they were able to be such responsible leaders.

'For a long time the Swahili New Testament was the text-book of Uganda; day after day the most intelligent of the Christians translated from it into their own language; day after day they discussed among themselves the proper rendering of terms, appealing to the European as to the exact force of the original; for years they were thus occupied in hammering out a version on a native anvil.'[3]

The men who had done that knew how to use the Bible, whether as preachers translating its message into vivid contemporary idiom, or as Christians confronting the ordinary secular problems of their daily lives. Frequently the Katikkiro and chiefs referred to the Bible for the solution of legal or political difficulties. On one occasion in the Great Lukiiko, or state council, of Buganda the leader of the Moslems brought a charge of blasphemy against one of their community who had given himself divine honours in response, as he said, to a vision. The Moslems would have put the man to death, but the Christians called for a Bible, and when it was brought they referred to Acts 5. 34-40 and 12. 21-24. The Lukiiko then decided that God must himself pass sentence on the man, if he would, but that it was not for them to do so; so they told him to return to his home and pray there. The man left the council in great triumph, believing that he had won his case, but on the threshold of his house he fell down and died almost immediately. This event caused great awe in the country.[4]

The Bible was even more the reference book of the church council in those days. Bishop Tucker records how the council decided that the time had come to build a more permanent cathedral; but brick, the only reliable material, seemed to be beyond the means of the church.

> 'A meeting of the chief and more prominent Christians was called by the Katikiro to consider the matter. As a matter of course a passage of Scripture was read, viz. I Chron. 29. The whole meeting was struck with David's question and its response: "Who then is willing to consecrate his service this day unto the Lord? Then the chief of the fathers and princes of the tribes of Israel, and the captains of thousands and of hundreds, with the rulers of the king's work, offered willingly." And so it was determined it should be in Uganda: every man should give according to his means.'[5]

Besides this practical application, there was a strong tradition of Bible study and expository preaching. Martin Hall noted that 'there is a kind of oral tradition of interpretation of parables, miracles, etc., which you meet with in all parts. . . . It is in some cases very quaint; its original source I know not.'[6]

Some of this indigenous exposition found its way into the first commentary published in Luganda, which was Ham Mukasa's remarkable *Gospel of St Matthew with Commentary*, published in 1900.

But from the time that portions of the Bible began to appear in the vernacular we find a new generation of Christians reading it superficially without the same penetrating search for its meaning, and without sufficient teachers to explain this to them. This was due at first to the enormous increase in the number of baptism candidates, each of whom had to read two gospels before being admitted.

> 'There is a growing danger of their coming to regard their New Testament as a mere class book . . . and of the teachers using it as such. . . . Such words as, "He that believeth on the Son hath ever-

lasting life" . . . are in grave danger of becoming a mere shibboleth.'

'In reading the Bible, the tendency is to wish to understand merely the literal meaning of the words, and not so much to take in the spiritual meaning. . . . There is, too, a tendency to look upon baptism and the Holy Communion as something to be worked for, as one works for an examination, and when anyone is passed for baptism all his friends congratulate him on having passed his examination.'[7]

At first the ill-effects of this indiscriminate, untutored dissemination of the Bible was countered by the continuation training of all the catechists. We have already seen how, in Kyagwe, they were recalled once a month to report and to receive instruction and inspiration. Moreover, the church workers and the intelligent lay leaders were equipped with a fine supply of literature to supplement their teaching of the Bible. The great translator after Pilkington's death was the Rev. F. Rowling, but Baskerville, Crabtree and others also contributed to the task, and in the early years of this century the commentaries of the Cambridge Bible for schools had been published in Luganda for the four Gospels, Acts, Romans, I Corinthians and I and II Thessalonians; and there were translations of the *Oxford Helps for the Study of the Bible*, Harmer's *Old Testament History*, Maclear's *New Testament History*, J. C. Robertson's *Sketches of Church History* in two volumes, and *The Pilgrim's Progress*, besides smaller textbooks on the life of Mahomet, the Levitical offerings, and the Roman Catholic Church. One of the sad mysteries of the years of disengagement is that all of these, except the Bunyan, were allowed to go out of print and are almost unobtainable today. The commentary on Acts has been republished since the Second World War, but otherwise the Christian literature produced in these days in Luganda is altogether slighter and more ephemeral than that which the Uganda Church enjoyed fifty years ago. Moreover, by 1910, the regular recall of catechists for refreshment at the pastorate centre had ceased to operate; they were left to become, gradually, blind leaders of the blind.

The church at the present time is dangerously out of touch with the Word of God. The Bible is widely distributed in the homes of the people, though in Buganda fewer are buying it today than before the last war. The simple village people struggle to read it but are baffled very easily by apparent contradictions. Among Christians who have some knowledge of the faith—catechists and clergy, devout laity, even those in the revival fellowship—the Bible is used more often to underline and illustrate familiar and stereotyped doctrines than as a living

Q

source of new knowledge and direction. Where it is read without comprehension it leads to discouragement; where there is some understanding it is used conservatively in much the same way as the traditional corpus of proverbial wisdom.

Three things seem to be urgently required. First, a continual process of Bible training should be made available to meet the various needs of different levels in the church. Among the more highly educated laity, Bible study groups may do much, but regular planned courses at the theological college or with the co-operation of Makerere College, along the lines of the Evangelical Academies in Europe, would more effectively help them to understand what it means for contemporary minds to learn to think in the light of the Bible. At the same time there is a need to recover some form of regular Bible teaching for catechists and others who have charge of parish, and village, churches. This can only be done with sufficient regularity by the clergy themselves. At one time the ordination course included, as a most important item, the thorough training of clergy to be teachers and fathers of the catechists in their charge. Then, when the effort was made to raise the academic standards of the ordinands, the training of catechists was removed from the central theological college. Today the situation is different, with the old style of catechist rapidly dying out; but there is at least a serious need once again to train all clergy so that they may better know how to work as heads of teams in their pastorates, and to give all who work under them the simple Bible teaching which they can pass on to their congregations.

Secondly, in order to support such a programme, the paralysis which has for so long lain over the production of Christian literature in the vernacular needs to be cured in order that the church of these days may be at least as well equipped with Bible commentaries for those who do not speak English as was the church in 1910. Thirdly, and closely linked with the second, is the need for some return to what was the basis of Bible study in the early days, namely a concentration of attention on the meaning of the text. In the communication of the Gospel nothing can exceed this in importance. The danger of the present time lies in the fact that the Scriptures are already in Luganda and therefore the immediate urge to search for meaning has gone, and teachers are tempted to the irreverence of imposing upon the Bible a neat doctrinal scheme instead of giving the Word of God free course. Perhaps the time has come when those who are responsible for theological training should seriously consider the oft-repeated demand of ordinands themselves to be given the opportunity to read, at least, the Old or the New Testament in the original tongue.

If the dissemination of the Word has been, perhaps, too unguarded, the very opposite is true of the church's use of the sacraments. In the early days the missionaries were divided over the question of the conditions of baptism for *adults*, some, like Mackay, and later Miller and Crabtree, urging the utmost caution, others, like Ashe, convinced that rigidity was impossible. For better or worse vast numbers were baptized in the ten years following the settlement of 1893. From that time the problem focused upon the conditions of *infant* baptism.

In 1902 the church council decided that if pagan parents placed their children under the care of a Christian chief, and if written pledges were given by the parents and the chief that the children were to remain in his care, then such children might be baptized. As a result the number of infants baptized rose from 1571 in 1902, to 2,829 in 1903. But when Bishop Tucker arrived back in Uganda in the following year he vetoed the decision of the church council on the grounds that such pledges, according to the Commissioner, would have no validity if the parents later claimed the child. This became the basis of the law of the Anglican Church; and since Christians who are not allowed Communion are regarded, in this context, as being on a par with pagans, it is now applied to the children of 87 per cent. of Anglican families, that is to say all families not married by the rites of the church, or in which monogamy has not been maintained; children of unmarried mothers are similarly excluded in practice on the grounds that, however repentant the mother may be, she is unlikely to resist the father should he claim the custody of the children.

There is from whatever motives, a deep-seated desire on the part of all Christian parents that their children should be baptized as infants. This is not only because of the social status which it undoubtedly confers, but far more because, as we have seen, such matters are not thought of in terms of individualistic decision but of communal solidarity. As many parents put it: 'If our child is not a Christian then what is he? Why should he be punished, or excluded, on account of his father's sin?' The official reply is to point out that baptism is only postponed until the child is old enough to enter an instruction class. But the parents know quite well that only a tiny proportion of the children who are refused infant baptism ever find themselves in such classes. Catechists, if they exist in that area, rarely go out of their way to search for such children and bring them in, and parents have often lost heart and do not make the effort by the time the children are older. There is everywhere, therefore, widespread concern over the Anglican attitude regarding infant baptism. The Roman Church, emphasizing the inherent power of baptismal grace rather than the human fulfilment of preliminary conditions, accepts all children for baptism, and those who are baptized in that church are usually followed up when they have grown older. Many Anglican parents are, therefore, taking their infants to be baptized by the Roman Catholic priests. The majority, however, avoid this expedient if they can because their sense of solidarity makes them reluctant for their children to 'change religion'. Instead they prefer to bribe Anglican clergy or senior catechists to disregard the practice of their church. It is not uncommon for a pastor to be offered several hundreds of shillings by a local chief if he will consent to baptize his baby. Naturally some of them administer baptism in such cases for the sake of a bribe. Others, including a few of the most sensitive pastors in the diocese, do so because they are convinced that the practice of their church is wrong.

For in practice the Anglican Church appears to apply quite rigidly the rule of thumb that no 'child of fornication' (which as we have seen, includes African customary marriage) may be baptized as an infant, whatever the circumstances. A widow, for example, who lives in Makindu parish and is a regular communicant, took charge of two orphans, aged six and one, the children born of an African customary marriage. Their father, her relative, had died and their mother had returned to her own people. The children are now growing up in the home of this widow, but when she asked for them to be baptized she was refused.

The same principle governs the practice of the Anglican Church with regard to Holy Communion. The rubric in the Prayer Book concerning the exclusion of the ' open and notorious evil liver' is applied to 87 per cent. of married men in the church, and about 80 per cent. of married women, and this quite irrespectively of the fact that in almost all parishes the congregation is not in the least 'offended' by what they have done. When the Holy Communion is celebrated in the parish churches it is only a small minority of those who have first attended Morning Prayer who are eligible to stay to partake of the sacrament. The trend of thought which this practice engenders can be seen in the case of a one-time Muganda prison-chaplain who would only celebrate the Communion on a few special occasions on the grounds that criminals were patently evil livers and therefore could not be admitted to the sacrament. The present chaplain does not hold that view, but it is easy to see that the universal practice of the church inevitably leads to the belief that the sacrament is a reward won by the righteous few.

Many Christians see beyond that crude misconception and say that the Communion is given not for the merits of the recipients, but because they have repented. Repentance, is, however, equated with amendment. A woman, for example, who married by African custom, should her husband die, may be readmitted to Holy Communion because she is now no longer in a state of sin. The children, however, having been born of a sinful union, may not be baptized except through attendance at a class. But, it is often asked, what is repentance for an Anglican who has married a Roman Catholic, or for a man who, having been left by his first wife, has married again?

Just as the practice concerning infant baptism leads to corruption, so also there are cases of chiefs who are admitted to Communion, though their marriages do not conform to the church's rule, while peasants in the same condition are excluded. The majority of people, however, including the chiefs, simply accept the prohibition of the church and withdraw themselves from the sacrament without any intervention from the catechist or pastor. This, while it simplifies the pastoral problems of the clergy, is a spiritually dangerous state of affairs, for not only is such excommunication taking place on a great scale without any particular reference to the bishops—how could the bishops responsibly discipline over 80 per cent. of their adult church members?—but it is accompanied by no proper ministry of penance, either to initiate the period of excommunication or to readmit the penitent to Communion. Apart from disciplinary measures in the schools among pupils and staff, excommunication in the Anglican church is unregulated, punitive rather than pastoral, and usually permanent.

The heart of the problem, however, lies not in isolated cases, nor even in the pastoral methods employed by the church, but in the fundamental conception of the sacraments as holy things needing above all to be guarded and fenced around. There is a good deal of evidence from other parts of the world Church that the sacraments of the Gospel, like the Lord who instituted them, far from needing to be protected from contamination, have a power of their own to do things to sinners when all else seems to have failed. In view of the anomaly of its present condition, in which the Holy Communion is retained for such a tiny minority of its baptized members, the church in Buganda might well take some cognizance of that evidence and consider, perhaps, whether some other means should not be found of disciplining offenders, in order that the sacraments may be offered, with less fear and more faith, to the whole body of the church for its healing.

In any case, if the Holy Communion is to be anything but the most esoteric and occasional rite in the life of the majority of communicants, some means need to be found to make it possible for a celebration to take place in every *muluka* parish church every Sunday. This can only happen if there is an ordained priest in every parish; but, though the output of new clergy from the theological centre is, for the first time in many years, greater than the losses from retirement, it is going to be a very long time before sufficient men have passed through the present courses of training to staff all the *miruka* churches. In view both of the need, and of the tradition of lay leadership in the Buganda Church, one is compelled to ask whether the new forms of ministry which are being seriously discussed elsewhere in the Anglican Communion may not be supremely well suited to this situation. The thorough theological grounding and training in exposition and pastoral responsibility which the present courses attempt to supply are clearly necessary for anyone who is to be a teacher of the Word or pastor of the flock; but are they essential for one who is to break the bread as head of the congregation on the Lord's day? Is there not a 'presidential' priesthood, a natural development of those heads of households who were the local leaders in the early church at Mengo, to which a layman, following a secular calling but endowed with the natural gifts of fatherly leadership in the local group, might be ordained? These are questions which lie beyond the competence of this study to answer, but which the facts are posing to the Uganda Church.

With regard to the recruitment and training of men for more traditional forms of ministry, much has already been written both in the *Survey of the Training of the Ministry in Africa*, Part I (I.M.C. 1950) and in Professor Sundkler's coming book *They Serve the Church in Africa*, and in earlier chapters of this work a good deal has been said about the catechists and clergy both of the old and new styles. It is impossible, at present, to generalize about the position in Uganda, for these are years of acute transition and in a short time the ordained ministry of the church is bound to present a very changed appearance. Already the first ordinands to have entered the theological centre from the highest class of a secondary school are in training, and the first graduate has offered for the ministry and is studying in a British university. The problem of recruitment still remains acute enough, however, to compel the church to explore seriously the possibilities of various types of lay ministry at all levels. It is to be hoped that in Buganda this will never again be regarded as a stop-gap, but that the riches of lay participation in the spiritual work of the church will be exploited for their own sake as a permanent possession.

The theological training centre should be the place *par excellence* where it is possible to work out the implications of the encounter between the Word of God, spoken in the Bible, and the traditional world-view of the people, such as was hinted at in Chapters 9 and 10 of this book. Such discussion, carried on for many years, must be the prolegomenon of any truly African expression of Christian theology or worship. Until the present time, however, any such conversation has been almost impossible owing, on the one side, to the ignorance of the European members of staff of the whole of that African background, through their lack of prolonged contact with life in the villages; and on the other side to the inhibitions, and sometimes the actual ignorance, of the African clergy and students themselves, which has prevented them from seeing that in the 'pagan' traditions there is a world-view and an attitude to life—a theology, in fact—which deserves to be examined seriously and objectively. The theological college is certainly the place where the old reactions towards 'paganism' of mingled antagonism, scorn and fear should be superseded by a new level of understanding, out of which the church may be equipped with a fresh insight into its own Gospel, and more effective pastoral methods.

Together with this should go the more thorough study of the text of the Bible, once again hammering out the meaning as the early church in Buganda had to do. The incentive to this kind of study can no longer be the need to produce a vernacular translation; but the need to communicate the Biblical message in terms which are relevant and actual to the lives and concerns of ordinary people still remains. 'Translation' in this sense must still be the primary objective of Bible study in the theological college.

If these two concerns are to be given priority in theological training, the main question confronting those who are responsible for it must be what they will dare to omit from the curriculum. Inevitably the pressure to attain better academic qualifications tempts people to model the curriculum more and more on European patterns, because only the known disciplines of classical theological studies can guarantee that the training is 'up to the same standard'. It will need great courage deliberately to excise large parts of the conventional curriculum in the fields, say, of Church History, Doctrine or Liturgy, in order to make room for other fields of study which have no counterpart in the European schools. Ultimately the solution must lie in the provision of alternative options in the curriculum, but this presupposes a staff that is beyond the bounds of possibility. The higher theological college proposed in Bishop Neill's report would go some way to meet the need; but it must not be supposed that the two concerns outlined above can be left to the higher grade students. They are needed most especially in the training of the men who will minister to the ordinary people at the lower levels of the church's life.

There remains the vexed question of the place of the missionary. The time has surely come for the full realization of Bishop Tucker's vision of a missionary body *wholly* incorporated into the Uganda Church. Owing to what Bishop Willis called the compromise of 1909, two elements in Tucker's dream still remain unfulfilled. The first was the active participation of every missionary as an ordinary but responsible member in the fabric of the church. As Willis described the proposal which he himself rejected:

'he laid it down that there must be no racial discrimination; all alike, European missionaries and African Christians must be equally members of the one church, Europeans sitting and voting with their native brethren, sitting not in virtue of their race but only as elected by the people; and bound, as the rest were bound, by any decisions of the Diocesan Synod.'[8]

This has been realized at the highest level: no missionary sits today *qua* missionary in the diocesan committees. But at the lower levels practically no missionary participates at all in the committees of the parish or pastorate in which he works. At that level he is entirely outside the fabric of the church, as Bishop Tucker feared he would be. This is a matter which missionaries cannot adjust by themselves. They, if they will, can try to exercise fully their membership, on a level with all other members, in the local congregation and its councils; the African church for its part, has a step to take by welcoming and making use of European church members at the parish and pastorate level.

The second element of Tucker's vision which is as yet not completely fulfilled was described by a sub-committee of the Church Missionary Society in London, in 1897 as

'putting the individual missionary under the direction and control of the governing body of the church, which is, of course, not subject to the C.M.S. . . . The C.M.S. would still govern them in matters of stipends, allowances, marriage regulations, furlough and so forth, but not in such matters as location, duties, development of work, and so forth. In these matters the authority would be with the governing body of the church.'⁹

This also has all but been fulfilled. There remains, however, the relics of that compromise whereby the Standing Committee which governs the missionaries and their location, though its decisions, like all others, are referred to the Diocesan Council, is not freely appointed by the Synod to do that work on behalf of the church, but is answerable rather to the C.M.S. headquarters. The office of Regional Secretary for C.M.S. in East Africa and the Sudan, while obviously fulfilling a valuable function, is a perpetuation of the dual control of missionaries which Tucker considered a threat to the ultimate responsibility of the local church. If his vision was a true one, then, perhaps the proper function of such a Regional Secretary is not to stand in direct relationship to the missionaries as such, or even to their Local Governing Body, but to act as a liaison between the London Headquarters of the C.M.S. and the Diocesan Councils in East Africa.

These are perhaps the minutiae of organization, and it would be easy either to discount their importance or to point out that the present regulations do in fact so nearly conform to Tucker's ideal as to make any further change unnecessary. Unfortunately the inherent attitudes of fifty years cannot be so easily transformed; and the fact remains, attested by many thoughtful African leaders in the church, that the majority of the clergy and catechists still think of themselves as being the employees of the Europeans who are on the headquarters staff of the church. Flagrantly incorrect as such a picture may be institutionally, it is nevertheless in these terms that Africans still describe the relationship of the mission to the church. It is believed that the decisive choices in the life of the church are taken by Europeans, and that the ultimate responsibility for the success or failure of the church does not rest on African shoulders. A proverb that is used to describe the danger of this situation is *Omuggo oguli ewa munno tegugoba ngo*—'The club in your friend's house won't do to beat off the leopard (that attacks you).' An unhealthy consequence of this attitude is the lack of trust and loyalty among the delegates to the highest councils of the church. Since so many committees are under the chairmanship and secretaryship of Europeans, African members tend to be watchful and defensive, often withholding their real opinions but going back to their deaneries or pastorates to report on the latest schemes of the Europeans and to arouse opposition to them. When this behaviour is frankly discussed it is surprising how often it appears that there is still a suspicion that the missionaries must, in the last resort, make common cause with the British Government. There can, therefore, be no complacency with regard to the organizational relationship of the church and mission.

Of even greater importance, however, is the missionaries' own conception of their function in the church at the present time. If it is true that the primary need of the church in Buganda is the recovery of integration—the bringing back into a single whole all the scattered and disengaged elements which make up the church—then that must be the process above all which the missionary body should try to foster. Looking back we have seen that there were two ways in which missionaries in the past contributed to the disengagement of the church—by always withdrawing upwards, and by the specialization of their function. Both these tendencies need now to be consciously put into reverse.

There is no longer any question of 'withdrawing sideways', as might once have been done. But it is still possible for a few missionaries to go back into categories of the church's ministry (in the widest, most Pauline, sense of that word) which were handed over *in toto* by a past generation. By doing so they would help to pull together elements in the fabric of the church that have become too widely stretched apart. It is, perhaps, still not too late for a realignment that would send some missionary clergy to the theological college, but more to take charge of *muluka* parish churches, where by consultation with their African neighbouring priests and fellow-workers they can make their contribution at some depth within the fabric of the church; a realignment that, for the same reason, would send some nurses to staff a hospital but others to work at the level of a local dispensary or as health visitors, some teachers to secondary schools or training colleges, but at least a few to primary day schools.

To say this is not to ignore the fact that the decision should rest not with the missionary body but with the local church. For in fact a widespread questioning of clergy and laity in various walks of life revealed that, so far from wanting to use missionaries in the stereotyped categories with a priority demand for teachers, a large majority would, if they had free choice, like to place from forty to fifty per cent. of missionaries in some direct contact with village congregations. 'To visit the people in their homes and know them' was the most constant request, together with many references to training men and women in family problems and child-welfare, starting Sunday School and Youth work at the *muluka* level and, very frequently, 'to preach the Gospel to ordinary people'. Another common request was for translators of books into the vernacular. The results of this questioning showed that, if the African church was made wholly responsible for the placing of all missionaries, once it had broken the fetters of habit, its decisions would be made with imagination and sympathy.

But while the missionaries, as such, would be serving an immensely important purpose in thus placing themselves wholly at the disposal of the church, other European servants of the church, especially, at present, in education, have a different, but also greatly needed function to fulfil, namely to help this church to accept without reserve or misgiving the fact that its bounds far exceed what is officially within its control. It was unfortunate that the recent realignment and development of the schools' system appeared to be done by *ex cathedra* decisions taken without the cognizance of the African church. This was not altogether so, and the process was in any case unavoidable; but it has left a legacy of regret and suspicion towards any educational and welfare activities that lie beyond the direct jurisdiction of the church. Christians, both European and African, who are engaged in such work have a particular opportunity to restore the lost confidence by the quality of their participation in the life of the local church, and at the same time to widen the horizons of the clergy so that these may more readily come to recognize spheres of service that lie beyond their competence as nevertheless being part of a total Christian enterprise embraced by, and included in, the caring of the one Church.

NOTES

1. Ashe's translation of St John was printed in England at his own expense in 1891. Pilkington knew only of Mackay's and Gordon's revision of this, which was incorporated eventually in the full New Testament. When, later, he heard rumours of Ashe's printing, he assumed that it was the First Epistle of John that he had done, and so omitted this from the New Testament which he sent home for publication. Gordon, therefore, being in England on furlough with Mika Sematimba, did the Epistle to fill the gap for the first edition.

2. C. F. Harford-Battersby, *Pilkington of Uganda*, pp. 192-3.

3. Ibid., p. 265.

4. Sir Apolo Kagwa: Article in *Mengo Notes*, Apr. 1901, quoted in *C.M.I.* 1901, pp. 545-6.

5. A. R. Tucker, *Eighteen Years in Uganda*, vol. ii, p. 283.

6. Martin Hall, Letter in *Proceedings of the C.M.S.* 1897, p. 119.

7. Martin Hall and Ernest Millar, Letters in *Proceedings of the C.M.S.* 1897, pp. 119, 122.

8. J. J. Willis, Unpublished memoirs in MS.

9. Report of a sub-committee appointed by the General Committee of the C.M.S. to confer with Bishop Tucker regarding the constitution of the Buganda Church, 25 Feb. 1898, in C.M.S. Archives.

14

Theological Questions:
Gospel, Religion and Society

A T almost every point in this study of the Buganda Church theological questions have been posed. It would be tempting to
follow them up immediately, and decide how far, in Mackay's
words, the unbiased examination of facts in this area of the church's
mission is 'destined to play as important a part in correcting the vagaries
of theologians, as practical engineering has done in the domain of
theoretical mechanics'. At this stage, however, any conclusions would
be superficial and unprofitable. The full theological implications can
only emerge when a sufficient number of other studies has been carried
out to enable us to see what are only local idiosyncrasies and what
general trends appear to be constant. In the meantime we can do no
more than notice some of the main theological issues which are raised
by this pilot study, or, it might be truer to say, the particular slant which
this study gives to some of the questions which are already being much
debated in the churches of the West.

We may take as a starting-point a question of communication. It
appears that there is an incalculable gap between the Gospel that is proclaimed and the Gospel that is heard, which has not always been taken
into account in discussions about evangelism. In the Anglican mission
in Buganda there can be no doubt that, from the time of C. T. Wilson
to the present day, the Christian message has been preached with all the
special emphases of Moravian and Anglican Evangelical theology—the
sinful condition of man, the Atonement and the Saviourhood of Christ,
the conversion of the individual through conscious repentance and
faith, and the offer of sanctification through the Holy Spirit conditioned
by the surrender of the believer's will. Yet the message which was
received and implanted and upon which the church in Buganda was
founded, was primarily news about the transcendent God. 'Katonda',
the unknown and scarcely heeded Creator, was proclaimed as the focus

of all life, who yet lay beyond and above the closed unity of all existence. This in itself was so catastrophic a concept that, for the majority of hearers, it appeared to be the sum of the new teaching. It was as though the missionaries preached Paul's gospel to Corinth, but their converts heard Paul's sermon to the Athenians mingled with Isaiah's message to the city of Jerusalem. Later on, as the same preaching was reiterated, a certain number in the church heard more of it. It is this which partly accounts for the successive revivals. So R. H. Leakey, writing of the 'mission' of 1893, reported:

> 'Many, who had long been looked upon as leading Christians, realized a new force and power in their Christian life. Some said to us, "Why have you been here so long and never told us this glad news before?" All we could say was, "You have been told, but have not believed it." '[1]

That, perhaps, is the truth which lies behind the concept of progressive revelation. But there is another aspect of this difference between the message proclaimed and the message heard. Clearly the missionaries preached from within the culture of nineteenth-century Evangelical Protestantism—or nineteenth-century Roman Catholicism—while the Baganda heard from within the culture of the traditional African world-view. Considered historically and sociologically, the communication of the Gospel is a matter of culture contacts; theologically it is more than that—'and in that more lies all her hopes of good'. But it is not easy to say precisely where the 'more' is to be found. By faith we believe that the preacher of the Gospel communicates the Word of God; yet he cannot himself distinguish the kernel of the Word from the cultural and historical husk in which he presents it. We believe that the convert receives the Word of God, but he can only hear it from within the 'auditorium' of his world, as he sees and knows it. It is not merely a question of relevance. The revelation of a transcendent, personal and righteous God was not relevant, but revolutionary, to the Baganda, yet that was the Word which they heard. The fact that they did hear it, and did not at that stage, for the most part, hear the message of the Saviourhood of Christ or the Power of the Spirit, though these were the themes that were being preached, suggests that this was the Word of God to them and it was independent of the word of the preacher. The preacher, therefore, can only speak from within his own culture; but, provided that he is faithful, according to the terms of I Corinthians 2, the Word of God will be made audible, though what is heard may not be the same as what is preached. The pentecostal experience, whereby the people heard, every man in his own language wherein he was born, was not primarily a linguistic miracle, but, rather, the unending mystery of preaching, through which the ineffable and creating Word, which is neither the word spoken nor the word heard, is made known and evokes faith.

Perhaps it is because this living Gospel can never be exclusively identified with the word spoken nor the word heard, both of which are conditioned by the particularities of culture and history, that Paul uses the ambiguous term ἡ ἀκοή to describe the crucial action which leads to faith. In Romans 10. 16-17, it means both the prophetic report and the hearing which begets belief. It is the passing of the Word from faith to faith. The Word submits both to the mouth that speaks and the ear that hears in all their temporal contingency, yet so far from being contained by them, it is the Word which contains and creates both the speaking and the hearing as a single redemptive process. Faith is ἐξ ἀκοῆς—born of the preaching-hearing process—and that process is activated by the utterance of God—διὰ ῥήματος Θεοῦ. So also, in I Thessalonians 2. 13, Paul gives thanks because in this speaking-hearing process which, like the sacraments, is an imperfect human action embodying the divine act—λόγον ἀκοῆς παρ' ἡμῶν τοῦ Θεοῦ—the thing which has actually been received and is still operative is not the meaning which men expressed but the meaning which God gave.

This truth should alleviate some of the anxieties with which the church of the West is haunted and inhibited as it grapples with the problems of communication. It should also give pause to preachers of the Gospel, wherever they may be, who finding that their hearers have not taken in what they said, assume too quickly that they have not received the Word of God. When, for example, those who seek to evangelize in Buganda meet many Christians who appear to be unresponsive to the message they preach, or who fail to reproduce in themselves the spiritual experience of the preachers, it is a false assumption for them to suppose that the Word of God has been rejected. It may have been, but the preachers are not in a position to know with certainty; for in the relativity of communication, they cannot tell what is in fact the Word which God is speaking to their hearers. The responses which are made to that Word are likely, therefore, to be for the most part out of sight and unrecognized, and, as we have seen, this is in fact the way in which the spiritual growth of the Buganda Church continues.

This relative and incalculable quality in the proclamation of, and response to, the Gospel raises the very difficult question of the real place and meaning of canonical standards in the church. What does it mean to proclaim 'one Faith, one Lord, one Baptism', if faith is a hidden response to a Word which is not the same as the word preached? What is the relationship between faith and creed? between obedience and law? If, in the church, there are some for whom effective revelation does not seem to include much more than the transcendent godhead of the Creator, while others appear to rejoice in the 'fulness' of the Gospel; if some 'good Christians' get drunk now and then, or marry without church rites, while others accept the same ethical norm as the pastor or missionary; what have they all in common as the cement of their fellowship? The answer can only be, their incompleteness and the grace of God. Those who appear to be more advanced in their understanding and discipleship, however much they may long to see their fellow Christians growing up into the fulness of the stature of Christ, can only know with certainty that they themselves have not yet attained it. Creeds and confessions have their place as a summary of what has been revealed, but they are not yet a statement of what most Christians actually live by. The same is true of the standards and codes of Christian behaviour. 'One Faith, one Lord' can only mean that there *is* an absolute Way and Truth and Life, but for those who follow him the different degrees of their attainment are far less noticeable than the similarity of their insufficiency, and their unity comes from the divine grace which makes up the short measure of each to a common completeness in Christ.

Such considerations, however, though they ease some of the tensions of the pastor and preacher, do not wholly answer the difficulties of the theologian. There still remains the inextricable confusion of the Gospel with the social patterns and culture of the West. To take but one example, there is the emphasis on the dominance of the male in traditional African marriage, exemplified in the standing orders which the husband is expected to give his bride on the marriage night. Much breakdown is due in these days to the new freedom of women and the men's inability any longer to enforce their superiority. It is easy to point out that in its fight for monogamy the church has been ignoring the real battleground, namely the conception of personality and the female rights inherent in Christianity. But this conception of individual personality is only a late fruit of Christian culture. For hundreds of years in Christendom there was no more recognition of the value of women's personality than there is in traditional African culture. In this respect some would say that the church of the twentieth century has outgrown Saint Paul.

But then, the question arises whether this is an essential element of Christianity or only one of a multitude of cultural accretions which has grown and changed through the centuries. Many, observing the blunders and confusions of the Christian mission in Africa, call for a return to simple essentials. A good gardener when transplanting a cutting deliberately prunes off all the flowers and fruit and leaves, and puts only the bare, clipped twig into the new soil. So, some would say, we are wrong to attempt to build a church, modelled on older churches, for a church involves a culture and a pattern of society. How much better to preach only the bare Gospel and let the new church, and its ethic and theology, grow up out of the encounter between that Gospel and the indigenous culture. Did not the Council of Jerusalem represent such a stripping off of the leaves of Judaism until nothing was left to be transplanted into the gentile world but the bare ethical essentials and the news of Christ?

Unfortunately such an argument is nostalgic and naive. The Gospel cannot be stripped bare and never has been. Even in the first century an incalculable amount of Jewish thought and morality came into the Roman world with Christ. For the Gospel is preached always, as it was in Buganda, by its fruits and in its preachers. It is true that the missionaries need not have imparted so many of the European patterns of behaviour, nor need the Gospel have been tied up to schools which, in African eyes, exist to give children the 'polish' of civilization. Christianity today need not be Western in every respect; but it cannot be anything but twentieth-century Christianity. The problem in Buganda, as in many parts of the world, is how to learn and live a twentieth-century Christianity in a third generation church; or, conversely, how to be a third generation church in a twentieth-century society. It is at this point that history is no help whatever, because this problem has never arisen before.

That is the chronological aspect of the problem of the Gospel and culture. The sociological aspect is even more acute. The church in Buganda is confronting the universal question of whether it is possible to build one church which is really the church of all strata of society. Nearly every town parish in Britain faces the same problem, and has found only the usual unsatisfactory solutions—Sunday morning and evening congregations representing different social levels; Sunday School and Children's Service catering for the two types of home background. Even deeper runs the divergence between the different kinds of ministry required in the urban and the rural parish. It seems that the more the church becomes indigenous to the society in which it exists, the deeper grow the differences between congregation and congregation, parish and parish, church and church. The difficulties of the ecumenical movement are cultural rather than theological more often than we care to admit.

The problem that is slowly building up for the church in Uganda is, how to be at the same time a church for peasants and cultivators attuned to the cycles of nature and rooted in an undifferentiated society, and also a church of the individualized and cosmopolitan middle class. The disconcerting fact is that Evangelical Christianity, with its Gospel of individual conversion, the good news of rescue and the power to be different, not only appeals to, but also creates, a *bourgeoisie*. The revival movement, for example, calls peasants and herdsmen to rise above the ruck, morally and spiritually. In a very short time they have inevitably risen above it socially. Money that was spent on drink or women or divination is put into the home. In a few years husband and wife are justifiably proud of their house and garden, of their children, and of their reputation. Even the simple, older village women in the movement have a new outlook; in relationship to the peasant society they are *évolués*. A new class is being created, fashioned by the Gospel in alliance with modern enlightenment.

The church in Buganda is now intensely conscious of the needs and responsibilities of this class, and the mission, through its policy of concentration on training leaders, is almost exclusively concerned with it. Because of the dominance of the bourgeois minority, there is a serious danger that thought and enthusiasm will be so devoted to developing the methods of ministry appropriate to that class that problems of the peasant congregation will be ignored. It is well known in Britain that the pastoral and evangelistic methods which are effective in a suburban parish—age-group clubs, evangelistic rallies, a simple, systematized presentation of salvation, special groups of the keener Christians—do not 'go down' successfully in a completely rural parish, where people dislike discriminatory groups and need a slower, more embracing ministry. The same contrast is far more acutely drawn in the church in Buganda.

But what is at stake is not merely a question of pastoral method but the whole relation of the Gospel to the peasant world. We have seen that in Buganda the village people have a deep sense of the need for

R

'religion', or *eddini*, which is compounded of custom, law, outward observance, beliefs held in common, all based on a recognition of the transcendent God and on some body of revealed truth. We have seen also that the idea of 'gospel' as something that challenges 'religion' and finds it wanting, goes against the grain of peasant culture, because of its inherent individualism and discrimination. We are compelled to ask whether there is any evidence, in the world today, or in the history of the church, that Evangelical Christianity—the Christianity of 'gospel'— can ever take firm hold of a peasant society. It was, perhaps, determin- ative of St Paul's theology that he was himself a cosmopolitan and exercised his apostolate towards the unrooted, urban populations of the Graeco-Roman world. The theological concept of the pilgrim and prophetic church seems only to arise in, and appeal to, an essentially homeless psychology. This may partly explain why only the so-called 'catholic' presentation of Christianity has taken a firm hold of peasant peoples in the past without changing them into something else, and why, in all such cases, the church has appeared to be socially un- prophetic and unprogressive. But the implications of this in the changing societies of Africa remain to be seen.

There is another, and more immediate, aspect of this question of the relation of the Gospel to peasant society. Has Christ come to fulfil or to destroy, to bring peace or a sword? The problem is felt most acutely in Buganda at the present time with regard to the serious breakdown of social stability in sex relations. If the church is really concerned with the health of society, then its weight must be thrown unequivocally on the side of stability; it must eschew whatever disrupts moral sanctions in society and it must support every phenomenon that stems the tide of dissolution. This means that the church should unreservedly honour and encourage faithfulness and stability wherever these are found, even where the marital pattern does not conform to what it regards as the Christian ideal. It means that the church should concern itself much less with punishing individual failures than with adjusting those factors in the social patterns which militate against the fulfilment of the Christian code. It means that the church must not permit itself, in the name of principle, to undermine any more of the structure of traditional authority, until new sanctions have been fully accepted in place of the old.

On the other hand it may be said emphatically that the stability of society is not, and never has been the concern of the church. Because of the inherent tendency to self-destruction in all human institutions,

Christians, it is said, are to expect the breakdown of societies. The Gospel, so far from shoring up the tottering fabric, is itself the most revolutionary factor in the process, for the new wine bursts the old bottles. Christ comes inevitably in judgment, but in the midst of breakdown and flux he stands as Saviour, and his Church offers the new society for all who will enter it.

It is the age-old dilemma of the Church confronting society. Is she to be, as the Epistle to Diognetus said, like the soul in the body, imprisoned by society yet holding society together? Or is she, rather, that βασιλεία ἀσάλευτος, the only unshakeable kingdom, standing apart from, and over against, the disintegrating systems and societies of mankind?

Richard Niebuhr[1] has shown that throughout the history of Western Christendom, Christian opinion has ranged between five classical answers to this question. At one extreme was the total rejection of responsibility for human society exemplified by Tertullian, the Montanist; at the other end was the total acceptance of human culture in the faith, as Abelard taught, that all is fulfilled in Christ. Between these extremes lie the synthesis of Aquinas; Luther's dual parallelism of the two realms; and what Niebuhr calls the 'conversionist' solution of Augustine, by whom the Church is seen to have a redemptive function towards society.

Yet neither the classical answers, nor the fumbling re-interpretations of the modern West, can wholly answer this question for the younger churches. What, for example, can our post-war utterances about the prophetic and confessing Church mean to Christians living in a society in which they are only one-half of one per cent. of the population? What, on the other hand, have we to say, with our 'Götterdämmerung' theology, to the church in Buganda, where hope is vigorous and naive, and where the solidarity of society, in spite of rapid change and breakdown, still means to the Christians who live in it something that we of the West lost centuries ago?

The question is, rather, whether in Buganda, and elsewhere in Africa, the church will be enabled by God's grace to discover a new synthesis between a saving Gospel and a total, unbroken unity of society. For there are many who feel that the spiritual sickness of the West, which reveals itself in the divorce of the sacred from the secular, of the cerebral from the instinctive, and in the loneliness and homelessness of individualism, may be healed through a recovery of the wisdom which Africa has not yet thrown away. The world Church awaits something new out of Africa. The church in Buganda, and in many other parts of the continent, by obedient response to God's calling, for all its sinfulness and bewilderment, may yet become the agent through whom the Holy Spirit will teach his people everywhere how to be in Christ without ceasing to be involved in mankind, how to be bound in the bundle of life, yet at one with the Lord their God.

NOTES

1. C. F. Harford-Battersby, *Pilkington of Uganda*, p. 229.
2. H. Richard Niebuhr, *Christ and Culture* (Faber, 1948).

APPENDIX A

A PARTIAL WHO'S WHO OF THE EARLY CHRISTIANS OF BUGANDA

The following material is not exhaustive by any means. There are bound to be some people of significance whose names have inadvertently been omitted. Of those who are included not all the available information is included. This has been deliberate, so that the few who are fortunate in having the events of their lives fairly thoroughly recorded in past accounts should not therefore stand out more than they merit above others who have no such memorial. Many of the members of the Roman Catholic Church have been recorded somewhat briefly here, mainly because they have been more fully described in Father Thoonen's admirable account, *Black Martyrs*. These notes, however, may serve as a preliminary aid to any who wish to study the history more fully and who find themselves confused by the haphazard references to names in the letters and books of missionaries, administrators and travellers. As far as possible the personal or clan name is given first, then other African names. Any baptismal name is given last. Dates of birth are only approximate.

ALIWONYA, Sirasi   One of Baskerville's catechists at Ngogwe from 1894. Licensed lay-reader 1896. Ordained deacon 1899 and went to Rakai in Koki.

BADZEKUKETTA, Athanasius   A baptized member of the Roman Catholic Church. First a page, then a soldier under Mutesa and Mwanga. Martyred at the foot of Mengo hill 26 May 1886.

BAJALIRWA, Yonasani   Head page to the Queen-Mother of Mwanga. Baptized at Anglican mission 25 April 1886. Put in stocks in June 1886, but escaped.

BAKUNGA, Nsubuga, Paulo   b. 1851. Appointed keeper of Mutesa's tomb. A very earnest pupil at the Anglican mission. One of the first church council 1885. A leader of Anglicans in Ankole 1888. Made a licensed lay-reader in 1891. Appointed Kaggo in 1892; and in 1897 followed Yona Waswa (q.v.) as Mukwenda of Singo.

BANABAKINTU, Luke   b. 1851. Servant to Mukwenda of Singo.

Regular pupil of Mackay in 1881. Baptized by White Fathers 28 May 1882. As a dependant of Kalemba (q.v.) taught a catechism class at Mityana. Martyred at Namugongo 3 June 1886.

BEKOKOTO, Shem   An Anglican of whom little is known until he appears as one of the first church council in 1885 living at the household of Walukaga (q.v.).

BUGEZA, Zefaniya   Pupil of Wilson. Baptized later by Anglicans. Appointed to chieftainship of Mukubankwata under the Mulondo in N. Kyagwe.

BUZABALIAWO (abbrev. BUZA), Henry Wright, later James   b. 1861. Son of Isaya Mayanja (q.v.). Attached to the Gabunga. Pupil of Wilson. One of first five Anglicans to be baptized 18 March 1882. Later attached to Andrew Kaggwa (q.v.) to learn to play cymbals. Baptized again by White Fathers. Martyred at Namugongo 3 June 1886.

BYEKWOLA, ?   Joined Anglican Mission to have ulcers treated in late 1882. Helped with cultivation. Was later baptized.

DAMULIRA   The first of the Anglicans to be baptized, in his last sickness by a pagan friend, in the autumn of 1881.

DOTI   A young girl from Buddu, ward of Nikodemo Sebwato (q.v.), who escaped from the harem of Mutesa I and attached herself to the Anglican mission early in 1883. Was married to Kibega (q.v.) when both were in catechumens' class. In Jan. 1884, when missionaries discovered she was the Kabaka's woman, they allowed her to be taken back to the palace.

DUTAMAGUZI (abbrev. DUTA), later Kitakule, Henry Wright   Large thick-set man. Nephew of Namalere, the Kangawo of Bulemezi. Became servant to the Mukwenda. Pupil of Wilson. Friend of Firipo Mukasa (q.v.), with whom he was imprisoned on an island in Lake Wamala for refusing to join in Moslem prayers (1880). Went with Pearson to the coast (1881). Became pupil of U.M.C.A. and was baptized there 25 March 1882. Returned up country in Bishop Hannington's first safari. Joined Anglican mission, but fled in 'Musisi' persecution in Jan. 1884. Returned June 1884. Member of first church council 1885. Attacked in persecution 1886, but escaped into Bulemezi and changed name to Kitakule. Lay-reader in 1891. Deacon 28 May 1893; priest 31 May 1896. Principal assistant to Pilkington for Bible translation. Served at Namirembe till death 11 June 1913.

EMBWA, Eriya   Was a page to Mwanga during Mutesa's reign. Given estate at Kisamula. Baptized by Anglicans Nov. 1885. In persecution of 1886 was mutilated and died on 29 May.

KABUNGA, Nuwa   When quite young was Mutesa's third Mukwenda. Pupil of Wilson, and befriended Anglicans though not willing for baptism. Banished by Mwanga for plotting to depose him in 1885. Baptized later.

KADOKO, Alexander   Brother of Serunkuma (q.v.). Page to Mutesa. Appointed as the Namfumbambi, sub-chief at Mpumu in Kyagwe. Baptized by Anglicans July 1883. Deposed and beaten by Sekibobo, his overlord, but later given Kitebe estate. An inconsistent Christian until Mwanga's persecution, when he boldly confessed and was martyred at Namugongo 3 June 1886.

KAGGWA, Andrew   A Munyoro. b. 1850; captured in raid 1865; page to Mutesa I, then became drummer under Toli. Given estate on Natete hill. Baptized by White Fathers 30 April 1882. Made Mugowa, or bandleader under Mwanga. Head of an important Christian 'cluster'. Martyred 26 May 1886.

KAGWA, Kalibala Gulemye, Apolo.   b 1865. ('Of passionate and at times rather childish disposition', but with immense powers of leadership.) Page to Mutesa I under Kolugi, the store-keeper. Severely gashed by Mwanga at time of persecution. Palace treasurer 1887; Mukwenda 1888 under Kiwewa; succeeded Nyonyintono (q.v.) as general of the Christian forces. Katikkiro from 1889 to 1929. Attended coronation of Edward VII in Britain. Knighted 5 June 1905.

KAIDZI, Yonasani   Sub-chief in Kyagwe. Among exiles in Ankole. Made a lay-reader some time after the first six. Ordained deacon 1893. Posted, with Ketula his wife, to Ziba with Baskerville. Remained in S. Kyagwe for eighteen years. Severe cataract in 1898 and suspected sleeping sickness in 1901, but recovered. Transferred to Buddu in 1912. His daughter Irene Drusilla married Kabaka Daudi Chwa 19 Sept. 1914.

KAKUMBA, Yusufu   b. 1870. Page to Mutesa I. Baptized by Anglicans 22 Dec. 1883. Transferred himself to Anglican mission on Mutesa's death. Martyred at Mpimerebera swamp 31 Jan. 1885.

KAKUNGURU, Lwakilenzi, Semei   Native of Koki, where he held chieftainship under Kamswaga, the king. Not as carefully taught as other Christians, because of frequent absence from capital. Baptized during persecution in 1886. Appointed Mulondo of N. Kyagwe in 1890. In March 1892 was made the Kimbugwe, Mugwanya, who held the title, being a refugee with Mwanga. Because he found this office involved him in continual strife with the Katikkiro, Apolo Kagwa (q.v.), he resigned, but was later made chief over newly acquired territories of Bugerere and Buruli, between Kyagwe and Bunyoro. Captured the fugitive Mwanga in Lango April 1899. Appointed agent of Government over the tribes as far to the N.E. as Mt. Elgon and became virtually king of the area known to the Baganda as Bukedi. Was later president of Busoga lukiiko. Retired in 1913 to estate at Mbale, and joined the new 'Malaki' movement. Died 1928.

KALEMBA, Matthias   A Musoga, b. 1840, taken as slave to Bulemezi. Later became the Mulumba, sub-chief under the Mukwenda of Singo, and was made his chief judge. Pupil of Wilson. Baptized by White Fathers 28 May 1882 and resigned judicial office. Leader of Roman Catholic 'cluster' at Mityana, with his wife Kikuvwa. Took up tanning and pottery. Martyred 30 May 1886.

KAMWAKABI, Samwili   ('A man of gigantic stature.') Was evangelist on Busi island in the Sese group in 1896. Ordained deacon 29 Jan. 1899. Priest 10 June 1900; remained as pastor on Busi.

KAMYA, Cyprian   One of earliest pupils of the White Fathers. Baptized 28 May 1882. Instructed Ngondwe and others at dead of night during first period of persecution under Mutesa I. Was taken to execution at Namugongo as a confessor, 1886, but was reprieved and imprisoned for a year.

KATE, Damulira, Yoswa   b. 1850. Quiet and introspective, but with strong influence over others. Made slow progress as a Christian, but was keen teacher. Was skilled tailor to Mwanga. Made Mugema of Busiro in 1889. Objected to introduction of medical work in the church in 1891. Sent own evangelists to Ankole in 1898. Co-founder of 'Malaki' Church in 1914. Died in exile 1929.

KAYA, ?   Called 'the boy admiral', because he was made Mutesa's Gabunga when very young. Pupil of Wilson. Baptized by Anglicans Dec. 1883. Killed on an expedition with five of his followers.

KIBEGA, Albert   brother to Edward Mukasa (q.v.). Page to Namasole until Jan. 1883, when he attached himself to Anglican mission. Married to Doti (q.v.). Escaped from capital during persecution. Made 'Mutesa' in 1888.

KIBUKA, Ambrose   b. 1873. Servant to Balamaze, steward to the Mukwenda. Joined Roman Catholic group at Mityana. Later sent as page to Mwanga. Martyred at Namugongo 3 June 1886.

KIDZA, Lubeli, Freddy Wigram   Was the Musali, or guide, to Bugala, the captain of the guard under Mwanga. A regular pupil of the

Anglican Mission during 1884. Baptized 21 Sept. 1884. Accompanied his master to the burning of the three boys 31 Jan. 1885, confessed at that time but was pardoned by his master. In 1886 Bugala warned him to escape, but he would not and was martyred at Namugongo, probably being clubbed to death, 3 June 1886.

KIFAMUNYANJA, ?   One of Anglican pages martyred at Namugongo 3 June 1886.

KIKWABANGA, Nuwa   Exiled with Christians in Ankole. Chosen to go with Stanley to coast in 1889. Joined Bishop Tucker's party at Frere Town for return trip, and taught Pilkington Luganda during the journey. In 1894 started evangelism in Busoga with Kiwavu (q.v.). Ordained deacon 1896. During Nubian revolt, 1897, rescued Weatherhead at Luba's and hid him in swamp. Priest 1899. In charge of work at Bukaleba 1901. Transferred to Makerere 1903. Died of sleeping sickness 1905.

KIRIGGWAJJO, Anatole   Page to Mwanga. Baptized by White Fathers c. 1884. Martyred at Namugongo 3 June 1886.

KIRIWAWANVU, Mukasa   Page to Mwanga. Pupil of White Fathers. Martyred at Namugongo 3 June 1886.

KISINGIRI, Kizito, Zakaliya   b. 1858. Made a *mutongole* at Kyango in Buddu. Frequent pupil at Anglican mission from 1882, but was at first refused baptism because he would not give up all his wives but one; eventually agreed to this and was baptized Dec. 1883. Was spokesman of exiles in Ankole, with Sebwato (q.v.). Made Kagoro or sub-chief in Buddu 1889. Kangawo in 1892 and was appointed one of three Regents when Mwanga fled in 1897. Lay-reader in 1891; ordained perpetual deacon 28 May 1893.

KISULE, Matthew   Gunsmith to Mutesa I. One of the earliest pupils of Lourdel. Baptized 14 May 1880. Had house at Natete, which was important centre for Roman Catholics during absence of the missionaries.

KIVEBULAYA, Apolo   b. 1864 in Singo. First came to Kampala after death of Mutesa I. Visited Anglican mission during 1885. Recalled to fight for Moslems, but rejoined Christian group in flight to Ankole in 1886. Baptized 1894. Volunteered to go to Toro with Petero Nsubuga and Sedulaka Makwata (q.v.) when they returned to their work there in 1895. Tabalo, chief of Mboga, was at that time in Toro and invited evangelists to his country. Apolo and Sedulaka went, but were later severely persecuted. In 1899 both were transferred to principality of Kitakwenda, between Toro and Ankole. Ordained deacon

1900. Back in Mboga 1901, but later that year sent to help Yakobo Kiwunyabungo at Butiti. Stationed there as pastor until replaced by Kitching in 1902. From 1905 was permanently in the Congo. Died 1933.

KIWANUKA, Achilles   Page to Mwanga. Martyred at Namugongo 3 June 1886.

KIWAVU, Yoswa   ('Above everything an evangelist . . . considerable preaching powers.') Pioneered evangelism in Busoga from 1894. Ordained deacon 28 May 1899. First pastor at Iganga.

KIWOBE, Samwili   Servant to Queen-Mother in Mwanga's reign. Baptized by Anglicans during persecution of 1886. Killed in battle in Buddu 1889.

KIZITO, ?   b. 1873. Page to Mwanga. The youngest of the martyrs at Namugongo 3 June 1886. A pupil of the Roman Catholic group in the palace under Charles Lwanga (q.v.), who baptized him a week before his death.

LUDIGO, Mukasa, Adolphus   A Munyoro. Page of Mutesa I, soldier under Mwanga. One of the Roman Catholic group at the palace. Martyred at Namugongo 3 June 1886.

LUGALAMA, Yusufu   b. 1874. A Muhima from Ankole. Captured in a raid by Nikodemo Sebwato (q.v.) and presented to Ashe on occasion of Sebwato's baptism. Himself baptized later in 1884. Martyred at Mpimerebera swamp 31 Jan. 1885.

LUWANDAGA, Andereya   b. 1860. Page at Mutesa's court. At time of Mwanga's persecution was in hiding in Mackay's house. Later exiled in Ankole. His wife Pulisikira died 1893. Succeeded Kakunguru (q.v.) as Kimbugwe and followed him also as chief of Bugerere. Helped him to capture Mwanga April 1899.

LWANGA, Lugajju, Charles   Page to Mutesa I. Became a favourite because he was a skilled wrestler. Joined White Fathers' catechism class 1882. Became head of Christian pages in the outer precincts of the palace in the time of Mwanga. Martyred alone on the way to Namugongo 3 June 1886.

LWANGA, ?   A dependant of chief Ngobya. Attached to Anglican mission when he was sent as page to the palace. Baptized shortly before first martyrdoms Jan. 1885. Martyred at Namugongo 3 June 1886.

MAGALI, Rebecca   Princess who joined O'Flaherty's class in 1883 and was baptized 16 March 1884. Gave much hidden support to the Christians in her enclosure.

MAKWATA, Zabuna, Sedulaka Evangelist who offered to go to Toro after the revival in early 1894. Returned to speak of the work 1895 and went back with Apolo Kivebulaya (q.v.).

MAWAGGALI, Noe b. 1850. Member of Mackay's class 1881. A dependant of Kalemba (q.v.). Expert potter and tanner. Attached to the Roman Catholic group at Mityana. Baptized 1 Nov. 1885 with 21 others. Martyred at Mityana 31 May 1886.

MAYANJA, Isaya Chief Munakulya and keeper of tomb of Kabaka Kamanya. Pupil of Wilson, and member of Mackay's class 1880. 'A great jolly giant.' Built a little hut for Christian prayer by his town house; but went back in first persecution in 1881. Recalled and taught by his slave Sembera Mackay (q.v.). Baptized 31 Oct. 1883 and had large community of Christians at his home. Deposed from office as Munakulya and feared that Mwanga plotted to kill all his followers.

MBAGA TUZINDE, ? Page of Mwanga. Baptized by Charles Lwanga (q.v.) 25 May 1886. Martyred at Namugongo 3 June 1886.

MUBULIRE, Fanny The first woman to join O'Flaherty's class in 1885. Was baptized with her two servant-girls, Ani Amanya and Webuzawaki. Later married Freddy Wigram Kidza (q.v.).

MUDEKA, Nasanaeri Fled to south of the lake with Mackay and became evangelist to the Wusukuma around Nassa. Ordained deacon 31 May 1896. Later sent to Ndeje in Bulemezi, where he remained many years.

MUGAGGA, ? Young Roman Catholic page to Mwanga. Martyred at Namugongo 3 June 1886.

MUGWANYA, Stanislas b. 1849. Leader of the Roman Catholic party from the time of the death of Nyonyintono. Made Kimbugwe 1889, but accompanied Mwanga when he was in the hands of the White Fathers after the Battle of Mengo 1892. Was made 2nd (R.C.) Katikkiro by treaty of 19 April 1893, but by Agreement of 1900 this arrangement ceased to operate and he became Mulamuzi, as well as being one of the three Regents.

MUKASA, Edward Brother of Kibega (q.v.). Page to Mutesa. Put in charge of the mosque in the palace compound, and so called 'Omu-zigiti'. Pupil of Wilson 1877. Pleased Mutesa by reading from the Bible in Swahili and was appointed special *Mutongole* to look after the mosque, now used as a Christian chapel, and to teach others there daily. One of first five Anglicans baptized 18 March 1882. Appointed Mulyagonja with a special charge to rebuild a new palace for Mutesa when his was burned. Killed in quarrel by another chief.

MUKASA, Firipo   Slave to Mukwenda. Pupil to Wilson. Married Sara
Nakima (q.v.). Baptized as one of first five Anglicans 18 March 1882.
Friend of Duta (q.v.), with whom he was imprisoned on an island in
Lake Wamala for refusing to participate in Moslem prayers (1880).
Stood firm during the 'Musisi' persecution Jan. 1884. Died of small-
pox in the autumn of that year. His son was called Balamu, and was
taken, with Sara, to the Mpimerebera swamp when the three boys
were burned, but was reprieved.

MUKASA, Ham   b. 1871, son of Zakaliya Makabugo Sensalire, the
Mujebejo. At Mutesa's request was sent as page to palace in 1883,
and learned to say Moslem prayers. Paid a few visits to Anglican
mission. At end of 1884 went back to father because of plague at
capital. Returned to palace at end of 1885 and was sent to collect
tribute; through other Christian pages was persuaded to lodge with
Walukaga (q.v.). In the big persecution of 1886 was hidden by
Yusufu Waswa the Kangawo and sent to take refuge at his estate at
Waluleta in Bulemezi. Later pardoned by Mwanga and made
Sabaddu over all the pages. Came under teaching of older Christians
and was baptized 1887. Joined rebellion against Mwanga. Became
Kiyoza at Nsagu. When Moslems seized power, went to Ankole. Sent
as envoy to Mwanga at Bukumbi. In war of 1889 played a decisive
part by destroying an Arab dhow and another boat that were
running arms for the Moslems, but was wounded in this engagement.
Became Sekibobo in 1905. Died 1956.

MUKASA, Henry   Remained at south of lake with Mackay in 1888.
Given chieftainship at Ziba in 1894. Worked as evangelist under
Baskerville and fought against Nubians at Luba's. Ordained deacon
31 May 1896 and sent to Bukasa Island. Transferred to Budo in 1904
and remained there many years.

MUKASA, Lukujuju Balikuddembe, Joseph, known as 'the long'
b. 1860. Page to Mutesa I from 1874. Pupil to Wilson in 1877 and
in Mackay's class 1881. Chosen by Mutesa as his nurse during his
sickness in 1880 and remained as his personal attendant and valet.
Baptized by White Fathers 30 April 1882. Became head of about 100
Roman Catholic adherents in the private apartments in the palace.
Retained as major-domo to Mwanga. Reprimanded him for the
murder of Bishop Hannington and for this was martyred 15 Nov.
1885.

MUKASA, Musa   Servant to Walukaga (q.v.). Taught Ham Mukasa
(q.v.) to read. For a time was assistant to Edward Mukasa (q.v.).

Baptized by Anglicans 15 Feb. 1885. Martyred at the door of Walukaga's house on the night of 25 May 1886.

MUKASA, Naganafa, Samwili (also called 'Muganzi Awongererwa') b. 1867. Page to Mutesa I when about 10 years old. Became pupil of Anglicans 1881 in spite of laughter of his fellows. Baptized 22 Dec. 1883. Taught his relatives and friends. Made member of first church council in 1885. Made Mulondo in succession to Kakunguru (q.v.) in 1894, but resigned in order to read for ordination. Ordained perpetual deacon 31 May 1896, posted to Bukoba in N. Kyagwe. Later accepted chieftainship at Kisitala in Bulemezi in 1898. Appointed Kangawo after Kisingiri (q.v.) in 1899. Fought in Nandi War 1900. Remained at Ndeje in Bulemezi for many years.

MUNYAGABYANJO, Robert   Page to Mutesa and chief gate-keeper to Mwanga. Attended Ashe's instruction and was baptized 22 June 1883. His wife and child lived at the Anglican mission for instruction. Member of church council in 1885; especially urged all converts to be evangelists. Bought Bishop Hannington's Bible from one of his murderers and presented it to the mission. Head of large 'cluster' of Christians in the outer courts of palace. Captured while praying at his home and martyred at Namugongo 3 June 1886.

MUSOKE, Zimbe, Batolomayo   Became a leader of the Anglicans after the persecution of 1886. One of those who baptized Ham Mukasa (q.v.). Appointed Sekiwala in 1889 and was signatory of the treaty with Mwanga 3 Feb. 1900. Was one of two who 'rescued' Mwanga from the White Fathers and brought him back to Mengo March 1892. Ordained deacon 31 May 1896 and sent to Kinakulya. Posted at Mengo in 1901 and remained for many years.

MUTAKIRAMBULE, Yakobo   Described as 'a lad of Mutambuza', i.e. Sembuzi (q.v.). A pupil of O'Flaherty. Baptized among first five 18 March 1882, but was a back-slider.

MUTAKYALA, Yairo   Was in exile in Ankole. Ordained deacon 28 May 1893. Priest 31 May 1896. Put in charge of church at Jungo, 16 miles from Mengo and left in sole charge of the work in that area. Called by Pilkington 'one of the brightest spots in Uganda.' Had 40 churches in his charge and 183 catechists. Remained there until 1916.

MUYINDA, Aloni   A Muhima from Ankole. Very short of stature. One of Baskerville's boys who became a catechist. Put in charge of district around Koja. Married Yokubezi, a Munyoro. Ordained deacon 10 June 1900 and posted to Ngogwe in place of Sirasi Ali-wonya (q.v.). Visited Ankole in autumn 1900 and saw the king burn his charms publicly. Remained at Ngogwe till 1903, when he was transferred to Toro.

MUZEYI, Jamari   b. 1862. Sold as a slave to one of palace officers. Later attached to Joseph Mukasa (q.v.) and was baptized by White Fathers 1 November 1885. Escaped main persecution in 1886, but was secretly murdered by the Katikkiro, probably on 27 Jan. 1887.

MWIRA, Yokana   Held chieftainship of Muwomba in Buddu. Joined O'Flaherty's class at the Anglican mission in Jan. 1883. Described himself as a climber exploring mountainous country. After some months brought his wife, and shortly after they were baptized as Yokana and Malyamu. Then retired to Buddu in 1884. One of first lay-readers 1891. Ordained deacon 1893 and worked at Mityana until 1904, when he was transferred to Mengo and served there for ten years.

NAKABANDWA, Daniel   Servant in the household of Mwanga's Queen-Mother. Baptized in Anglican mission April 1885. Martyred with two others of that household 6 June 1886.

NAKIMA, Sara   Came to Anglican mission about August 1881; wife of Firipo Mukasa (q.v.), and married him by Christian rite after the baptism of herself and her child Balamu in 1883. Taught several of the princesses secretly and so was apprehended with the three boys and taken with them to execution 31 Jan. 1885, but reprieved at the last moment. After her husband's death from smallpox she married his friend Henry Duta (q.v.). One of the first three women elected to the church council in 1887.

NAKIWAFU, Nuwa   ('Spiritually minded; very earnest and pains-taking.') One of the early evangelists in Singo. Ordained deacon 28 May 1899. Opened up work in Bunyoro with Thomas Semfuma (q.v.) and was pastor at Masindi, and, after being priested, at Hoima (1901).

NASIBU, ?   A skilled tailor to Mwanga. Attached to the Anglican group in the palace. A confessor and arrested in the persecution, but later was reprieved.

NGONDWE, Pontian   A man of Kyagwe presented as page to Mutesa I about 1875. Later made a soldier and given an estate at Kitibwa near to that of Andrew Kaggwa (q.v.). Baptized by the White Fathers. Martyred on the road to Namugongo 26 May 1886.

NKANGI, Timoteo   Attached to Anglican mission from 1887. Did translation work with Cyril Gordon. In 1892 accompanied Sebwato from Buddu to Kyagwe and was appointed as Katenda, sub-chief at

Ziba. Assisted the start of the mission at Ziba and preached in surrounding area. Was implicated in the abortive rebellion of May 1897
with other chiefs, mainly from Buddu, and banished.

NYAKUTUNGA, ? Was keeper of Mwanga's fireplace who confessed
during persecution, as a member of the Anglican group in the palace,
and was arrested, but later reprieved.

NYONYINTONO, Honorat Page to Mwanga, who had become a
leading Roman Catholic under Joseph Mukasa (q.v.). Appointed
major-domo 7 Dec. 1885. Arrested by order of Mwanga and shamefully mutilated 25 May 1886, but survived. Confirmed by Lourdel
while still in prison. Reinstated in the autumn of 1886; urged to
become Moslem but refused. Made commander-in-chief. After
revolt became Kiwewa's Katikkiro, and when Kalema seized throne,
was head of Roman Catholic party in Ankole. Led the whole Christian
force back into Buddu, but was killed in battle early in 1889.

SEBBOWA, Alexis Chief of Kitabazi under Mwanga. In persecution
gave himself up to captain of the guard, but was saved by pleading of
Katikkiro Mukasa. Made Sekibobo of Kyagwe 1889, but exchanged
with Sebwato (q.v.) after settlement of 1892 and became Pokino. Was
leader of the Roman Catholic faction after death of Nyonyintono
(q.v.).

SEBUGGWAWO, Musajjamukulu, Denis b. 1869. Nephew of Katikkiro Mukasa, who presented him as page to Mwanga. Pupil of Joseph
Mukasa (q.v.). Because he taught Christianity to other pages was
first to be martyred in the outbreak of persecution, being killed outside palace enclosure on 25 May 1886.

SEBULIMBA, Rachel (Lakeri) A member of the Ngogwe congregation
who, with three other women, offered to go in 1903 to evangelize the
islands on which the whole population was condemned to sleeping
sickness. Returned in 1904 to report, then went back for a second
spell, contracted the disease, and died at Mengo hospital.

SEBWATO, Nikodemo b. 1840. A sub-chief of Buddu under Mukasa
the Katikkiro. First approached O'Flaherty in Oct. 1882 as result
of a debate between the missionaries and the Arabs at the palace.
Later was instructed in his own house at the capital, with his women
and his spirit-medium; all became Christian. Then went back to
estate in Buddu, but returned to Mengo at end of 1883. Baptized
23 March 1884 (his medium was baptized six months later). Gave up
all his wives but one, who was baptized Julia. Mwanga ordered his
death in 1886, but Katikkiro only had him publicly flogged. Leader

of first church council. Made Pokino of Buddu in 1889, but after settlement of 1892 exhanged offices with Sebbowa (q.v.) the Sekibobo. Ordained perpetual deacon 1893. Moved headquarters from Mukono to Ngogwe to assist Baskerville. Died 30 March 1895.

SEMATIMBA, Mika b. 1860 in Singo. Given as page to Queen-Mother when 8 years old. Became pupil to Moslems in 1873, but became attached to Lourdel after arrival of White Fathers. Dissatisfied because he did not teach him to read. At end of 1882 was sent to Zanzibar with gift from Mutesa to Seyyid Bargash, met Duta at U.M.C.A. mission, and was persuaded to go to Anglican mission on his return to Buganda. Baptized Dec. 1883. Member of the first church council 1885. Sent by Mwanga to meet Bishop Hannington and take him to south of lake, but missed him. One of the Anglican leaders in Ankole 1888. Went with Walker to England in 1892. Sent to the coast again to buy goods for the Regents 1899. Appointed chief of Busiri Island in the Buvuma group 1900. Also in charge of the district surrounding his estate 12 miles from Mengo.

SEMBERA, Kamumbo, Mackay A Musoga slave belonging to Isaya Mayanja (q.v.), whom he taught Christianity. Pupil to Wilson. Asked Mackay for baptism in 1881. Baptized among first five 18 March 1882. One of the Anglican leaders in Ankole. Later went to be with Mackay at south of lake, and was with him when he died. Refused chieftainship in order to be an evangelist. Was not required to have church marriage to his wife before 1890. Lay-reader 1891. Killed in Battle of Mengo 23 Jan. 1892.

SEMFUMA, Tomasi ('A grave-faced, scholarly man.') Servant to Princess Nalumansi, Mutesa's sister. Became a pupil of the Anglican mission during 1884. Attached himself to Christian 'cluster' in house of Isaya Mayanja (q.v.) at Kasengeji, and was made member of first church council in 1885. On 22 May 1886 took Ashe news of the action of Nalumansi in burning her fetishes, which precipitated the next persecution. Captured and condemned to execution, but redeemed by Mackay for two tusks of ivory. One of Anglican leaders in Ankole 1888. In battle of Mengo, 1892, his chest was ripped by a bullet. One of first lay-readers in 1891, he was rejected from ordination as unready in 1893. Went as evangelist to Koki in 1895. Sent to Masindi to lead new work in Bunyoro in 1898. Ordained deacon 1899. Moved to north Bulemezi in 1901, where he remained for fifteen years.

SEMUKASA, Tomasi Appointed Kayima in 1889. In May 1893 was reported to have stopped and robbed Sudanese troops on their way to Bunyoro and was condemned to banishment in Kikuyu. But Mwanga, and the Anglican mission, redeemed him from Portal for 700 lb. of ivory. When resettlement gave his county to the Roman Catholic party he, as an Anglican, was transferred to Kikabya royal estate in N. Kyagwe. In April 1894 he settled at Nyakanonyi and was of great help to Baskerville.

SERUNKUMA, Bruno Half-brother to Kadoko (q.v.). Page to Mutesa and later a soldier of Mwanga's bodyguard. Baptized by the White Fathers. Was martyred at Namugongo 3 June 1886.

SERWANGA, Nuwa Page to Mutesa. Attached to the Anglican mission as a servant in 1884 and baptized. Martyred with the other two boys at Mpimerebera swamp 31 Jan. 1885. Ashe reported that, though the boys may not have sung at their martyrdom, it was in keeping with what he knew of Serwanga.

WALUKAGA, Nuwa Chief blacksmith to Mutesa, his name was a title of that office. Ordered to help Mackay build copper coffin for Mutesa's Queen-Mother and, attracted to Christianity as a result of this contact, was baptized 21 Sept. 1884. A man of exceptional intelligence, his estate at Kasengeji became an important Christian centre. One of the first seven elders of the church and a member of the first church council. When persecution broke out in 1886 he sent away his wife and children and all Christians living with him and sat awaiting the arrival of the executioners. Martyred at Namugongo 3 June 1886.

WAMALA, Yoeri ('A slow but devoted man.') A lay-reader for many years, he was one of the early evangelists to the islands. Ordained deacon 1900, he was put in charge of the pastorate on Kome Island by Cyril Gordon. In 1904 he moved to Jungo with Yairo Mutakyala (q.v.).

WASWA, Yona One of the earliest Anglican converts after arrival of Mackay, but because he was constantly away from the capital he made very slow progress. After sharing exile in Ankole was made Mukwenda of Singo. But in 1897 he was convicted of serious immorality and deposed, his place being taken by Paulo Bakunga (q.v.).

S

APPENDIX B

THREE GENERATIONS OF BADAMA DESCENDE) FROM A BROTHER AND SISTER, SHOWING HO' THE GREATER PART OF A FAMILY MIGRATE TO ONE PLACE (*see page* 114)

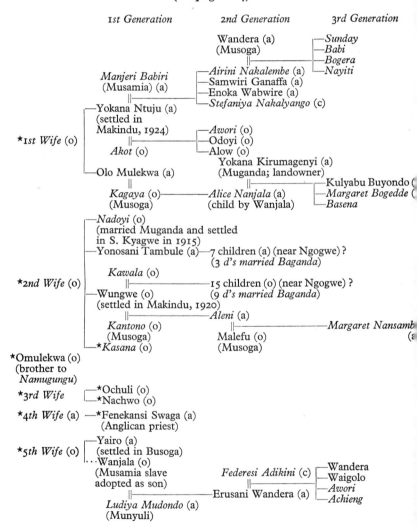

| *1st Generation* | *2nd Generation* | *3rd Generation* |

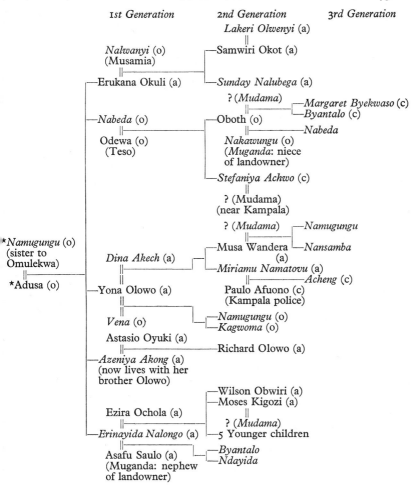

1st Generation   2nd Generation   3rd Generation

Lakeri Olwenyi (a)

Nalwanyi (o)   —Samwiri Okot (a)
(Musamia)

—Erukana Okuli (a)   —Sunday Nalubega (a)

? (Mudama)   —Margaret Byekwaso (c)
—Nabeda (o)   —Oboth (o)   —Byantalo (c)
Odewa (o)   Nakawungu (o)   —Nabeda
(Teso)   (Muganda: niece
of landowner)

—Stefaniya Achwo (c)

? (Mudama)
(near Kampala)

? (Mudama)   —Namugungu
—Musa Wandera   —Nansamba
Dina Akech (a)   (a)
—Miriamu Namatovu (a)
—Acheng (c)
—Yona Olowo (a)   Paulo Afuono (c)
(Kampala police)

*Namugungu (o)
(sister to
Omulekwa)   Vena (o)   —Namugungu (o)
—Kagwoma (o)
*Adusa (o)   Astasio Oyuki (a)
—Richard Olowo (a)
—Azeniya Akong (a)
(now lives with her
brother Olowo)

—Wilson Obwiri (a)
—Moses Kigozi (a)
Ezira Ochola (a)
? (Mudama)
—Erinayida Nalongo (a)   —5 Younger children

Asafu Saulo (a)   —Byantalo
(Muganda: nephew   —Ndayida
of landowner)

Note.—Those in Roman type are male, those in *italics*, female. Unless
another tribe is mentioned, all are Badama. (a) indicates that a person is Anglican,
(c) a Roman Catholic, and (o) an animist or of no religion. Where there is no
such indication this means that the person is still a child unbaptized. Those
marked * have never migrated from Budama. All the others, unless otherwise
stated are in Makindu parish.

DATA PROVIDED BY A STUDY OF 177 BOYS IN FIVE EDUCATIONAL CENTRES (*see Chapter 8*)

The following tables have been drawn up as the result of a questionnaire that was answered by 177 boys in Junior Secondary classes, or the equivalent educational standard, in 1956. In every case plenty of time was allowed for a preliminary discussion with each group of boys in order to gain their confidence and explain the purpose and manner of the questioning, and in order to give an absolute guarantee of anonymity. After this the questions were put and answered; any boy was then free to withhold his paper if he did not care to give it in, or if he had not answered truthfully. In every case the group asked for a further interview in order that they might continue a discussion in an atmosphere of frankness, and ask their own questions which were put with equal seriousness. (Apart from its value as providing information, this study showed clearly the pastoral possibilities of such an approach.)

King's College, Budo, is the oldest of the Full Secondary boarding-schools, of an English 'public-school' pattern, in Uganda, and has a high proportion of boys from professional homes. Busoga College, Mwiri, is a similar school in Busoga. Both these are self-governing schools affiliated to the Anglican Church. The school at Kasawo is one of those newly supported and governed by the Buganda (African) Administration. Kabubiro is typical of the smaller, struggling private schools, receiving no grants and failing in every respect to qualify for official recognition, yet attempting to offer a so-called 'secondary' education for which there is an overwhelming demand. The Teacher Training Centre at Iganga is one of several regional centres supported by the Protectorate Government though affiliated to the Anglican Church. Students go there from Primary schools, so educationally they are of the same level as the Junior Secondary standards, but they are older than the schoolboys.

For convenience the various tribes from the north-east of Uganda are grouped together in this survey, and the few boys from the other districts are omitted altogether from the results.

School	The Schools divided by tribes					
	Average age	Baganda	Basoga	N.E. Tribes	Others	Total
Budo . .	15	48	—	—	1	49
Mwiri . .	16	4	40	1	2	47
Kasawo .	16	27	2	11	1	41
Iganga P.T.T.C. }	20·5	1	15	—	—	16
Kabubiro .	17	2	3	19	—	24
Total .		82	60	31	4	177

Very often it is impossible to tell whether a particular feature is due to tribal differences, or to the difference between the mainly traditional home background and the more Westernized homes. The sample was therefore divided also between the boys whose fathers were in salaried or comparable jobs, and those whose work indicated that their pattern of life fitted the traditional village background. This is how the whole sample was made up.

Professional

Teachers . . .	12
Chiefs	9
Clergy	7
Administrators . .	7
Medical . . .	7
Clerks	3
Business . . .	3
Coffee estate . . .	1
Journalist . . .	1
Police	1
Railway . . .	1
Bus driver . . .	1
	52

Non-Professional

Cultivators . . .	107
Traders . . .	6
Muluka chiefs . .	5
Artisans . . .	3
Catechists . . .	2
Fisherman . . .	1
	124

One did not indicate his father's work.

The Schools divided according to the father's work			
	Professional	Non-Professional	% which is Professional
Budo . . .	27	21	56
Mwiri . . .	14	33	30
Kasawo . .	9	32	22
Iganga . .	1	15	6·25
Kabubiro . .	1	23	4

As will be seen, however, it is usually impossible to tell whether a particular feature is, for example, due to the boy being a Muganda or due to his coming from a professional background, since both these influences tend to operate together.

The following tables should now be self-explanatory. It must be remembered, in the case of Budo and Mwiri, that only the Junior Secondary classes (i.e. the first three standards) of the school were included in this study.

I. PREVALENCE OF SENDING CHILDREN FROM HOME

	Percentage sent away before 12th birthday	% who express dislike of the custom	DURATION OF STAY (Years) 0–1	1–2	2–3	3–4	4–5	5–6	6+	Length of stay of median average boy (Years)	AGE AT WHICH SENT (Years old) 0–2	2	3	4	5	6	7	8	9	10	11	Age at which median average boy was sent	RELATIONSHIP OF PERSON TO WHOM SENT: Grandfather	Grandmother	Paternal Uncle	Maternal Uncle	Paternal Aunt	Maternal Aunt	Brother or Cousin	Sister	No relation
By Tribes:																															
Baganda .	53·6	12	8	11	4	12	4	6	8	3	3	1	4	4	3	7	5	4	5	7	–	7½	13	7	13	3	7	3	5	2	2
Basoga .	66	15	8	9	12	7	2	1	5	2¼	1	–	2	7	10	3	7	3	3	3	1	6½	14	2	13	2	3	2	5	3	5
N.E. Tribes .	38·7	7	2	3	4	1	1	1	5	2½	–	1	1	–	–	3	2	1	3	–	1	9	–	–	5	5	2	1	2	1	1
TOTAL .	52·6	11	18	23	20	20	7	8	18	2½	4	2	7	11	13	13	14	8	11	10	2	7½	27	9	31	10	12	6	12	6	8
By Schools:																															
Budo . .	54	12	5	4	–	4	1	3	6	3¼	3	1	3	2	2	2	1	2	1	1	–	7	6	5	6	1	4	1	3	2	–
Mwiri . .	63	12	7	6	12	3	2	–	5	2¼	–	–	2	6	10	3	4	4	2	3	1	6	5	2	16	1	6	2	4	1	4
Kasawo .	55	16	3	8	5	8	2	4	3	3	1	–	1	2	1	6	4	1	5	4	–	9	8	2	7	4	2	2	2	1	3
Iganga . .	55	0	2	4	1	3	1	1	–	1½	–	–	–	1	–	–	4	1	2	2	–	8	6	–	–	1	–	–	1	1	1
Kabubiro .	37	18	1	1	2	2	1	–	4	3	–	1	1	–	–	2	1	–	1	–	1	9	2	–	2	3	–	1	2	1	–
By Home background:																															
Professional .	46	10	4	6	3	4	3	4	6	3¼	1	1	2	4	1	2	1	3	2	4	1	7½	3	3	8	1	2	4	3	2	4
Non-Professional .	59·6	13	14	17	17	16	4	4	12	2¾	3	1	5	7	12	11	13	5	9	6	1	7¼	24	6	23	9	10	2	9	4	4

2. AUTHORITY AND PUNISHMENTS IN THE HOME

	Baganda	Basoga	N.E. Tribes	Boys from Professional homes
Boys who feared their father in childhood .	% 24	% 28	% 67	% 29
OFFENCES FOR WHICH THE HEAVIEST PUNISHMENT WAS GIVEN				
Laziness				
Refusal of home chores	14	18	37	8
Non - attendance at school . . .	14	17	17	14
Nonconformity				
Not washing, eating, removing jiggers, etc.	2·6	8	—	2
Impudence, disobedience . . .	14	33	13	18
Truancy, staying from home . . .	4	1·7	—	6
Nuisance				
Damage to property .	18	8	17	14
Fighting, playfulness	13	5	3	14
Crying . . .	9	—	—	4
Improbity				
Lying . . .	6·4	1·7	—	8
Stealing . . .	4	1·7	13	6
Bullying younger children . . .	2·6	1·7	—	4
Unchastity . .	—	3·3	7	4
Slandering parents .	3	—	7	4
TYPES OF PUNISHMENT MOST COMMONLY INFLICTED				
Beating . . .	77	62	83	82
Refusal of food . .	25·6	52	26	20
Binding, locking up .	18	12	—	10
Detention at home .	9	8	—	4
Enforced digging .	1·3	5	3	2
Other manual tasks .	10	5	—	6
Shutting out at night .	2·6	5	—	2

3. SEXUAL EXPERIENCE OF BOYS OF 14-17 IN RELATION TO BEHAVIOUR PATTERNS AT HOME

a. Percentage of boys who have had intercourse :

By Schools: Budo 39·5; Mwiri 57·5; Kasawo 48; Kabubiro 94.
(All at Iganga were over 18 years old)

By Tribes: Baganda 43; Basoga 56; N.E. Tribes (mainly migrant) 77.

By Home background: Professional 46·6; Non-professional 59.

Note.—Of those who have had intercourse, about one-third had it with one girl only, and one-third with more than three; there was almost no difference in this respect between boys from the professional and non-professional homes. But while only 39 per cent. of the girls involved with boys of non-professional homes were school pupils, in the case of boys from professional homes 70 per cent. of the girls were at school.

b. Significant differences in patterns of behaviour in the homes of boys who have remained continent and those who have not

	Of boys who remained continent	Of boys who have had intercourse
	%	%
Afraid of father as a child .	20	41
Parents pleased or indifferent if the boy had girl friends	6	18
Child not taught to pray .	19	36
Mother no longer in home	18	29
Child sent away before 10th birthday . . .	42	56
Parents of mixed religious affiliations . . .	9	16
Parents not regular church-goers	61	74·5
Other wives joined home during child's life .	45	53
Family prayers not practised	34	45
Beating, starving or binding used as punishment in home	78	96

GLOSSARY

Words not explained where they occur

NOTE. Bantu tribal and similar designations normally consist of a root to which differing prefixes are attached. Thus, *-ganda* is the Luganda root from which are formed *Buganda*, the country of the tribe, *Baganda*, the people of the tribe; *Muganda*, a person of the tribe; and *Luganda*, their language. *Kiganda*, and in more recent literary usage *Ganda*, are adjectival forms.

Uganda is the Swahili form applied to the country by the first explorers. In modern usage Buganda is the kingdom of Buganda, which is only one of the four provinces (some non-Bantu) comprising the much larger political unit, the Uganda Protectorate, which last is commonly referred to as Uganda.

bakongozi, see *mukongozi*.
bakopi (sing. *mukopi*), peasants.
balaguzi, see *mulaguzi*.
balokole, members of the recent revival movement.
balubaale, see *lubaale*.
bataka (sing. *mutaka*), owners of land, particularly of clanland or *butaka*. The Kabaka as overlord of the *bataka* is *Sabataka*.
batongole (sing. *mutongole*), administrative chiefs appointed by the Kabaka. Land held by them was *butongole*.
Bazungu (sing. *Muzungu*), Europeans.
bitambo, see *kitambo*.
buzimbi, funds for church-building.
byalo (sing. *kyalo*), cultivated estates.
eddini, religion.
emibala (sing. *omubala*), recognized drum-beats.
Futabangi, 'hemp-smokers', a rebel movement intent on restoring the old religion.
gombolola, subdivision of a county.
Kabaka, title of the ruler or king of Buganda.
Kabejja, a subordinate wife of the Kabaka.
kabina, society.
Kaddulubaale, chief wife of the Kabaka.
Kangawo, title of the county chief of Bulemezi.
Katikkiro, title of the Kabaka's chief minister.
Killa siku tuusifu (Swahili), 'Every day we praise thee'; first words of hymn based on S. Baring-Gould's 'Daily, daily sing the praises'.
Kimbugwe, title of one of the Kabaka's great functionaries.
kitambo (pl. *bitambo*), familiar spirit.
lubaale (pl. *balubaale*), hero-god: recorded as *lubare* or *lubari* by early writers.
Lubuga, Royal Sister.
Lukiiko, the Kabaka's council of state.
masiro, royal shrines.
miruka, see *muluka*.
mmandwa, spirit-medium.
mugalagala, boy-page of the Kabaka's household.
Mugema, title of county chief of Busiro, in which lay many of the *masiro*.
mukongozi, official bearer (on his shoulders) of the Kabaka; a person so designated is attached as medium to every royal shrine.
Mukwenda, title of county chief of Singo.
mulaguzi (pl. *balaguzi*), diviner.
mulangira (pl. *balangira*), prince.

mulogo, sorcerer.
muluka (pl. *miruka*), administrative subdivision equivalent to a parish.
Mulumba, title of subordinate chieftainship.
Munakulya, title of subordinate chieftainship.
musawo, nature healer; adopted by early missionaries for a European doctor.
musezi, night-prowling wizard.
mutaka, see *bataka*.
Mutambuza, title of subordinate chieftainship.
mutongole, see *batongole*.
Muwanga, title of subordinate chieftainship.
muzimu (pl. *mizimu*), the human spirit.
Namasole, Queen Mother.
Nasaza, a subordinate wife of the Kabaka.
nsaasi, gourd rattle.
okwalula abaana, child-naming ceremony.
omubala, see *emibala*.
omusomesa, teacher (of reading), catechist; cf. *soma Luganda*.
Sabataka, see *bataka*.
Sekibobo, county chief of Kyagwe.
senga, join a new master.
soma Luganda, 'read Luganda'.
ssenga, one's father's eldest sister.
Tukutendereza, 'We praise thee'; hymn chorus adopted by *balokole* revivalists.

INDEX OF PERSONAL NAMES

INDEX OF SUBJECTS

Railway Line from Kampala

BUIKWE

River

Sezibwa

Kisala

Malongwe

River M.

Nam.

Bwoya

Wakabuzi

Ziba

NGOGWE

✝ = Anglican Church
⚲ = Roman Catholic Church

To Bukunja

Scale 1 = 50,000

0   ¼ ½   1   2

Part of Kyagwe County, Uganda